THE
UNEXCEPTIONAL
CASE OF HAITI

Cover image: A *machann* on Route des Dalles. The postcolonial gaze might see class in the race of the street vendor walking anonymously up the road, while race is subsumed in intersecting genealogies of privilege beyond the enclosure to the left. The site was the colonial estate of Pauline Leclerc and her husband, Charles, who was sent to Saint-Domingue by Napoleon in 1801 to restore slavery in the colony. (Black) US anthropologist and dancer Katherine Dunham purchased the property in the 1940s as her second home. In the 1970s, she leased it to a (white) French entrepreneur, who built the luxury resort Habitation Leclerc, home to Hippopotamus, sister nightclub to a noted discothèque of the same name operated in New York City by the same entrepreneur. Before her death in 2006, Dunham donated the property for a botanical garden. Fokal, the Haitian NGO funded by Hungarian-US billionaire George Soros, combined the estate with that of renowned (mulatto) architect Albert Mangonès together with another Dunham property across the road to create the *Parc de Martissant*. Photo by the author.

CARIBBEAN
STUDIES
SERIES

Anton L. Allahar and Natasha Barnes
Series Editors

THE UNEXCEPTIONAL CASE OF HAITI

RACE AND CLASS PRIVILEGE IN POSTCOLONIAL BOURGEOIS SOCIETY

Philippe-Richard Marius

University Press of Mississippi / Jackson

The University Press of Mississippi is the scholarly publishing agency of
the Mississippi Institutions of Higher Learning: Alcorn State University,
Delta State University, Jackson State University, Mississippi State University,
Mississippi University for Women, Mississippi Valley State University,
University of Mississippi, and University of Southern Mississippi.

www.upress.state.ms.us

The University Press of Mississippi is a member
of the Association of University Presses.

First printing 2022
∞

Library of Congress Cataloging-in-Publication Data

Names: Marius, Philippe-Richard, author.
Title: The unexceptional case of Haiti : race and class privilege in
postcolonial bourgeois society / Philippe-Richard Marius.
Other titles: Caribbean studies series (Jackson, Miss.)
Description: Jackson : University Press of Mississippi, 2022. | Series:
Caribbean studies series | Includes bibliographical references and
index.
Identifiers: LCCN 2021062300 (print) | LCCN 2021062301 (ebook) | ISBN
9781496839077 (hardback) | ISBN 9781496839084 (trade paperback) | ISBN
9781496839046 (epub) | ISBN 9781496839039 (epub) | ISBN 9781496839060
(pdf) | ISBN 9781496839053 (pdf)
Subjects: LCSH: Haiti—History. | Haiti—Race relations. | BISAC: SOCIAL
SCIENCE / Ethnic Studies / Caribbean & Latin American Studies | HISTORY
/ Caribbean & West Indies / General
Classification: LCC F1921 .M38 2022 (print) | LCC F1921 (ebook) | DDC
305.80097294—dc23/eng/20220110
LC record available at https://lccn.loc.gov/2021062300
LC ebook record available at https://lccn.loc.gov/2021062301

British Library Cataloging-in-Publication Data available

In Memoriam

Michel-Rolph Trouillot

Map 1. Hispaniola, known in Haiti as l'Île d'Haïti, with Cuba, Jamaica, and Puerto Rico as the Greater Antilles. Google Maps.

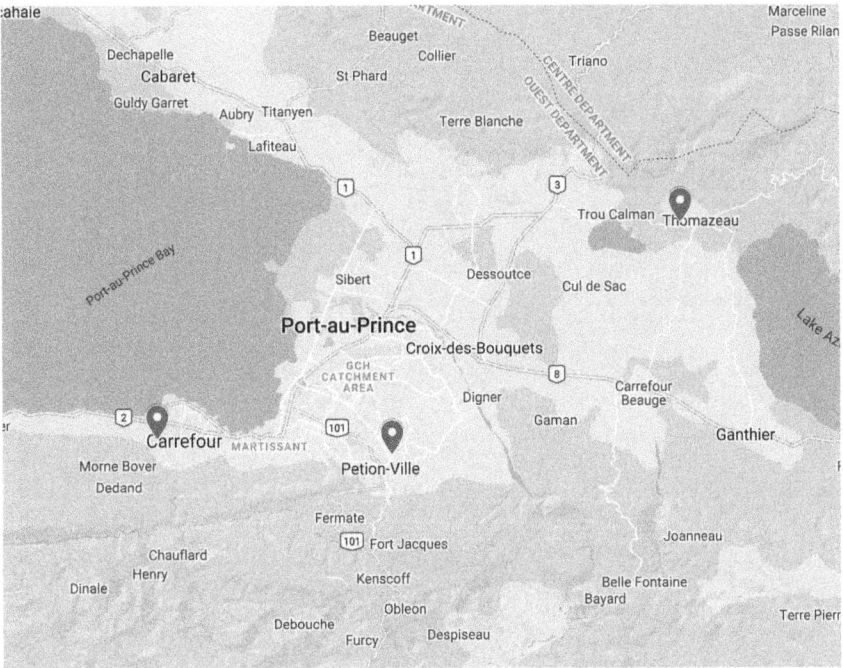

Map 2. Port-au-Prince and surrounding municipalities. Google Maps.

CONTENTS

ACKNOWLEDGMENTS

Haitians of enormous generosity of spirit gave me access to minutiae of their everyday life and to their most private thoughts, in which I sought and found societal significance, and which are thus the foundation of this book. I owe them a considerable debt because without them this work would not have been possible. They were active collaborators, to whom I promised anonymity. I wish I could thank them individually in acknowledging their contribution here.

Don Robotham, as a fellow Caribbeanist and as a friend, was a constant source of guidance with his scholarship and practical wisdom over the years that I brought this project to fruition; I thank him very deeply. I shared my earliest thoughts of a research project on privilege and nationalist ideologies in the Haitian elites with him, Marc Edelman, Ida Susser, Jeff Maskovsky, Mark Schuller, and the late Leith Mullings. I thank them all for their critical remarks, which were crucial to my earliest mental map of the present study. I also thank Mark for a long telephone conversation that was most helpful to my imagining of Haiti as "field" of inquiry rather than "home" in the months before I left for Port-au-Prince, and I am grateful to the Wenner-Gren Foundation for funding the fieldwork.

I thank Deborah Thomas for her thorough critique of a detailed outline of the study in the summer of 2016, after I had completed an early draft of the manuscript. I began to envision the final shape of the book from her remarks. Several colleagues in and out of anthropology read the first draft that I submitted for review to the University Press of Mississippi. The critical remarks of Don Robotham, Jane Schneider, Anton Allahar, Kalli Valadakis, and Garvey Musumunu considerably helped my subsequent revisions. Mark Schuller helped me tighten the thematic focus of the analysis; Michel DeGraff helped me contextualize my transcription of privileged Haitians' Creole speech, which does not conform to academic Haitian Creole orthography; and Alex Dupuy helped me clarify a problematic of positionality that I delineate in the preface. I am grateful as well to the anonymous UPM reviewers. Their critique was immensely helpful to me, especially a set of comments on my engagement with gender and Haitian exceptionalism.

Throughout the time that I worked on the book, I drew valuable insight as well on Caribbean history and postcolonial society in impromptu chats with my steadfast friends Calvin Holder, David Traboulay, and Ismael Garcia-Colón at the College of Staten Island. As a career administrator on the campus, I am also forever appreciative of the paths they created for me to feel at home with the CSI faculty. Edward Sammons is quite likely unaware of how much my thought on Haiti owes to our myriad conversations in New York and at conferences of the Caribbean Studies Association between 2011 and 2014. Of course, while I am indebted to all these scholars for their critical advice, I remain solely responsible for the use I made of it.

To help me ground an important section of the manuscript that I was working on at the time, Marcus Plaisimond re-created for my benefit the entire ritual of the raising of the flag on weekday mornings in Haiti during the Duvalier dictatorship. His inspired performance of François Duvalier's Oath of Fidelity to the Flag was spot-on, with a rendition of both Duvalier's voice and that of his alter ego echoing his words. I thank him very much. Anton Allahar's early interest in this work was priceless encouragement to carry it through completion amidst myriad responsibilities as a parent and as head of a major administrative department at the College of Staten Island. I thank him and Natasha Barnes for their support as coeditors of the Caribbean Studies Series at UPM. For their patient guidance, I thank Vijay Shah, the series' acquisitions editor, associate editor Lisa McMurtray, who continued to shepherd the project after Vijay left the press, and project editor Valerie Jones.

Finally, and not least, my thanks to my soulmate and life partner, Marie Étienne Benoit; my daughter, Joanne Anaïse; and my twin sons, Philippe-Edner and Richard-Olivier. They were a reliable—perhaps I should say, a stoic—sounding board for my thoughts on race and class, on Haiti and Haitians, and on the human condition, throughout the years that I worked on the book.

LIST OF ABBREVIATIONS
AND ACRONYMS

AAA—American Anthropological Association
BNC—Banque nationale de crédit
BNRH—Banque nationale de la République d'Haïti
BRH—Banque de la République d'Haïti
CEP—Conseil électoral provisoire
CIMO—Corps d'intervention et de maintien de l'ordre
CSI—College of Staten Island
FAd'H—Forces armées d'Haïti
FNCD—Front national pour le changement et la démocratie
Fokal—Fondasyon konesans ak libète
FRAPH—Front pour l'avancement et le progrès haïtien
IDP—Internally Displaced Person
ISPAN—Institut de sauvegarde du patrimoine national
MINUSTAH—Mission des Nations Unies pour la stabilité en Haïti
NGO—Non-governmental organization
PAIN—Parti agricole industriel national
PL—Parti libéral
PN—Parti national
UFDC—University of Florida Digital Collections
UN—United Nations
VSN—Volontaires de la sécurité nationale

POSITIONALITY, METHOD, AND THE HAITIAN VOCABULARY OF COLOR

Themes that percolate in this work of social science percolate in my personal history, and I could not help but be mindful of my situation in the research field. My paternal great-grandfather, Septimus Marius, was a black man, a jurist, a statesman, and an army general. In letters and other documents dating to the nineteenth century, his penmanship and command of the French language are as fluid and effortless as one would expect from a privileged Haitian. In the late 1890s, he was minister of war and the navy for President Tirésias Simon Sam of the Parti national. He also served in the administration of Sam's successor, Nord Alexis, after which he shortly lived in exile in Jamaica. After he returned to Haiti, he served again as minister of war and the navy, and in an interim during this tenure was also "charged with the Departments of Finance and Commerce," for President Antoine Simon (1908–1911) of the Parti libéral, the Parti national's archrival (Pan American Union 1911, 365). He appears in that role in Zora Neale Hurston's (1990) allegorical-ethnographic account of Simon's rise and fall.

At the onset of the American Occupation of 1915–1934, one of Septimus's sons, my grandfather, was married to a cousin-in-law of Sudre Dartiguenave, a mulatto installed as president (1915–1922) by the Occupiers "whose name is anathema to Haitian nationalists" (Trouillot 1990a, 30–31). Dartiguenave's cousin was my paternal grandmother. In the late 1940s, a white US heiress

visiting Haiti met two of my father's brothers "at a party [for] a sprinkling of
Americans and members of the Haitian *élite*" (Miller 1981, 19). As she recounts
in her memoirs, "one [was] short and light-complexioned, the other tall and
dark" (20). The tall and dark one, "uncle" Arsène, "an upper-class educated
Haitian" (97), was a contributor to the journal of cultural criticism *Les Griots*,
the quasi-official organ of "noirisme," a black-nationalist current that would
become the ideological backbone of the political action of François Duvalier, Haiti's infamous dictator. The US heiress married uncle Arsène not long
after they met. Before they divorced in the 1950s, they lived in the US and
Mexico, where he received a PhD in social anthropology. During that time,
Paul Eugène Magloire was president of Haiti (1950–1956), my father traveled
on an official passport, and the first lady was matron of honor at his first
wedding. Upon becoming president in 1957, Duvalier stripped Magloire of his
citizenship and exiled him. My father and his siblings nonetheless retained
access to state power as Duvalier had long been a good friend of the family.

In the 1970s, my father, who began his career at the Banque nationale de la
République d'Haïti (BNRH) in the 1940s, was concurrently—on distinct lines
of employment and compensation—director of the state sugar monopoly
and treasurer of the international airport.[1] In my recollection of conversations with him when such things began to be of interest to me in secondary
school, he told me he did both those jobs on behalf of the BNRH, where he
drew a third salary as an officer of the bank. At his death in January of 1985,
when I was twenty-two years old and had recently completed my studies
for a Bachelor of Fine Arts in film at New York University, he was a retiree
of the Banque nationale de crédit (BNC), a BNRH spin-off. His last formal
title at BNC, *Fondé de pouvoir* (Vested with Power), indicates an embodiment of institutional powers. While he lay dying at Canapé Vert hospital in
Port-au-Prince, my former pediatrician—a cousin—came to visit. He was
now the pediatrician of the children of François Duvalier's son Jean-Claude,
the current dictator, and his mulatto wife, Michelle. Shortly afterward came a
retired BNRH *Président-Directeur Général*, who spoke of how fast the years
had passed since he last saw me.

Thus, in investigating social relations and practices around color in the
privileged classes of Haiti, I was very much a "native" anthropologist, to a
significant extent studying milieus in which I grew up. I consequently gave
due thought to my relationship to the field of study before I arrived there,
throughout the time I was there, and after I had returned home in New York

to write up my interpretations of it. I revisited disciplinary lessons learned in anthropology's postmodern moment nearly two generations earlier, when the discipline confronted the "problematic of representation" that would inhere in any enterprise that proposed to tell itself and the world who and what *other* people were. Throughout the project, objective moments of my family history such as those I sketch above reminded me, the *anthropologist*, that in the field I, too, was a privileged *Haitian* among the privileged subjects of my study. I also was a black, and black-nationalist, Haitian. None of all this, of course, in and of itself would have prevented me from also being an ethnographer. In this particular field, I nonetheless had to be aware of the Haitian I was, if I were to become what an ethnographer should be. I indeed was continually able, I believe, to keep anthropology's "canonical . . . distance" from the object of study (Narayan 1993, 680).

In this work, I sometimes rename and reframe my *Haitian* experience of Haiti through the anthropological lens (Narayan 1993), my engagement taking at such times an auto-ethnographic dimension. Occasionally, I not only am a native ethnographer "talking back" to anthropology (Jacobs-Huey 2002, 792), I am also an anthropologist talking back to other disciplines, which, like anthropology in general, have taken the paradigmatic Blackness of the Haitian nation at face value. To understand how color operates in the politics of class privilege in Haiti, I have fruitfully adapted the argument that it is more useful to apprehend the "*work* race does" than to define its content and note its presence in social organization (Holt 2002, 27). In the field, I found "*a* world" (Merleau-Ponty 1999, xi), which "furnishes the text" this ethnography relates "to *the* world" (xiii; emphasis added), whereupon the ethnographic method cannot but lead me to a "moral anthropology" (Fassin 2012).[2] In their African origins, Haiti's founders were black people. They nonetheless fashioned a society in which inheres an intense oppression of other black people for the reproduction of a black elite. I could not shrink from a rigorous interrogation of their legacy simply because they founded their nation-state in epochal defiance of white supremacy.

The Haitians who allowed me to make sense of a Haitian condition by observing and participating in their public and private lives did not merely provide me with *information*. They actively collaborated with me on the formation of my understanding of Haiti that I bring to this monograph. I sought to let all of their voices transpire in the study to ensure a substantial polyvocality that might do justice to the complexity of their everyday realities. In a place of such immense gaps in all forms of wealth between the privileged and the nonprivileged, social injustice and the forces that produce them could seem atemporal.[3] While I sought to apprehend ethnographic significance in a temporally and spatially specific present (Sanjek 1991), I also constantly sought to keep the present ethnographic encounter in diachronic linkages to local and global social histories. I remained alert that neither collaborator nor ethnographer owned the reality of the encounter but inevitably negotiated its meanings in the intersubjective space (Crapanzano 1985). I maintained the analytic distance in the transparency of the moment, which I sought to produce by bracketing my collaborator's presence between an acknowledgment of my own critical presence and an awareness of my interpretive choices as I turned the lived experience of the field into text. Always, I remained engaged with anthropology's historic commitment to demystifying social inequalities.

I conducted the investigation through participant-observation, interviews, and documentary analyses of public and private histories. My field collaborators were mostly from Haiti's political, economic, and intellectual elites, and from the middle classes. I analytically collapsed elite and middle-class experiences together to arrive at a study of relations between and within formations of privilege. These collaborators did not always control significant financial capital. Some in fact lived precarious lives. However, they invariably enjoyed definite access to the upper reaches of social and political power. My research subjects represented the full range of Haiti's social colors and political spectrum. They included cabinet members, civil servants, a former president of the Republic, members of the Duvalier family, former presidential candidates, a former prime minister, parliamentarians, entrepreneurs, liberal professionals, leaders of iconic business enterprises, a director of the country's largest private bank, a director of the Banque de la République d'Haïti (BRH), and leading writers, artists, and intellectuals.[4] They also included collaborators whose everyday lives were well outside the elites and middle classes and whose often contrapuntal perspectives helped elucidate the effective meanings of what privileged Haitians think, say, and do.

I did the principal work in the field in the Port-au-Prince metropolitan area over approximately seven weeks during three trips from my base in New York City in March–April 2011, December 2011, and October–November 2012. By the time I first arrived, I had secured the commitment of the majority of a core group of over a dozen collaborators. I was intimately competent in the vocabularies of contemporary Haitian social relations, and I knew my way around the social geography of Haiti's elites. Arriving in the field, I had minimal need to dedicate time to subject recruitment or acculturation, and the compact periods on the ground were intensely productive. The better to capture the range of thought and action of privileged Haitians as subjects of the global West, the fieldwork became multisited (Marcus 1995). The Caribbean Studies Association annual conference was a fruitful site of participant-observation in the Haitian intellectual elite in Curaçao (2011), Guadeloupe (2012), and Grenada (2013).

To a lesser extent, I spent time on the ground with collaborators realizing their privilege in trips to the New York area and at the 2012 edition of the art fair Art Basel Miami, or who maintained their privileged lives after relocating in the diaspora. I researched genealogies in the digital collections of the Association de généalogie d'Haïti. I read primary sources of the colonial era in the Mangonès Collections of the University of Florida Digital Collections (UFDC), and of the nineteenth and twentieth centuries in the Kurt Fisher and Eugène Maximillien Collections of the Schomburg Center for Research in Black Culture in New York City. In the UFDC, I read issues of *Le Nouvelliste*, Haiti's newspaper of record, published between August 1, 1899, and December 15, 1979; and of *Haiti Sun* (an English-language weekly published in Port-au-Prince between 1950 and 1962), *Revue indigène* (July 1927–January 1928), and *Les Griots* (July 1938–March 1940).

Given the global context of the production of the meanings of social color in Haiti, where conditions elsewhere in the Caribbean or the Western postcolony were significant to my interpretation of the ethnographic field, I sought to make the significance transparent. More specifically, wherever in the postcolony I find racial or color identities being deployed toward the reproduction of class privilege in similar ways as in Haiti, I tease out the similarities within the analysis of the Haitian case. Altogether, in apprehending the ethnographic field, I conjugated the case of the Haitian postcolonial bourgeois society with others in the Atlantic world, when it seemed the conjugation might elucidate the articulation of race and class as foundational global phenomena of Western modernity. I drew my analytic approach from the argument that socioeconomic inequality in the twenty-first century should ideally be addressed in a coordinated global response because it is produced by global processes of late capitalism (Piketty 2013).

The ethnographic interpretive endeavor on privileged life in Haiti entailed speaking to my positionality as an organic actor in the field of privilege. It

Figure P.1. Jean Price-Mars presided over the historic First Congress of Black Writers and Artists, held at the Sorbonne September 19–22, 1956. This much-reproduced print image of an apparently lost photograph shows the participants in the courtyard of the university. Of the eleven in the front row, four are Haitians: Emile Saint-Lot, third from the left; Mrs. Price-Mars (so identified in the official program), fifth; Price-Mars, sixth; and Jacques Stéphen Alexis, ninth. René Piquion (behind Price-Mars in the white suit), the architect Albert Mangonès (in profile behind Piquion), René Dépestre (behind Saint-Lot with arms crossed) and Gérard Bissainthe (tall figure in the center at the far back, aligned with Mrs. Price-Mars) are also among the notable Haitian presence. Among the key figures who originated *négritude*, Leopold Sedar Senghor is seated to the right of Alexis, and Alioune Diop, who organized the conference, is to the left of Saint-Lot and directly in front of Aimé Césaire. Among other major black writers of the twentieth century, Frantz Fanon is second from the left in the third row, and US novelist Richard Wright is the second standing to the left of Piquion. Image courtesy of Gérard Bissainthe.

also entailed speaking to entwined epistemic and ontological positionalities in the global production of knowledge on Haiti and Haitians. Scholars and activists globally imagine and theorize the significance of Haiti's Blackness. As they do, they generally tend to remain unaware that they are reproducing their own positions of privilege in articulation with *classes* of Haitians who operationalize the trope of Blackness in the reproduction of *their* privilege. In this articulation, Haiti's elites are forever aware of the engagement of Atlantic imaginaries with the making of their nation, and the nation's world-historical significance has in turn informed the meanings of these elites to themselves. On the one hand, for example, founding authors of the French black Atlantic *négritude* movement saw its roots in the thought of Haitian ethnologist Jean Price-Mars.[5] On the other, from the 1960s to the 1980s, négritude was central to elite and middle-class Haitians' understanding of what it meant to be *black* in Haiti and on the global stage (fig. P.1).

On the whole, scholars and activists generally engage with conditions of poverty in Haiti from within the epistemic enterprise of seeing and reproducing the nation's Blackness. They generally do this while they concomitantly remain with Haiti's elites and middle classes in an ontological universe of people educated in dominant histories of the Atlantic. Haitians of this world generally speak and write fluently, and "properly," the dominant form of at least one major European language, typically French, alongside their native competence in Haitian Creole. It is a universe that is radically shut from the country's vast majority population of poor people. Not surprisingly, poor monolingual Creole-speaking Haitians do not give much of a hoot about the nation's Blackness projected from above. Alertness to this epistemic problematic of positionality, I suggest, would be helpful to a critical engagement with the condition of the "Black Republic."

I should note here that the importance of French as class demarcation line in the Haitian praxis of privilege had a methodological effect on the making of this monograph. There is an academically sanctioned orthography of the Haitian Creole language. However, in quoting Creole speech of the privileged Haitian throughout the study, I do not use the academically correct spelling. The formally correct written language generally reflects the speech of rural, working-class, and "uneducated" Haitians. Rather, for ethnographic integrity, I use an orthographic inflection that reflects the Frenchified speech of privileged Haitians. In fact, I make this contextual note because a few colleagues who read earlier drafts of the manuscript remarked that I often misspelled Creole words. In one of my reported conversations conducted in Creole, for example, I use the French "neuf" rather than the academically correct Creole "nèf" to reproduce my interlocutor's pronunciation of the word for the English "nine," and "suicidè," approximating the French "suicidaire," rather than the formally correct "swisidè" for the word that means "suicidal." This methodological strategy reflects the French-inflected pronunciation of Haitian Creole as an unmistakable marker of a Haitian's [relatively] privileged class situation.

I can easily grasp why anthropologists would presumptively see a Black Republic upon arriving in Haiti to study conditions and cultures of the country. However, the most apprehensible of my findings on the ground in Port-au-Prince was probably the deep indifference of Haiti's poor majority population to the conceit of the country's blackness authored by privileged people.

Since I left the field, I have not ceased to wonder *why* anthropologists can still so consistently imagine Haiti as a *Black* place *after* their fieldwork. I do not know the answer, but it might reveal that the anthropological imagination is organically impermeable to challenges to the constellation of meanings that the discipline of anthropology has elaborated in the Western cosmologies of race and class. Perhaps the answer might also lie in the epistemic production of the self. In a foundationally racist Western modernity, discourses and practices of blackness can reasonably become sites of resistance to white supremacy and bourgeois capitalist rapaciousness. Thus, blackness might become a technique of making and performing a righteously *radical* self as much as a technique of knowing and representing social phenomena. Scholars or activists who imagine blackness fundamentally as a modality of antiracism, anti-imperialism, or anti-oppression, will *become* righteous and radical in firmly standing up for *blacks*, at which point a due interrogation of blackness can become fundamentally incomprehensible to them.

I should also contextualize my use of the Haitian vocabulary of social color. Jean Price-Mars, one of the most astute thinkers on color and class in Haitian intellectual history, was stymied by its complexity. Having met President Boisrond Canal once, Price-Mars could not decide whether he was a *griffe* or a "mulatto." The distinction between these two particular colors is generally measured in hair texture rather than skin tone. Both being of a relatively light complexion, the griffe would have more or less "nappy" ("black") hair, while the mulatto's hair would be supple. Unable to assign Canal a color by empirical observation, Price-Mars followed historiographic tradition and counted him as a mulatto (Price-Mars 1967). At that point, he was no longer seeing Canal in his somatic appearance but in his class belonging. "Mulatto" indicates here not the social color of Boisrond Canal the person but the color of his social formation in the elite.

Had Canal's somatic characteristics been nearly indistinguishable from that of a "white," Price-Mars would have read his personal color also as "mulatto" without hesitation (cf. Labelle 1987). However, being a mulatto—belonging to the mulatto formation—in contemporary Haiti is not a simple matter of mixed-race ancestry as was the case in Saint-Domingue. It is in the conjugation of complexion—presumably indicating some degree of "white" ancestry, when relatively light—hair texture, and values such as wealth, income, and genealogy. Relatively dark-skinned children of "black" parents might yet arrive at the mulattoization of their persons, and an elite mulatto family's relatively dark-skinned child does not ipso facto cease being a mulatto.

The meanings of "black" are also determined in the social context. Informed by its historic resonance from the race of the nation's Founding Fathers, the term is used to denote a social formation of relatively dark-skinned national subjects that stands in contradistinction to the *mulatto* formation. This is a priori a formation of relatively privileged people because only Haitians in the privileged classes are situated or situate themselves imaginatively in one of the two colorized social formations. To embody a claim on the nation in social and political arenas, subjects of the formation also routinely appropriate "black" in its historic resonance as the color of their persons. Otherwise, in general, constituent subjects of the black formation of privilege systematically avoid using "black" in the description of their persons. They reserve "black" to indicate the social color of the poor person, and they draw on alternative terms for themselves. A *marabou*, for example, is dark-skinned, but with "supple" hair. A *brun* (feminine *brune*), a particularly elastic term, will have skin complexion ranging from dark to just short of what elsewhere might be "white," its elasticity such that it can be used for persons of drastically contrasting complexions across the two formations of color.

Given the complexity of contextual everyday usage, for analytic clarity I avoid using the Haitian descriptive terminology of color in its details, and I describe here only the terms that appear in the text. In general, I use three terms to refer to the social color of the person—*black, clair,* and *mulatto*. Additionally, brun, marabou, and griffe appear in sources with which I engage. In speaking of my collaborators or other privileged subjects, I use "black" to refer to a constituent of the black formation of privilege, although I may also use the term contextually to indicate more generally a relatively dark-skinned Haitian. Similarly, I use a lower case "b" in referring to Haiti as a black country or a black nation, because then I am invoking its foundational population of black people. I capitalize it when referring to the color ascribed to Haiti as a Black Republic in the historiographic literature. Blackness here distinguishes the world-historical significance of the Haitian nation-state. The importance of the Republic in modern global history is found in the race of the historical population that achieved the unprecedented, and still unique, feat of an enslaved people liberating itself by the force of arms and asserting its sovereignty in the very world of its former masters. In the capitalization, this work continually acknowledges the magnitude of the achievement without ceasing to interrogate the political uses of the color ascribed to it.

While mulatto and clair can be used interchangeably as a person's color, in everyday practice both blacks and mulattoes tend to eschew the former in favor of the latter. In the text, I use "clair" descriptively for a mulatto of relatively darker skin tone—someone who would decidedly be "black" in North Atlantic centers of whiteness—and "mulatto" for one whose somatic appearance begins to approach the point where she or he might "pass" for white in the global North. I also use "clair" to describe individuals who would not subjectively see themselves as mulattoes but who by appearance and various forms of capital, including family pedigree, could circulate as such in the mulatto formation. In speaking of nationalists, I use the phrase "black-nationalist" as a noun (with the hyphen) to refer to a black-nationalist subject without giving significance to the person's social color. For all that, as may be evident by now, "color" obtains its local significance in Haiti from the significance of the white-black racial binary of the North Atlantic. Thus, when the analysis engages with global processes around whiteness and its alterities, the language of color may become the language of race.

THE
UNEXCEPTIONAL
CASE OF HAITI

PRIVILEGE IN HAITI AND THE CARIBBEAN'S MODERNITY

I arrived in Port-au-Prince to begin fieldwork on this ethnography on March 24, 2011. I was there to study how ideologies of race and class influence privileged Haitians' engagement with the national condition. I was going to do that empirically as a participant-observer in the lives of my privileged research subjects. I landed at Aéroport Toussaint Louverture in what was axiomatically the first Black Republic to legions of learned people globally, myself included at the time. In my case, I had learned that from my primary and secondary schooling during the dictatorship started by François Duvalier (1957–1971) and inherited by his son, Jean-Claude (1971–1986), and from about a dozen years of postsecondary studies in New York City, the whole augmented by decades of independent reading in popular and learned literatures. A week and a day after my arrival, the field of my investigation shifted significantly.

I was with a black physician, an obstetrician-gynecologist, at Kay Atizan (Artisans House), a trendy bistro in Pétion-Ville, a wealthy suburb in the hills southeast of Port-au-Prince. The questions of interest to me did not change. I still aimed to learn who contested the formation of Haiti's elites, and how. If elite Haitians constituted themselves in a Blackness vs. Mulattoness opposition, what were the political consequences? However, it dawned on me that French-speaking blacks and mulattoes in Haiti's elites and middle classes—*privileged* Haitians—were quite innocuously bourgeois subjects

Figure I.1. A supermarket billboard advertisement on Delmas Road in October 2012, marketing stuff of a modern life in aspirational French to people of Haiti who can afford it. Photo by the author.

of the modern West. I awakened to the fact that I was studying a Western bourgeois society. It also struck me then that billboards throughout Port-au-Prince pitch the slick modernity of the West to a privileged minority of relatively light-skinned and relatively dark-skinned people (fig. I.1), who live among a vast—and vastly dark-skinned—majority population mired in grinding poverty. More or less simultaneously, it seemed to me that to see Haiti as the *Black* Republic in this study was as viable as attempting empirical observation in a labyrinth of smoke and mirrors.

This ethnography's central thesis is that in contemporary Haiti, and throughout the history of the country, class, not color or race, has been the principal site of unity among Haitians. I do not wish to speak of a *national* unity here. I wish rather to say that, in Haiti, class "is the primary vector through which patterns of social inclusion and exclusion are drawn," to borrow Deborah Thomas's so precise formulation (private communication). The work's ultimate ambition as engaged scholarship is to contribute clarity on the political uses of race, color, and nation as symbolic operators in socioeconomic stratification in Haiti and other Western postcolonial bourgeois societies.

Haiti was the first postcolonial place in the West in which nonwhites attained privileges that had categorically been exclusive domains of whites. In fact, when that first happened before the turn of the nineteenth century, the place was neither "Haiti" nor "postcolonial." It was ruled as the French colony of Saint-Domingue by the black military leader Toussaint Louverture. Today, postcolonial *elite* subjects throughout the global West routinely hold powers that reproduce elite privilege and concomitant social inequalities, while becoming in elite discourses *racial* subjects whose "race" is presumptively a formation of oppressed people. How do we reveal who is doing what to whom beyond the race discourse? How do we speak to race and racism, when oppressors "of color" *can* experience racism while coherently standing in solidarity with "white" oppressors, and political resistance by the oppressed below remains fragmented in racialism? In Haiti, a Western place of late capitalism, I found questions such as these the ones worth asking, when the answer worth seeking is a *social* justice *beyond* racial justice (see Scott 2004 on "problem-space").

The Black Republic trope being pervasive as contextual pivot—the fundamental framework of analysis—in the literature on Haiti and Haitians, I write against it throughout this ethnography in order to make the story of Haiti that I found on the ground comprehensible. Below, I first relate the ethnographic encounter with the black physician at Kay Atizan for what it reveals about class, belonging, and identity. I then engage critically with an exceptionalism that obtains in the epistemological veneration of Haiti's presumptive Blackness. I unpack the Black Republic trope, and its reproduction by a global intelligentsia, against historiographic facts of the Haitian experience and of the Revolution that founded it. I do so first in a long historical view, then more directly in relation to the present work as I posit Haiti as a bourgeois society at its foundation.

❧   ❧   ❧

Chatting with the black physician that Friday evening at Kay Atizan as I began my second week in the field, I initially grasped the fallacious exceptionality that obtains from the axiomatic Blackness ascribed to the Haitian nation. The place very much conformed to the construction of Haiti as a locus of transcendent blackness. Its Haitian Creole name, its decorative artifacts and the house band were all evocative of Haiti's vernaculars bequeathed by the African past.[1] Yet it is where it began to transpire to me that *blacks* and *mulattoes* constituting the truly rich and the relatively comfortable educated middle classes share a common "style of being together" (Linnet 2011, 21). It is a cohesive sociality, generally bilingual in French and Haitian Creole, in which Haitians express and cultivate privilege across boundaries of color. More significantly, I also began to grasp, the vast majority of Haiti's population was an object, not a subject, of the national identity in blackness.

Haiti, it already seemed to me at Kay Atizan, was not after all particularly different from other places in the Caribbean or the broader Western postcolony, which I see comprising societies distinctively inflected by an end of European colonization since the late eighteenth century. Behind a dominant narrative that effectively posits a unity in blackness, I began to glimpse a sociopolitical economic stratification, in which class boundaries did not conform to social colors derived from Western racialism. Sociopolitically, I was to find, the indeed generally dark-skinned majority of Haitians is much more meaningfully a formation of monolingual Haitian Creole speakers than a formation of "blacks." They are "about 95%" of the population (DeGraff 2017, 178). When this monolingual majority is conflated with dark-skinned privileged people in the presumptive Blackness of the Republic, their radical sociopolitical marginalization is actively mystified.

I attended kindergarten through high school with the black physician. I left Haiti for college in the USA; he went on to the School of Medicine of the State University of Haiti, followed by stints of specialization in France and at Columbia University in New York. We had not communicated in the intervening decades until I randomly came across his contact information on Facebook the January before I arrived in the field. When he picked me up at home earlier in the evening to go to Kay Atizan, he drove a late-model four-wheel-drive hatchback. He had stopped by the house yet earlier in the afternoon; then, he drove a sedan. On our way to the restaurant, I asked him whether one of the two vehicles was his wife's. It was not. His wife generally drove a third car of the family. Because of its higher clearance off the ground, they use the hatchback at night or when security is otherwise an issue: "Si w bezwen monte twotwa a pou w debloke tèt ou" [If you need to drive over the sidewalk to get yourself out], the physician explained.

Figure I.2. Citadelle Laferrière, also known as Citadelle Henri Christophe after the Founding Father who built it in his Kingdom of the North. Photo by Alex E. Proimos.

As the black physician and I spoke about Haiti and shared news of our private and professional lives at the restaurant, the inconsequential stories of his everyday amounted to a portrait of privileged life. Some were also tales of variously becoming a bourgeois middle-class subject, a Haitian, or a *black* Haitian. They were all told in experiential vocabularies of the modern West. The story of his teenaged daughter setting the agenda of the family's most recent vacation would have a familiar ring to many a middle-class household in the global North. Perusing the Internet, she found a cruise out of a port in Florida and enlisted her younger sister to convince their parents to make that their destination. The physician and his wife eventually made the appropriate reservations to fly to Miami, cruise the Caribbean Sea, and return home. In a simpler mode of family recreation, the physician occasionally takes early morning drives with the children to the rural interior. On these impromptu excursions, they leave at dawn, and the destination is what random town or hamlet they reach from which he can return to Port-au-Prince by late morning to attend to the business of the day. His father did the same with him, when he was a boy, and, as it happened, so did mine with me. The physician specifically placed those outings in the context of acquainting his children with Haiti. He furthers the acquaintance with planned trips to such landmarks of the national past as the Citadelle Laferrière (fig. I.2), a massive stone fortress built on a mountaintop near the coastal city of Cap Haitien by Henri Christophe.

Figure I.3. A community fountain in the mountainous rural interior of the South-East Department, about a twenty-minute walk from the last section of the adjacent road accessible by car. Photo by the author.

The day before the physician told me of the excursions with his children, a wealthy fair-complexioned executive, a direct descendant of a mid-eighteenth-century white native of Saint-Domingue, also told me of taking her teenaged son to see the Citadelle. She told me she took him there in the wake of the 1994 US military occupation, which brought President Jean-Bertrand Aristide back from exile. She had been adamantly opposed to Aristide's return. She wanted to show her son the grandeur of his country's past, she told me. Incidentally, the black physician was no fan of Aristide either. In the same conversation, the fair-complexioned executive alluded to herself as *white*, and, as I discuss further in chapter 5, she remains the only native of Haiti of Haitian parents living in Haiti I have ever known to think of herself as a white Haitian. For her nonetheless, as for the black physician, the visits to the countryside and to the national patrimony were effectively journeys of becoming Haitian in the momentary encounter with the rural place and the glory of the imagined past (fig. I.3).

During our evening at Kay Atizan, the physician also recalled a family dinner with bemused paternal affection. He and his wife were eating with their
children at La Plantation, an upscale restaurant in Pétion-Ville where the cost
of dinner for two can easily reach upwards of US$100.[2] As they perused the
menu, their younger daughter insistently asserted her desire for "mayi moulen"
(cornmeal), her general preference also at home. The dishes at La Plantation
are heavily inflected by French culinary traditions. In popular memory, mayi
moulen was served to the slaves of the colony. It remains a staple in the diet of
the peasantry and the urban poor in lieu of the more expensive "diri" (rice).
In telling me the story, the physician let it be clear that neither he nor his wife
objected to their daughter's predilection for mayi moulen. Their concern at
the restaurant was to convince her to settle for what was available. Thus, a
family—the daughter in her taste for mayi moulen, her parents in legitimating
that taste—found a populist commonality with the poor Haitian, a pivotal
preoccupation of what I refer to as Haitian black nationalism, the discourses
and practices which in aggregate posit Haiti as a black nation.

In the physician's telling of the family's meal at La Plantation, he, his wife,
and his children became *black* Haitians inasmuch as they affirmed the validity
of the cultural vernacular of the nation's *poor* black majority and inasmuch
as they practiced—selectively, in context—ways of being that are evocative of
the life of *those* blacks. However, at Kay Atizan, as it had been at La Plantation,
the physician realized the ideological identity in blackness at an unbreachable
social distance from the nation's immense majority of poor subjects.

The physician, whose late father was an entrepreneur, is also an incidental
landlord. He is the owner-developer of an impressive office building with
prime frontage on a major thoroughfare in the vicinity of the international
airport in Port-au-Prince. He told me how that came to be also that Friday
evening at Kay Atizan.

A commercial group once wanted to buy a parcel of land, which the physician's father owned in downtown Port-au-Prince. The group was controlled
by a wealthy mulatto businessman, whose father had been one of numerous
mulattoes to serve as high-level officials in the Duvalier dictatorship.[3] The
sale of the downtown lot was negotiated at the physician's house (his childhood home). During the meeting, small talk came to another parcel that his
father owned in another commercially vibrant part of the city. The mulatto
businessman suggested to the physician's father that he develop it. However,

the physician's family did not have the means to do so. The businessman also controlled a bank. To solidify the relationship with the physician's father, he arranged for a mortgage through his bank. He made the mortgage possible by waiving a bewildering array of conditions through which the economic elite has controlled access to credit and the business terrain.[4] Leading the project for his family, the physician hastily ordered architectural plans, closed on the mortgage loan, and broke ground. The resulting building is now a notable hub of professional offices. Its value stood at well above a million US dollars, and the remaining amount on the mortgage a third of that, at the time I was in the field. It is a store of social and economic capital passed on by the physician's father to his children and potentially to his grandchildren.

So it was that well before I could fully contextualize in a broader set of social relations the tidbits the physician shared with me over beer, wine, and snacks at Kay Atizan, before we even left the restaurant, two basic facts seemed to transpire about the politics of color in Haiti. On the one hand, it seemed, the colorized fragments of the nation's privileged subjects actually recover societal cohesion in the practice and reproduction of privilege, notwithstanding the political fact of the fragmentation over nearly the entire history of the country. On the other, I also began to think, privileged dark-skinned Haitians do not live a common blackness with the country's socio-politically marginalized blacks. These preliminary insights effectively became twin working hypotheses. In the event, they were correct. Laura Nader (1972) wondered what might be found through an anthropological study of elites rather than the poor. After indeed doing just that in Haiti, I found without a doubt a Western bourgeois society in which cultures of power and afflu-ence reproduce *classes* of relatively powerful and affluent people, whom they simultaneously separate from classes of powerless and poor people. The experience of privilege amongst colorized Haitians suggests that race is indeed "the modality through which" one lives one's class situation in racial-ized Western structures of dominance (Hall 1980, 341).

❧   ❧   ❧

An interrogation of what I call the Black Republic narrative eventually became the lynchpin of this study. It undergirds my apprehension of the operations of color and class in the reproduction of social privilege and inequality in Haiti. In the broad outlines of the country's history, slaves in the north of Saint-Domingue began a *soulèvement général* in August of 1791, and the massive insurrection transformed itself into an implacable revolutionary confrontation with the colonial system of slavery. "Freedmen" and "freeborn" eventually joined the movement and significantly inflected it. The freedmen had been granted freedom from slavery over the years; the freeborn, descendants of slaves, were mostly of racially mixed ancestry but not exclusively. After a dozen years of turbulent conversation with the French Revolution of 1789 around the themes of liberty and equality, the Saint-Domingue Revolution defeated an expeditionary French army, the remnants of which evacuated the colony in November 1803. On January 1, 1804, the Revolutionaries renamed the land Haiti and declared their political sovereignty in the Independence of a new nation-state.

The historiography retains four *Pères fondateurs* (Founding Fathers) of the nation, preeminently Jean-Jacques Dessalines, a former slave last owned by a black man. Of the other three, Toussaint Louverture, a black freedman, had become a slaveholder by the time of the insurrection (Girard 2012, 2016; Johnson 2014; Bell 2007; de Cauna 2004), but he nonetheless took control of the Revolutionary colonial state as an uncompromising foe of slavery; Henri Christophe, also a black freedman, was born in Grenada; and Alexandre Pétion, the freeborn son of a wealthy white man and a free mixed-race woman, was educated in Paris. The four indeed led a black people to crush Napoleon Bonaparte's plan to restore slavery in Saint-Domingue. Through boundless heroism and creativity, they vanquished white supremacy at the dawn of the bourgeois capitalist West.

The Black Republic narrative is nonetheless an origin story that draws on the historiography to canonize the blackness of Haiti's Founding Fathers. The tale essentializes the Founders' race to make of it a transcendent symbol of resistance to racist-imperialist aggression by dominant (white capitalist) powers of the modern West. That is understandable. However, as I aim to frame the Founders as sociopolitical actors actually *being* in the eighteenth-century Atlantic, it is not too fine a point to make that Jean-Jacques Dessalines's last male owner, the black man Janvier Dessalines, was the second husband of Toussaint Louverture's daughter Marie-Marthe (Girard 2016, 76; 2012, 555); the next to last, Philippe Jasmin Désir, "an affluent free black" (Girard 2016, 63), was her first. Between the two, the slave Jean-Jacques, who was his owners' most valuable human property "at 1,500 livres" (Girard 2016, 72), worked for Louverture the slavemaster after Désir leased his small coffee plantation to his father-in-law in August of 1779. Louverture eventually returned the estate, and Marie-Marthe inherited it upon Desir's death in 1784. After she subsequently married Janvier Dessalines, the latter gave Jean-Jacques his surname.

Besides eliding indelicacies of the Founding Fathers' pre-Revolutionary positional relations, the narrative of Haiti's Blackness, a product of political and intellectual elites, is very bad at capturing the fact, and the implications of the fact, that the Founders did foundational violence within the Revolution to *other* black people, generally African-born, who did not share their vision of a nation-state. Quite remarkably, in that origin story as in the historiographic scholarship proper, there is an absolute silence on a yet more crucial fact. The Founding Fathers and the Revolutionary elites who triumphed over the French were generally *creoles*, born in Saint-Domingue or, in the case of Christophe, elsewhere in the Americas. Between the text and the context of the Haitian Act of Independence, which I read in the historical contextualization of the study in chapter 1, they clearly did not extend citizenship to the natives of Africa present at the creation of the new nation, about half of the total population, perhaps more.[5]

Today's peasantry and its migrants in towns and cities are, sociopolitically and culturally, descendant formations of Saint-Domingue's enslaved native Africans, who generally lacked the creole slave's residual acquaintance with European cultures. As Leslie Manigat, a scion of the black political elite and former President of the Republic, would confidently assert in the twenty-first century, in Haiti the "'poor is that person who does not have access to Western culture'" (Ribeiro Thomaz 2005, 144). Those who bear the brunt of deep sociopolitical economic injustice in the country do in fact live at a more or less absolute distance from the dominant cultural modes of the West. Their historical condition and its genealogy are continually mystified in the dominant tale of the nation as a seminal site of triumphant blackness. The fetishism of national Blackness in the narrative thus aligns with the uses of fetishized race in sociopolitical organization by white-supremacist colonial regimes. In line with what Alex Dupuy has said of the fetishism of race in Saint-Domingue, the fetishized Blackness of Haiti is an ideology born of exclusionary social relations and a deeply inequitable division of labor (Dupuy 2015).

For the coherence of my critique of the Black Republic narrative with the history of the anticolonial African-born insurgents, throughout the text I speak of the *Saint-Domingue* rather than the *Haitian* Revolution. In this methodological choice, I evoke two facts about the genesis of Haiti. The first is that people of the colony of Saint-Domingue made the revolution that resulted in the founding of Haiti. The second is that not all the people who made the revolution wanted to express their sovereignty in the form of the nation-state.

The African natives generally fought for radical freedom from slavery and *any* central state authority (Barthélémy 1989). In addition to their campaigns against the French army, they insistently waged a losing war on the eventual Founding Fathers' political vision of Independence. Their dissent and defeat are no small historic details. On the one hand, making the Revolution *Haitian* delegitimizes the dissenting African agency within the Revolutionary project. On the other, it does symbolic violence to the memory of the African dissenters and to their sociopolitical descendants in contemporary Haiti. When the phrase appears—in quotes—in the text, I use it solely to represent the usage of other scholars whom I invoke. I do speak of the Haitian *War of Independence*, because the phrase refers to the battles that Dessalines, Pétion, and Christophe fought against the French from the middle of 1802 to their conclusive victory in November of the following year. It is the war through which those three Founding Fathers realized their distinctly creole project of a sovereign nation-state in the Atlantic world that prefigured the West.

If this study entails an unpacking of Haitian black nationalism, it in no way can diminish the enormity of the achievement of the enslaved people of Saint-Domingue in successively destroying slavery in the colony and the Napoleonic army sent to restore it. However, the political meanings of the achievement locally must be apprehended in its due global context. The modes of social privilege and social inequality in contemporary Haiti are closely bound to the fact that, upon winning the War of Independence with France, the Founding Founders realized their political sovereignty in the nation-state, a quintessential invention of European modernity. In doing so, they effectively committed themselves to approximate in the new nation social features of colonial Saint-Domingue—nodal features—that articulated with the political, economic, and cultural requirements of the emergent bourgeois capitalist global order. That arguably was the beginning of the tragic dissipation of the promises of the anticolonial struggle in postcolonial geopolitical realities (Scott 2004).

Not surprisingly, the Saint-Domingue Revolutionaries' sovereign state adopted a protocapitalist mode of socioeconomic organization, which stretched the brutalities of the nation's productive mechanisms to the limits

countenanced by norms of the day. Racialism, another defining feature of the
Atlantic political economy, also unsurprisingly remained politically instrumental in the Revolutionaries' new society, and its uses by the dominant
groups remained historically adaptive. Also quite logically, to negotiate their
position on the global terrain efficiently, the new nation's elite appropriated
European cultures that dominated the Atlantic global order. The Revolutionary elites' descendant formations have inherited the requisite articulation of
the nation's social, political, and economic organization with the requirements of the global order. Considering this existential reality, I seek to create
in this ethnography an investigative "problem-space" where the interest is not
so much in "particular problems" of sociopolitics, including the problematic
of race, but in the urgency to imagine answers that "seem worth" imagining,
if we are to pose "questions . . . worth asking" in light of our postcolonial
historical detritus (Scott 2004, 4).

In anthropology's defining tradition of the ethnographic gaze destabilizing
the taken-for-granted, this report emerged from the field in critical conversation with a vast array of foreign and Haitian thinkers who have analyzed
Haiti's privileged classes from theoretical premises. Michel-Rolph Trouillot's
(1990a) historical anthropology of the Haitian state standing against the
nation is essential reading for a social science of contemporary Haiti. It is
an exhaustive investigation of the social, political, and economic contexts
of class privileges and related, exceedingly deep inequalities. Trouillot links
the immiseration of the majority of the population to antiblack racialist
thought and practice. The sociologist Jean Casimir reprises this thesis yet
more forcefully in speaking of the elites' suppression of the African cultural
heritage in national expression (2000; 2009b). Yet Trouillot's and Casimir's
understanding of social relations in Haiti's elites—as that of most foreign
and Haitian scholars—is limited by a lack of critical inclination to link the
nation's Founding Fathers systematically to the debilitating conditions of the
nation's oppressed people.

In both Trouillot and Casimir, the investigation is duly critical of the reproductive structures of inequality at the foundation of the state. The investigation also problematizes actions of the nation's founders in both their
lifestyles as social subjects and their modes of governance as political actors.
However, the analysis generally comprises these two investigative moments
as two distinct lines of critique. The distinctively elite ways of pre- and post-
Independence elites, their tactical and strategic actions as people of power

in politics and economy, and the life conditions of the nation's powerless are read as disaggregated phenomena in the critique. When the inquiry arrives at the condition of the nation today, it remains incisive on the deployment of the state as instrument of sociopolitical economic oppression. However, because of the prior critical disaggregation, there is a mystification of the sociohistoric links between contemporary inequalities produced or facilitated by state agency and the Founding Fathers. Almost inevitably, the Founding Fathers, the poor, and the contemporary formation of privileged dark-skinned subjects are collapsed together in the fictional Blackness of the Republic, to be imagined as a singular people of fundamentally common interests.

Both Trouillot and Casimir, and the global intelligentsia's thinking on Haiti in general, work in an epistemological current that is hugely influenced by C. L. R. James's study of *The Black Jacobins: Toussaint Louverture and the San Domingo Revolution* (Garrigus 2006). Although James (1963) is amply justified in asserting the world-historical significance of the Revolution, he conflates antiracism and antislavery with antiexploitation. The conflation leads him to read promises of justice and liberation that in fact the Revolutionaries never made, and it is central to his legacy in the historiographic tradition on Haiti. Trouillot, in particular, is emblematic of anthropologists and scholars in other disciplines working within James's understanding of the meanings of the Saint-Domingue Revolution. Their scholarship may unequivocally show that the Revolutionary state disciplined formally freed agricultural workers in a regime of labor extraction that considerably resembled their previous working conditions as enslaved people. Yet, with the evidence stated, they generally cannot arrive at an unambiguous conclusion that the Revolution, while assertively defeating slavery and white power, showed no interest in undoing the gross social inequalities that conditioned class privileges of the Revolutionary and post-Independence elites.

As James reproduces stereotypes of mulatto selfishness (Garrigus 2006), his influence is perhaps also present in the frequent reading of political agency through color, which has considerably contributed to the fragmentation and incoherence of liberalism in Haitian politics. That the conflation of color and political position is analytically chimerical is cogently clear in Trouillot's wholesale dismissal of Haitian liberalism at its formal roots in the nineteenth-century Parti libéral (Trouillot 1990a, 126–27). The PL membership consisted mostly of well-off mulattoes, and its slogan, *le pouvoir au plus capable* [power to the most capable], was a theme that underlay

nineteenth-century mulatto nationalism since the early 1800s. Trouillot
nonetheless reads the Parti libéral through its two best remembered theo-
reticians, Anténor Firmin, an intellectual and politician, and Edmond Paul, an
economist, both black men from distinctly black families. Yet Trouillot concludes dismissively that the PL was the definitive mulatto party. He also reads
the PL in contrast to the Parti national, headed by Lysius Salomon, another
black. The PN's slogan was *le pouvoir au plus grand nombre* [power to the
majority], alluding to Haiti's majority *black* population, and both the party
and Salomon are the nineteenth-century wellspring of today's black nationalism. However, Salomon's genealogical presence is not visible in contemporary
Haiti's mulatto elite only because of gender conventions. His only child, Ida,
was a girl.[6] He had her with the second of his two white French wives, and
both of Ida Salomon's own marriages were to light-skinned Haitian men.

As a public personality, Salomon's daughter is remembered as the poet
Ida Faubert, bearing the surname of her second husband, whose name was
also borne by their son. In his marriages, Salomon, the father of modern
Haitian noiriste thought, concretely advanced the lightening of privilege in
Haiti and his mulatto daughter, in her mulatto son, effectively attended to
the mulatto preoccupation with reproducing lightness of complexion in the
lineage.[7] I thus do not approach *la question de couleur* [the color question] as
a "cultural" problematic of color and identity but as a material web of social,
political, and economic relations.

❧   ❧   ❧

To make sense of the operations of color and class amongst the privileged of
Port-au-Prince, I had—so to speak—to unlearn the historical sketch of the
Haitian nation that has become a canonical template in many an introduction
to popular and scholarly texts on Haiti and Haitians. That story, the Black
Republic narrative, inflected by themes and theses of the given author, may
very well be aware of class lines amongst Africans and African descendants
who transformed the general slave insurrection in Saint-Domingue into a
sustained revolutionary process. However, it collapses class distinctions in a
commonality of race or color. Fick (1990), for example, speaks of privileged
positions in the division of slave labor, including the enslaved commander
who supervised the vast majority of other enslaved laborers. Yet, when the
analysis moves from the slaves on the plantation to the formerly enslaved

on the Revolutionary field, class drops off the analytic frame. Fick is wholly uninterested in what class continuities from the colonial order might obtain in what she calls with good reason the "Revolution from Below."

The economist Leslie Péan's (2003) *Haïti, économie politique de la corruption* is the rare work that resolutely holds in the one and same moment of critical scrutiny—across boundaries of color—the nation's Founding Fathers together with the reproductive systems of inequality they embedded in the state. I reread the Saint-Domingue Revolution through Péan's analytic paradigm. Perhaps not surprisingly, the historiography does not particularly note that Haiti's Founding Fathers created for the first time in the postcolonial Atlantic a sovereign Enlightenment domain, in which classes of universally *free* people labored for the accumulation of capital controlled by determinate elite classes. I do, and in doing so I take Haiti to be the first postcolonial *bourgeois* nation-state of the West.

In speaking of "bourgeois," "liberalism" or "bourgeois liberalism" throughout this work, I evoke or speak of the European Enlightenment ideology that underpinned the French Revolution by postulating liberty and equality as core values of all human existence. Moreover, I take a bourgeois society to be one that formally defines itself in these values as universal principles within a capitalist political economy, notwithstanding customary practices to the contrary that may prevail. I use political scientist Andrew Hacker's practical definitions of "liberal" to indicate a political will to support remediation of social ills to the extent that the remedy would not significantly diminish the socioeconomic standing of the political actor. I make no attempt to assess the efficacy of liberalism as praxis of social equity. However, in using the term I do generally refer to a substantive politics, emblematically expressed in the post–World War II welfare state of the dominant Western nations, through which elites expand the distribution of political, economic, and social privileges for varying degrees of social peace. Thus, when I speak of "progressive" politics and the "left" in this study, I do readily see these modes of political thought and action within the historical scope of bourgeois liberalism (Rosenblatt 2018). Furthermore, I see modern liberal elites as actors in the sort of moral economy that engaged the "crowd," the aristocracy and the emergent bourgeoisie in eighteenth-century England (Thompson 1971).[8]

Liberal politics emerged as an object of the study incidentally. At the time I first arrived in the field in March of 2011, moving about in Haiti's civil society were two former presidents—Jean-Claude Duvalier and Jean-Bertrand

Aristide—representing arguably the two most polarizing moments of Haitian
politics since the turn of the twentieth century. Outgoing President René
Préval, ideologically situated somewhere between those two, was also headed
toward civil life, not exile. Soon, far from a usual moment in Haiti's history,
there would be three former presidents in civil life and one sitting president—
Michel Martelly—in chronically obstreperous dispute with a recalcitrant
legislature. I took the moment to be a significant historical expression of
Haitian political liberalism. I found it important for two reasons. On the one
hand, visions of revolutionary postcolonial socialism had been giving in to
geopolitical realities well before the fall of the Duvalier dictatorship (Scott
2014), leaving liberal democracy as an increasingly respectable object of postcolonial aspirational politics. On the other, since at least the late nineteenth
century, black-nationalist students of Haiti had tended to dismiss the liberal
tradition in Haitian political history as mulatto shenanigans. I thus made the
privileged liberal subject the locus of the overarching research questions. I
sought to understand how color mediates liberal political thought and action
on the nation in the privileged classes.

This work is effectively an "anthropology of Western hegemony." It situates the genesis of Haiti's privileged classes in a Revolution through which
Africans and descendants of Africans, in a transmutation that obtained from
their defeat of the slavery system, reinvented themselves in modes of social
power and knowledge produced by European colonization (Asad 1991). It
is not, or should not be, difficult to fathom that, post-Independence, Saint-
Domingue's blacks and mulattoes, freeborn and freedmen, and slaves and
slaveholders, transformed themselves into national elite classes as adept as
Europeans at mastering European cultures, as adept as Europeans at resolutely extracting surplus labor from rigorously disciplined working people,
and as adept as elites elsewhere in the global bourgeois West at deploying
discourses and practices that manage the political instrumentality of race.
I seek to grasp historically the new privileged sociopolitical subjectivities
informed by the colonial experience that the Revolutionary elites bequeathed
to their descendant formations.

If I argue that class, not color or race, primarily produces the unity of distinctive Haitian socioeconomic formations, I do not argue that color does not
matter in Haitian social organization. Color is of fundamental importance
precisely for the ways in which it shadows operations of class in the contestation of privilege. The fact of the Haitian nation was asserted by towering

figures the likes of whom—by their somatic appearance and the geographic origins of their ancestors—were not expected to be towering figures in the global order, much less towering figures who forced their sovereign entry into the system on their own power.

Justifiably, to people who give voice to the Haitian nation locally and globally, Haiti's Founding Fathers have never ceased to be of world-historical significance in a global context of deeply ingrained racism originating in Europe and its diaspora. In Haitian social relations, this history makes for a complex entanglement of class and color (relative to elite Haitians' internal relations), or of class and race (relative to the nation in the racialist West). In any event, although color remains a powerful vector of belonging, the distinctively black and mulatto groups that it does produce are secondary to a prior formation generated by inclusionary/exclusionary logics of class. For example, according to their socioeconomic situation, privileged Haitians gravitate toward the same types of residence in the same neighborhoods, and they send their children to the same schools, whereupon lines of color emerge. Haiti's privileged subjects may be politically fragmented in color, but they in fact share systematic social relations across color boundaries in public and private spheres to reproduce their respective class situations.

The everyday routines and life trajectory that the black physician shared with me at Kay Atizan were hardly exceptional in the Caribbean context, because they conform to social organization in the region (see Charles 2002). Yet the Blackness of the Haitian Republic, a taken-for-granted reproduced globally, makes Haiti a priori an exceptional nation-state, because no other Caribbean (or Western) country is distinctly and qualitatively imagined "Black" by learned people, whatever its politics or demographics. This exceptionality, in mystifying complexities of Haitian social relations, has led to a crisis in the representation of Haiti and requires due theoretical attention (Clitandre 2011). To take a "theoretical leap" out of Haitian exceptionalism as Trouillot recommends (1990b, 6), I simply write Haiti out of the Blackness of the Republic and into the bourgeois modernity of the Atlantic. In chapter 2, I sketch the country's contemporary privileged classes in the cross-currents of color and class as modern Western phenomena, and I speak to their dehistoricization as a society of the bourgeois West by Buck-Morss (2009).

Historian Ronald Angelo Johnson implicitly acknowledges that Haiti's Founders intended to situate their sovereignty in the political world of the Atlantic. In his history of diplomacy from 1798 to 1801 between Toussaint

Louverture and US President John Adams, Johnson sees their engagement as an Atlantic World Alliance. He nonetheless draws the pathos of the tale from an exceptionalism inscribed in the blackness of Louverture against the backdrop "of the eighteenth century Atlantic world" (Johnson 2014, 94). However, the exceptionality in blackness bears epistemic effects. Like narrators of the Blackness of the Haitian Republic in general, Johnson knows the fact that Louverture was a slave who became a freedman, and then became a slaveholder, but he does not seem to know what analytically to make of the fact. He also grasps that Louverture and his officers became wealthy while commanding "a counterrevolutionary economic program" (2014, 91), a system of plantation agriculture much like that of slavery. Yet, keeping with the discursive schema of the Black Republic narrative, Johnson takes Louverture's words at face value, when he "proclaimed, 'I want liberty and equality to reign in Saint-Domingue'" (107).

In situating Haiti in the history of the Atlantic, I read the political agency of the nation's founding elites not in their race or color but in historical technologies, including discourses of race and color, deployed by dominant Atlantic elites to discipline working people and articulate other processes of social organization. That seemed particularly advisable in light of the "modern blackness" that Thomas (2004) maps in Jamaica, a demographically similar Caribbean island nation. In the 1970s, challenging from below the nationalism of Jamaica's anticolonial creole elites, sociopolitically marginalized black Jamaicans defined their blackness and national belonging at a distance from the Jamaican state (Thomas 2004). By contrast, in 1805 the state itself formally made all Haitians "black" irrespective of complexion. With this measure, Jean-Jacques Dessalines sought to preempt formations of "blacks" and "mulattoes" in the new nation's elite by making it homogeneous in blackness (see Trouillot 1990a, 45–46). However, the nation being engaged in the Atlantic world, national sovereignty did not preempt local refraction of the global significance of whiteness and, through the twenty-first century, mulattoes could not be made to give up the derivative currency of their approximations of somatic whiteness in local social economies.

In a place with a long history of politically operative racial typologies, Dessalines's singular race in answer to politicized color heterogeneity created a potential space for the construction of an *ideal type* of Haitian, particularly one that would negate mulattoes' enduring colorism. That in fact began to happen in the last quarter of the nineteenth century, when a faction of the political elite flipped Dessalines's logic on its head. It claimed power distinctly in the name of the nation's dark-skinned people—the *blacks*—because they constituted the most numerous segment of the national population. Explicitly politicizing their blackness in the contestation of the political terrain with privileged mulattoes, black privileged Haitians made their color the fundamental argument for control of state power. By the middle of the twentieth century, the movement had produced its cultural and political coherence in *noirisme*, a Haitian nationalism that makes the *black* Haitian the ideal national subject, and which I investigate in chapter 3. It culminated with the 1957 election of President François Duvalier, whose dictatorship lasted twenty-nine years, with any number of mulattoes serving it in top positions.

Thus, unlike the phenomenon that Thomas (2004) documents in Jamaica, from the birth of their nation onward, blackness has been historically instrumental in social relations of *privileged* Haitians, and it has articulated from above with state agency. If one remembers that race entails a racial ideology that articulates with conditions of political economy (Dupuy 2015), one will have to wonder what exactly Haiti's black and mulatto elites have been up to with the supposed Blackness of the Republic.

Nationalism being the deployment of symbolic operators around the theme of nation (Verdery 1993), nationalist engagement is a fruitful site in which to engage with Haiti's politics of color and class. Haitian black nationalism—the aggregate of thought and action ideologically positing Haiti as a black nation—remains a focal point of critical analysis, and mulatto nationalism is not, because *mulâtrisme* (mulattoism), the ensemble of distinctively *mulatto* worldviews among privileged Haitians, has been reduced to an ideology of bodily aesthetics that seeks its ideals in the white body. However, as I unpack Haitian exceptionalism in the course of interrogating the Black Republic narrative, I occasionally engage critically with the exceptionality of the mulatto besides the exceptionality in blackness.

The narrative of the nation from a distinctly mulatto viewpoint began to be elaborated in the early 1800s. Mulattoes had entered the postcolonial period in greater numbers than blacks with a French education acquired from colonial positions of privilege, and their nationalist narrative came of age in the middle of the century. It pivoted on a claim that mulattoes constituted the *éclairé* (enlightened) segment of the national population by virtue of their education. Mulatto intellectuals constructed a schema of national history that foregrounded the founding of the *Republic* in 1806 by Alexandre Pétion, the mulatto Founding Father. They posited Pétion as bearer of [Western] civilizational values, in contrast to the purported perfidy of Louverture and the cruelty of Dessalines and Christophe. Thus, the mulatto becomes positively an exceptional subject of the nation.

For much of the nineteenth century, to mulâtriste subjects, the mulatto's most distinctive value to the nation was in being "the civilized representative of the black race" to the white world (Dalencour 1944, 322). However, by the turn of the twentieth century, black formations of privilege had considerably closed the gap in education, and, with masterly agility in European cultural domains, they were increasingly challenging mulatto nationalist discourses. Not surprisingly, sometime around the midpoint of the last century, mulatto nationalism as public discourse and political project lapsed into irrelevance. Among a relatively large black middle class, commanding fluency in and preference for Western cultural ways became as banal as it was among privileged mulattoes. Today, the *mulâtre*'s distinction in aesthetic judgment amounts to an obsession with measuring and reproducing bodily traits of the person that approximate European ideals. This obsession—expressed in mulatto colorism—along with the persistent mulattoness of the upper echelons of economic power, generates a chronically percolating anger among privileged blacks. Mulattoes become collectively a negation of the [Black] nation, generating a negative mulatto exceptionalism in the black-nationalist imaginary. In chapter 4, I explore critically a black qua black sociality of privilege that arises to challenge that negation and reproduces the Blackness of the nation.

The critique of black nationalism is not predicated on a postracial or postcolor vision of Haiti. In chapter 5, the ethnographic moment reveals the mulatto's concrete appreciation of such materialities of somatic whiteness as "good" hair, "straight" nose, and thin lips in addition to lightness of complexion. The moment thus also reveals global white racism inflecting the social economy of a nonwhite people in the valuation of approximations of somatic whiteness. Light skin being a social value in Haiti, as it is in many a postcolonial society produced in the orbit of the West, mulatto Haitians manage it with as much vigilance as they manage other material dimensions of wealth. A black-nationalist mulatto Haitian is not particularly rare, nor is a mulatto who earnestly condemns mulatto color prejudice. What is rather unusual is a black-nationalist mulatto, or a mulatto disavowing color prejudice, who is married to a black person. A mulatto qua mulatto sociality obtains from endogamous practices that reproduce lightness of complexion parallel to the reproduction of economic power in the elite and middle classes.

We ultimately find among the privileged of Haiti "a sexual substructure" that regulates color and class in social mobility, and where mulatto mothers in particular stand guard at "'ethnosexual frontiers'" (Nagel 2000, 109, 113). It comprises gendered modes of managing social color and lightness of complexion in the family. The female body being the conclusive site of the biological reproduction of color, premarital mulatto female sexuality becomes the object of particularly attentive parental surveillance at the boundary of color. The relatively light-skinned Haitian female body is ultimately instrumentalized in an economy of color, a tidemark of colonial racialism that articulates with the political economy of privilege. Blacks operate alongside mulattoes in the economy of color, and the endogamy becomes permeable to external mobility, because of the exchangeability of color for other forms of capital in marriage alliances. Lightness of complexion is but one of the values operating in the negotiation of a privileged class situation. This leads me to apprehend mulatto color prejudice through its material logic, which is the transactional logic of a social economy. In chapter 6, I show that, although mulatto color prejudice does affective violence to black privileged Haitians, and blacks are loath to extend political goodwill to mulattoes, colorism and other class ideologies unite them toward the social, political, and economic marginalization of the poor Haitian.

In chapter 7, I sketch a cross-color unity in the practice and reproduction of privilege. Parallel to the black and mulatto circuits of privileged social experience, there exists a transcendent sociality, in which blacks and mulattoes realize and reproduce their privilege alongside one another. Competencies in dominant Western cultures remain the irreducible barrier to monolingual Haitian Creole speakers. As with the two colorized circuits, even in national vernaculars, Western cultural modalities are the vectors through which social actors enact the "proper forms" of belonging to trans-color spheres of privilege (Bruun et al. 2011), filtering their Haitian Creole speech, for example, through a normative competence in French diction. In chapter 8, I delineate a veritable political economy of Western—particularly French—cultural competence, which I call "knowing white." In the conclusion, I note that, within the competence in Western culture, liberal blacks and liberal mulattoes share a bourgeois sense of the political self that can be spurred to relatively ethical action by social conditions. Yet the liberal black and the liberal mulatto talk past each other, as it were, on the national condition, because one defines the nation in a language of color, which the other steadfastly resists. In a conundrum of hermeneutics, they effectively fail to realize the commonalities of their respective bourgeois experience of the historical moment. I consider what it might take to repair the rupture of liberalism at the boundary of color.

CHAPTER ONE

HISTORICAL CONTEXT

Class, Race, and Nation

The *Acte de l'Indépendance* of Haiti is a most sensible point of departure for the historical contextualization of a work that apprehends Haiti's social conditions not in the triumphs and travails of blackness in the nation's history, but in processes that reproduce the nation's two social formations of color as united classes of privileged people. The two groupings generally constitute a bilingual minority of French and Haitian Creole speakers. As Deborah Thomas points out (private communication), processes of unity should be expected to produce a corollary disunity, and the reproduction of the unified bilingual minority does also reproduce its corollary disunity from the country's vast monolingual Creole-speaking majority. Thus, if so historic a document as the Act of Independence may efface Africans from the national polity, it is a primordial point of historical context for this study. In this chapter, I first undertake an exegesis of the act in its use of the *indigène* (indigenous) to define citizenship. I then trace the historical imbrication of Haiti's elites in the Atlantic and their historical instrumentalization of color in the nation's politics.

The first of the three sections of the act is an official document of the *Armée Indigène*, the Indigenous Army of blacks and mulattoes that won the War of Independence, the final phase of the Saint-Domingue Revolution. In it, the thirty-six signatories formally attest that Dessalines, as "Général en

Chef de l'armée Indigène" [Chief General of the Indigenous army], assembled its highest ranked officers to let them know his earnest intentions to guarantee a stable government to the "*Indigènes* d'Hayti" (emphasis added). At the time, the native populations of Hispaniola, the island that Saint-Domingue shared with the Spanish colony to the east, had long been exterminated in the aftermath of the European invasions that began with Columbus's arrival in the final decade of the fifteenth century. The "indigenous" people referred to in the act are the natives of Saint-Domingue. The second section of the act, the only one of the three signed solely by Dessalines, leaves no doubt about that. It is a Proclamation Au Peuple d'Hayti, whom he greets as "Citoyens" (Citizens). In the one-sentence first paragraph of the section, he states explicitly what he means by "indigenous," when he exhorts the citizens to ensure forever "l'empire de la liberté dans *le pays qui nous a vu naître*" [the hold of liberty in the *country that saw us being born*] (emphasis added). Dessalines then addresses the new citizenry interchangeably as "Citoyens" [Citizens], "Citoyens Indigènes," or "Indigènes d'Hayti."

I do not read Dessalines's definition of citizenship in the Act of Independence in an epistemic vacuum. The leadership of the Indigenous Army comprised colonial native freeborn and freedpeople, former slaves and former slaveholders; it was an alliance of creoles. There were other black armies engaged in the confrontation with the slavery system, the so-called *bandes rebelles* [rebel bands]. They were the African-born bossales, who fought as distinct factions—relative to the colonial natives—from the time the insurrection broke out in 1791. In slavery, they were scorned by the creole freedpeople, who helped transform them from African "captives into slaves" (Casimir 2009b, 25),[1] and by the creole slaves. In the Revolution, they were at war against both the French and the creole alliance uniting blacks and mulattoes from disparate pre-Revolutionary sociopolitical categories. While the creoles eventually fought for Independence, the bossale factions, bearing memories of their native African nonstate societies, fought a war of *liberation*, seeking to be free of state control altogether (Barthélémy 1989).

In January 1802, expeditionary forces sent by Napoleon arrived in the colony under the command of General Charles Leclerc, whose secret mission was to restore slavery. With them were Alexandre Pétion and other mulatto officers who had gone into exile in France following a confrontation with Toussaint Louverture. At the time Leclerc arrived, Louverture, who had established a relatively flourishing but brutal agrarian regime as master of

Saint-Domingue in the late 1790s, was significantly unpopular among both his troops and the civilian population. Initially, it appeared that the mission of the French expedition was to stabilize the Louverturian order. Jean-Jacques Dessalines, Louverture's chief lieutenant, aligned himself with the expedition in April 1802. Henri Christophe and other black military leaders also took their troops to the French army.

The black and mulatto officers who joined the French forces were generally creoles, including freeborn, freedmen, and former slaves emancipated in 1793. They were variously heterogeneous. The freedmen had gained freedom from enslavement through various mechanisms before the abolition of slavery in February 1793; some had also become slaveholders. Together with the freeborn, they were the "free coloreds," for whom mulattoes were the "reference group" even though they included blacks (Dupuy 2004, 8). Within this formation, mulattoes were endogamous and "practiced their own racism against" the blacks, and the latter could not own mulatto slaves (Dupuy 2004, 9). As *anciens libres* [formerly free], the free coloreds nonetheless constituted a grouping that was sociopolitically distinct from the *nouveaux libres* [newly free]. The latter had had none of the degrees of privilege experienced by the *anciens libres* within the slavery system. The black officers who joined the French army with their troops included *anciens* and *nouveaux libres*. The mulatto officers were generally freeborn. Relative to the blacks born in Africa, they all nonetheless together formed a distinct sociopolitico cultural creole group as natives of Saint-Domingue.[2]

The bossales adamantly refused to lay down arms or to join Leclerc's forces. They pressed on with their fight against the French, while also fighting the mulatto and black troops in the French army. The mulatto and black officers in Leclerc's army fought the African armies on behalf of the French from June to October 1802 (Trouillot 1995). When Paris's intent to restore slavery transpired to Dessalines and the other creole officers, they broke with the French to launch the War of Independence proper (October 1802). Alexandre Pétion, the most important of the mulatto officers, recognized Dessalines as the supreme leader of the reconstituted creole army, now christened the *Armée indigène*. The bossales refused to accept Dessalines's authority as they had refused to bow to Leclerc's. Dessalines and his creole alliance fought them again starting in November 1802 and this time defeated them, in April 1803 (see Trouillot 1995, 40). The alliance eventually finished off the French in the Battle of Vertières on November 18, 1803.

It is thus preponderantly clear in the historiography that at the conclusion of the Saint-Domingue Revolution with the defeat of the French at Vertières, mere weeks before Dessalines offered citizenship specifically to the indigènes, the bossales were the indigènes' *other*. It thus also seems preponderantly clear that, in expressly extending citizenship solely to the native-born population of the new country, Jean-Jacques Dessalines withheld citizenship from the African natives. No subsequent official act of the Haitian state ever revisited the position of the bossales relative to the indigeneity of citizenship in The Act of Independence, and I have found no sign of a public conversation on the matter in Haiti's civil society since the founding of the nation.[3]

On the whole, the founding of Haiti was a *creole* project. On January 1, 1804, Dessalines orally proclaimed the founding of the sovereign nation to local populations in the colonial creole lingua franca. At the time of the 1791 general uprising, bossales constituted two-thirds of the total slave population, and over 10 percent of them had arrived the year before (Dubois 2012, 21).[4] They represented up to twenty-four ethnicities, and "blacks" and "Africans" would have been meaningless as indices of human subjects in their native lands (Casimir 2009b, 26). It is eminently imaginable that any number of bossales had not much of an idea what in the world Dessalines was talking about, when he proclaimed the Haitian nation. Ultimately, where the creole victors entered the global world of the Atlantic as sovereign nationals, the defeated bossales dispersed in the interior of the new nation to lay the foundation of the peasantry (Barthélémy 1989, 23–26). Haitian rural folks, quintessential monolingual Haitian Creole speakers, eventually came to see their existential space as *peyi andeyò* (the country on the outside) and themselves as *moun andeyò* (people on the outside).

The Revolutionary elites' apparent denial of citizenship to native Africans is significant to the historical contextualization of this ethnography because it lays bare the fallacy of any notion of a Haitian unity in blackness. As significant is the absolute silence in the extensive scholarship on Haiti and Haitians on the possible meanings of Dessalines's "indigène" vocabulary in defining Haiti's founding citizenry. All three sections of the *Acte de l'Indépendance* were published in their entirety in the initial 1849 edition of Thomas Madiou's *Histoire d'Haïti*, tome 3 (see Madiou 1988b, 146–51), but no scholar of Haiti and no Haitian intellectual in learned or popular literature seem to have ever reflected over the significance of "indigène" in the first two.[5] Madiou does not, but he does reproduce the sociopolitical marginalization of the Africans and their descendants by arguing that the bossales, with faith in "African fetishism," confronted in the creole alliance a "system more civilizing than theirs" (Madiou 1988b, 43). Yet more remarkably, in a recent volume dedicated to the creation, context, and legacy of the Act of Independence (Gaffield 2016), among twelve essays by thirteen authors, including some of the most prominently active historians of Haiti, there is no trace of any interest whatsoever in Dessalines's choice of words to define the Haitian citizen. This epistemological silencing of the apparent denial of citizenship to the bossales by the nation's founding elite facilitates the orthodoxy of national Blackness in Haitian studies, and, among Haitians, the orthodoxy is meaningful only to privileged people.

❧   ❧   ❧

The Saint-Domingue Revolution disrupted the political economy of the Atlantic world (Geggus 2014), but the triumphant Revolutionaries hardly repudiated that global system. They entered it *intentionally* as a sovereign people. As they did, they redrew in the history of Western capitalist modernity the boundaries of who could apprehend and redeploy the ways of thinking and acting that produced and defined its elites. The Revolutionary elites were implacable enemies of white supremacy and its system of slavery, but they nonetheless did not conflate slavery with labor extraction in their radical confrontation with the incipient West, or after Independence. Moreover, in their international negotiations to make the Revolution and to create their nation-state, they were informed navigators of the global racial terrain. Altogether, if one lucidly apprehends the imbrication of Haiti in the Western global order as the intention of its Founding Founders, one begins to see material logics in the contemporary nation, where one might see paradoxes in the Black Republic narrative.

A mulatto-rights movement with no interest in the slaves' conditions lasted from the middle of the 1780s until it was overtaken by the 1791 insurrection. The historian John D. Garrigus (2006, 2009) links it to the historical flow of the Revolution without usurping the dominant significance of the black leaders who came on the scene in the wake of the slaves' uprising. His work is helpful to tease out of the established historiography the historical-material origins of modern Haiti's sociopolitical topography.

The wealthy mulatto slaveholding planter Julien Raymond was "no abolitionist" (Garrigus 2006, 234) when he established himself in Paris in the mid-1780s to advocate for official recognition of political equality between free people of color, particularly the propertied class, and whites.[6] He and other mulatto planters invoked their wealth, enterprise, and loyalty to France in pressing their case. They effectively argued, one might say, that they were no less capable than the white colonists to be architects and custodians of a system that appropriates the labor of a class of working people to enrich a propertied class above them in the social hierarchy. The group tactically recruited blacks as members, and by early 1790 free blacks constituted almost half the membership (Garrigus 2006, 237–40).

While the institution of slavery was never questioned, free blacks were conflated with mulattoes in various decrees from metropolitan France that granted rights of citizenship to the colony's *gens de couleur* [people of color] between March 1790 and May 1791, and free blacks joined mulattoes in the armed campaigns to force their application in the colony after a civil war broke out within the planter class in October 1790 (see Fick 1990, 83, 118–34). Expanding on the work of Carolyn Fick (1990), Garrigus argues that, to destabilize the racial supremacy of their white peers, mulatto planters were actively complicit in a limited slave insurrection in the southern peninsula in early 1791 (2006, 250–52). In August, the massive insurrection broke out in the north. In 1793, acknowledging the fact of the slaves' self-liberation on the ground, the first French Republic decreed the abolition of slavery. By 1796, Toussaint Louverture was increasingly the dominant political and military figure in the colony; by the close of the century, he was its undisputed ruler. Leading the first state in the control of the Revolution, he had revived the plantation economy from its devastation in the first half of the decade. A former freedman slaveholder, he considerably expanded his land holdings after the general emancipation (see Turnier 1989), and his state ruthlessly disciplined former slaves who were now laboring as formally liberated *cultivateurs* (cultivators).

Louverture nonetheless claimed Republican France's ideals of *liberté* for all and *egalité* of all. Julien Raymond, the mulatto slaveholder who had not yet been an abolitionist in the 1780s, joined nine white planters to constitute an assembly that drew up the Constitution of 1801. The document consistently employed the French Republican calendar, and it made Louverture *Gouverneur general à vie* (Governor General for Life) with the right to name his successor. While stating the colony's political autonomy de facto, it also expressly stated that Saint-Domingue remained part of France. One might again say, having restored much of the colony's economic luster, Louverture, in effect, asserted to metropolitan France that blacks of power no less than mulattoes were as capable as whites in orchestrating the accumulation and circulation of capital from a class of working people with no control over wealth that their labor produced.

Dessalines, who was illiterate and monolingual, ordered the formal *Acte de l'Indépendance* in addition to his oral statement of the nation to the population on January 1, 1804. That was not merely an act of formally recording national history at its inception; that was an engagement with the political logic of the global order. The Act of Independence is one of several texts written in French before and after January 1 that announce the nation, the first being a statement issued on November 29, 1803, that has been called a "'proclamation of independence'" (Jenson 2009, 76). Although the overwhelming majority of the population was illiterate, that they are *written* texts is of secondary sociopolitical significance to the fact of their expression in a European language. They certainly spoke to the minority of local French-speaking colonials, whether or not they had supported the Revolution. However, more significantly, those texts spoke the arrival of Haiti in the global political economy to the complex of symbolic, political, and economic powers that articulated the Atlantic world.[7] In announcing its sovereign entry therein, for the announcement to be significant to the powers of that world, the new nation-state needed to express itself in dominant languages, and in dominant modes of stately communication, of the Atlantic.[8]

In the year following Independence, the state adapted Louverture's economic project and its ruthless agricultural labor policies (cf. Trouillot 1990a, 73, 76). Sociopolitical economic organization in the sovereign nation mirrors that of the Louverturian colonial society. The "freedom" of working people is formally asserted in the proclamation of universal liberty in the nation, but the labor force is subjugated by capital at the control of an elite class. Sugar, coffee, cotton, and cocoa, the principal export crops of the revived plantation system, are as labor-intensive as they were prior to Independence, and the agricultural labor force is pushed to produce annually a minimum of a thousand pounds of the given commodity per worker (Madiou 1988b, 204, 279–80). Ada Ferrer speaks of "dilemmas around labor and autonomy" appearing in Haiti for the first time in a postslavery nation (2012, 65). I would speak more specifically of dilemmas around wage labor and personal agency of "free" working people who do not control the product of their labor, while a post-Independence elite reproduces itself off of that product. In the New World, it is evidently in Haiti that these dilemmas emerged for the first time, and they have arguably remained a defining leitmotif in the last instance of all politics of modern bourgeois capitalism. Thus, the founding of Haiti bore the first instantiation of the signal political economy of a bourgeois society in the Americas.

In seeking to understand Haiti's historical condition, it is difficult to over-state the fact that the Revolution's elites moved on relatively promptly from their triumph over the French and maneuvered to situate their sovereignty in the Atlantic world as it existed. In grounding the new nation's sovereign economy in the plantation, a form of production that would be a political-economic absurdity without global commerce, Dessalines reprised Louver-ture's claim of a stake in the international order constructed by white powers. Notwithstanding his massacre of the remaining French whites in the new country, Dessalines cultivated close relations with Frenchmen who could help to renew channels of commercial exchange from the colonial era. Far from repudiating sociopolitical economic policies prevalent in the Atlantic, he modeled his after them (Girard 2012, 553–54). Post-Independence, the Revolutionary creole alliance intended the new nation to be a node of the global system, much as colonial Saint-Domingue had been. Like Louverture before him, Dessalines used a Joseph Bunel, a French planter married to a black freedwoman, as de facto ambassador to the US on trade and defense matters (Girard 2010).

The Constitution of 1805 made the nation an Empire, and it made all Haitians "blacks" irrespective of skin shade or colorized belonging, officially ushering Haiti's presumptive Blackness in the national narrative. The same year, Dessalines also undertook the nationalization of plantations abandoned by their French owners. Not incidentally, the Emperor, who as a *nouveau libre* had not owned property in the colony, held extensive leasehold interests in state plantations and bore on his person expensive jewelry and other markers of elite personhood.[9] On October 17, 1805, he was assassinated amidst wide-spread discontent not only among senior black and mulatto army officers but also among the masses (Trouillot 1990a, 46–47; Dubois 2012, 50). General Henri Christophe, the army's second in command and a black *ancien libre* who controlled the North province, succeeded him. In December 1806, the political establishment of the West province interfered intensively in the ratification of a new Constitution that favored the mulatto general Alexandre Pétion, the provincial commander and the army's third-ranked officer. A civil war broke out between Christophe and Pétion, and the two split the nation between two distinct states.

On February 17, 1807, the North formally seceded under a Constitution that made Christophe *Président et Généralissime* of the State of Haiti (1807–1811), which he eventually made the Kingdom of the North (1811–1820). The following March, Pétion was elected President of the *Republic* of Haiti, and he remained in office until his death in 1818. The first article of Pétion's Constitution of 1806 invokes the "territory of the Republic," and the second speaks of "The Republic of Haiti." Christophe's Constitution of 1807 altogether side-steps the form of the nation by speaking solely of The Government of Haiti, "known [as] the State of Haiti." Both Pétion's and Christophe's respective Constitutions repeat Dessalines's Constitutional abolishment of slavery, but both dispense with Dessalines's coloring of the nation. The experiment of universal blackness had lapsed with the implosion of the Empire after Dessalines's assassination. While Pétion, the mulatto, reprises Dessalines's limitation of Haitian nationality to specific categories of whites and the prohibition of property ownership by any "white of any nation," the Government of Christophe, the black, "solemnly guarantees" the safety of foreign merchants and their property. Yet, if Christophe's Constitution implicitly lifts the prohibition on whites as property owners, it says nothing at all about whites as nationals.

Thus, of the three authors of Haiti's *Indépendance* who became the nation's initial heads of state, the first, a black *nouveau libre*, made it a black Empire and the third, a mulatto *ancien libre*, made it a Republic of no particular color. Both nonetheless agreed on formally curbing whiteness within the nation. The second, a black *ancien libre*, showed no interest in the form of the nation in the four years before he made it a kingdom, or in its color, and no apparent reservation in countenancing whiteness. While Christophe's State and subsequent monarchy rested on yet another brutal regime of plantation labor extraction, Pétion shifted the taxation burden disproportionately onto small agricultural producers (Trouillot 1990a), indirectly grinding surplus labor out of rural populations, which would support the reproduction of the political and economic elites throughout the history of the country (cf. Trouillot 1990a; Fass 2004).

If Pétion's regime favored a young postcolonial national "business bourgeoisie" (Fanon 1991, 198), those of Dessalines and Christophe actualized "a bourgeoisie of state functionaries" (221). Ultimately, on the one hand, between Dessalines, Christophe, and Pétion, it is clear that the ideation of Haiti as the "Black Republic" is grounded neither in a singular event nor in a coherent suite of events in the nation's genealogy but in an amalgam of political maneuvers that, at their inception, were in no way intended to cohere. On the other, between the three, the country saw the emergence of a "caste of privileged subjects" (Fanon 1991, 242). As cultivators' resistance to plantation work eventually led to the demise of the export-oriented plantation economy and a definite turn to small-scale farming (Dupuy 1989), large landholdings in the elite became stores of value of limited productive capacities. Meanwhile, over the course of the nineteenth century into the early decades of the twentieth, a *bord de mer* (seaside) import-export economy enriched US and European commercial agents established in port cities to broker exchange with their native countries (Trouillot 1990a). They and their descendants married into Haiti's mulatto bourgeois society, transforming the mulatto elite into a merchant bourgeoisie of much greater economic power than the landed black elite (cf. Dupuy 1989).

Jean-Pierre Boyer, another mulatto officer of the Revolutionary army, became president upon Pétion's death in 1818. He made the last systematic attempt at reestablishing plantation agriculture in Haiti by way of a project to secure the nation's sovereignty. This moment of his presidency provides a revealing window on the country's imbrication in the history of the bourgeois West.

Boyer reunited the nation in 1820 after Christophe committed suicide amidst widespread popular discontent in his Kingdom. In 1825, he signed an agreement with French King Charles X to indemnify France for the loss of the colony of Saint-Domingue. In 1826, to raise revenues that would pay the indemnity, he devised the Code Rural, which codified and considerably intensified the extraction of rural surplus labor by binding landless peasants to agricultural estates. Boyer entrusted enforcement of the Code Rural to Balthazar Inginac, another former officer of the Revolutionary army, who decades earlier had led Dessalines's plantation nationalization project.

While there has been critical attention to the crippling financial cost of the indemnity that Boyer agreed to pay France in exchange of recognition of Haiti's Independence, there has hardly been due scholarly consideration of the global context of the agreement. Originally 150 million francs, later reduced to 90 million francs, exclusive of fees and interest on its financing, the indemnity was undoubtedly a debilitating economic burden on Haiti's development capacities. Haitian nationalists have long indignantly argued that in paying the indemnity the country was forced to pay again for an Independence already won on the battlefield. However, in the creation of Boyer's Code Rural and in its ultimate failure, post-Independence Haitian elites evidently presumed, but overestimated, their ability to pass the cost of the indemnity to an overwhelmingly peasant working class. Yet, if the country's elites miscalculated their political sway over the rural "masses," their pact with Charles X articulated Haitian national history with a broader dialectical history of the Atlantic.

Vast numbers of aristocrats were among *émigrés* who fled the revolution of 1789 in France, and the revolutionary state confiscated their properties. After Napoleon's protracted fall (1814–1815), the First Republic, which he had thoroughly repressed, remained defeated. The *ancien* monarchy and its aristocracy returned from exile to begin the Restauration regime in Paris. The new king, Louis XVIII, was the younger brother of the last, Louis XVI, who was executed in January 1793 by the revolutionary Republic proclaimed in September 1792. Louis XVIII's first significant legislation, in 1814, gave back to returning émigrés confiscated properties still held by the state. After Louis's death in 1824, another of his brothers succeeded him as Charles X. In April 1825, Charles X's law of "le milliard aux émigrés" [the billion to the emigrants] held the people of France liable for a billion francs budgeted to indemnify returned émigrés, the vast majority aristocrats, whose confiscated properties had been sold by the Republican state.[10] Nine days after passage of that law, on May 4, 1825, a diplomatic mission left France for Haiti with Charles X's demand of a parallel indemnity for properties lost by the colonial plantocracy in the Revolution of Saint-Domingue.

Charles X's formulation of the indemnity included recognition of Haiti's sovereignty. The diplomats nonetheless arrived in Port-au-Prince on vessels of the French navy. Although they were very cordial in their meetings with Haitian officials, as Boyer and his government considered Charles X's proposal, a "French flotilla [with] 538 cannons" was moored in the bay of Port-au-Prince (Madiou 1988c, 462). The French First Republic had been the first state to consecrate the principle of universal political emancipation of the person in the history of Western modernity, and it had ceased to exist in May 1804, mere months after Haiti had become the second state to do so.

On July 11, 1825, in the nascent West, Haiti was thus the only extant instantiation of the Republican vision birthed by the revolution of 1789 in France.

And it remained so on that day, when its senate approved the pact imposed by Charles X for recognition of its sovereignty. In France, except for the *Cent-Jours* [Hundred Days] of Napoleon's return to power (March 20–July 8, 1815) and the brief interlude of the Second Republic (1848–1851), the Restauration and successor aristocratic regimes would successfully repress the French Republican project until its third iteration in 1870. It would still take the Third Republic (1870–1940) another thirty-five years to impose its power conclusively on the Catholic Church, the monarchy's historic ally. *La loi de 1905* (the law of 1905), making *laïcité* (secularity) the cornerstone of French governmentality, finally inscribed the defeat of the Ancien Régime in French history. Thus, while there may not yet be a scholarship that duly examines the world of Boyer's pact with Charles X, it can be said that the project of the Saint-Domingue Revolution came to terms with the persisting French old order more than three-quarters of a century before that of the French Revolution of 1789. Incidentally, the July Monarchy of King Louis-Philippe I, a cousin of Charles X, received Boyer in exile after his fall in 1843. He died in July of 1850 during the Second Republic and was interred in Père Lachaise cemetery in Paris.

✤   ✤   ✤

Over the course of Pétion's presidency (1806–1818) and that of Boyer (1818–1843), mulatto intellectuals and politicians developed a distinctive nationalist discourse that operationalized color identity in political partisanship (see Nicholls 1974b). This nationalism, legitimizing mulatto claims on leadership of the state, was multidimensional. It was existential in its embrace of dominant European cultural values as the nation's civilizational compass; it was political in its claims on the nation-state. The political dimension turned on two central theses. I call the competence thesis—after Trouillot's (1990a) analysis—the argument that mulattoes should lead the nation by virtue of their education in European thought and practice dating to their privileged social situation in the colonial era. The argument was further anchored in a presumption that, in their mixed racial origins, mulattoes were the embodiment of European civilization by a black race (Dalencour 1944; Trouillot 1990a, 126). I call the Pétion-authorship thesis the construction of a historical memory that glorified Alexandre Pétion specifically as *the* "Père fondateur," who founded the *Republic*. Mulatto nationalism duly acknowledged bravery and intelligence in black leaders of the Revolution, particularly Toussaint Louverture, Jean-Jacques Dessalines, and Henri Christophe. However, it also found them unfortunately deceitful and cruel, while lauding Pétion as a paragon of republican virtues and thus effectively the ultimate author of the *modern* nation.

A forceful counternarrative emerged by the final decades of the nineteenth century. It reasserted the unqualified centrality of Dessalines's leadership in the forging of the nation, and it posited that representatives of the most numerous segment of the population ought to lead the nation. By the middle of the twentieth century, the mulatto-nationalist Pétion authorship thesis had lost its last shred of public resonance under the weight of a modern historiography that attributes the Revolution's strategic genius to Toussaint Louverture and its conclusive military sweep to Dessalines's bravado. The competence thesis must have begun to lapse into obsolescence well before the close of the nineteenth century due to a rising number of prominent blacks well versed in French intellectual traditions. If it is not surprising that the Parti libéral, founded in 1870, had a mostly mulatto membership, because it represented elite interests, it is no more surprising that two elite blacks, Anténor Firmin and Edmond Paul, were among the most eloquent and prominent members to make the party's central argument that Haiti ought to be led by its most competent citizens (fig. 1.1, fig. 1.2).

Louis Joseph Janvier, a point of departure of modern intellectual noirisme, became one of the most fervent ideologues of the Parti national, the party claiming power in the name of the country's blacks as its majority population (see Nicholls 1996, 113–16, 311). Janvier, who left Haiti in 1877 to study medicine in France, took his host country to be "the capital of humanity" (Janvier 1883, 57). He sponsored the membership of Anténor Firmin, the black theorist of the Parti libéral, in the Society of Anthropology of Paris, and Firmin's work at the Society led him to write *De l'égalité des races humaines* [On the Equality of the Human Races] (1885), an assertive response to a French "scientific" racist. In the course of his counterargument to scientific racism, Firmin confidently proposed that "the white race of Europe" represented the greatest ideal of human beauty (1885, 278).

Janvier's and Firmin's robust competence in the universalization of European normative thought was happening in the context of a relatively expansive black political elite. On the one hand, the Parti national, Janvier's ideological home, was led by President Lysius Salomon (1879–1888), idol

Figure 1.1. Anténor Firmin, a black anthropologist and statesman and the author of *On the Equality of the Human Races*. His Parti libéral remains a mulatto party for black nationalists.

Figure 1.2. Edmond Paul, a black economist and statesman, and, like Anténor Firmin, a leading figure of the Parti libéral. He embraced the PL's argument for "power to the most capable."

of contemporary noiristes and the first in a run of six black heads of state through the second decade of the twentieth century. On the other, Firmin was in Paris in self-imposed exile from the autocratic Salomon. A black man of advanced education in dominant French cultural ways, he had come to sociopolitical prominence—and had become Salomon's antagonist—as leader of the Parti libéral, still today the emblematic mulatto party in the black-nationalist imagination. As it happens, since theorists of the PL included a few of the most iconic black thinkers in Haitian intellectual history, the tradition of reading the PL as a mulatto party suggests the capacity of Haiti's colorized formations to produce an intersubjective space of engagement on the national condition.

In 1904, for the nation's centenary, the state adopted "La Dessalinienne" as its anthem. In expressly referencing Jean-Jacques Dessalines among "Les Héros de l'Indépendance," it settled the question of the nation's authorship.[11] Significantly, color is absent from the hymn, which thus stays with the spirit if not the tactic of Dessalines's intent of a national society undifferentiated in social color.[12] No less remarkably, President Nord Alexis, a black, utilized—perhaps introduced—a discursive innovation in addressing the nation solemnly (in French) for the occasion: "I thus invite you all, my fellow compatriots, to Unity, in order to preserve our Fatherland, our Race, and our Independence."[13] Although Alexis gave an ostensibly national address, he in fact spoke to the small minority of the nation's subjects who could understand both French and the historical reference that he made.

Alexis was speaking to privileged Haitians. "La Race" [the Race]—big "R," no color—is a transcendent vocabulary that contemporary black privileged Haitians and mulatto privileged Haitians continue to use across the boundary of color, when, on more or less solemn occasions, they wish to evoke together the ancestors' triumph over white supremacy, while also asserting to themselves that they are *not* white. The discursive tactic allows them to commune in the glory of the national past, which turns on the decisive defeat of European racism, while simultaneously sidestepping the discomfort of the "color question." In availing himself of this rhetorical conceit, Alexis could proudly assert to Haiti's privileged blacks and privileged mulattoes, and to the world, that they were a nonwhite people. At one and the same time, he also sidestepped the ascription of a universal blackness to Haitians, which the mulatto formation effectively sees as a problematic practice. Much like Dessalines in making all Haitians black, Alexis in his vocabulary was managing a problem among privileged people of the nation, not a problem of the national population.

A few decades after the centennial, in the midst of the US Occupation of 1915–1934, the black elite began to deploy its deep competence in European cultural skills to assert the validity of the African heritage. During that period, Jean Price-Mars profoundly marked Haitian intellectual history. With close family ties to the political elite and the grandson of an important export merchant (Price-Mars 1967), at the start of the Occupation, he was posted as a diplomat in Paris. As a medical student there at the turn of the century, he had been influenced by the socialist Jean Jaurès (Shannon 1996).

Price-Mars returned to Haiti toward the end of 1916 and spent the next decade in critical conversation with what he believed was one elite comprising both colorized formations of the country (Gaillard 1998). He remained aware that he and his privileged interlocutors lived at a distance from the formation of poor Haitians, whose ways of being in the world he would explicate and validate in his most famous work, *Ainsi parla l'Oncle* (Price-Mars 1998). Much later, Leopold Sedar Senghor, president of the Republic of

Senegal and a founder of the *négritude* movement, which validated Africa's cultural traditions, would introduce Price-Mars as "'le père de la Négritude'" [the father of Négritude] to the French Minister of Culture André Malraux in Paris (Price-Mars 1967, 7). In the moment, French culture mediated the global articulation of postcolonial Atlantic elites in a seat of global Western power.

In the first decade of the US Occupation, Haiti's mulatto elite engaged in conversation with Price-Mars on the national condition, which, not incidentally, he refused to read through the "color question" (Gaillard 1998). The French language and other dominant cultural domains of France mediated that engagement as well. Price-Mars was not oblivious to mulatto colorism. He spoke directly to mulatto color prejudice, which he saw as one mental stupidity among other "aberrations of judgement" in the mulatto formation of the nation's unitary elite (Price-Mars 1998, xxxviii). The nationalism that animated his conversation with mulattoes could not have been a *mulâtriste* nationalism, that is, one distinctive of the mulatto formation. Like the nationalism that united blacks and mulattoes of the Parti libéral in the nineteenth century, the one that united Price-Mars and the mulatto elite was a local iteration of Western liberal bourgeois nationalism.

A group of young mulatto intellectuals at the core of *Indigénisme*, a literary school that linked fierce opposition to the Occupation and validation of national vernaculars, founded *La Revue indigène* expressly in the lineage of Price-Mars's thought. In the mulatto intellectual tradition, they did not read Haiti through a blackness. The six issues of the review that they published, between July 1927 and January 1928, nevertheless celebrated the nation's popular cultures to such an extent that, in certain elite circles, they were disdainfully "dubbed 'The Indigestible Review'" (Meehan and Léticée 2000, 1377). The first edition envisioned a "terrain d'entente et d'union" [a space of understanding and unity] of all Haitians and called for teaching "the people . . . the French language and civilization [through] our Creole dialect" (Sylvain 1927, 1). Jacques Roumain, a founder of the Haitian Communist Party in the 1930s, became the most influential writer of the *Revue* group with his novel *Gouverneurs de la rosée* [Masters of the Dew], which critically probed the material condition of Haiti's rural poor. Price-Mars himself published the last chapter of *Ainsi parla l'Oncle*, a forcefully argued legitimation of the cultural ways of the Haitian peasantry, in *La Revue indigène*. The publication of that seminal monograph in 1928 marked the start of the "ethnological movement" in Haiti.

In 1932, three urban, Westernized young black intellectuals from the middle classes—François Duvalier, Lorimer Denis, and Louis Diaquoi—formed the "Groupe des Griots" and began appropriating Price-Mars's work to assert the "multiple and tight linkages that unite the Haitian people with Africa" (Duvalier 1969, 141).[14] Although Price-Mars unequivocally denied any centrality to the color question in Haiti's sociopolitical-economic condition, the Griots Group claimed his thought as "our gospel'" (Nicholls 1974a, 5), while asserting that mulatto prejudice was Haiti's fundamental sociopolitical problem (Nicholls 1974a, 7).

In 1938, with Duvalier and Denis at its core (Diaquoi having died in 1932), an enlarged membership of the Groupe became "l'École historico-culturelle Les Griots" [The Historico-Cultural School Les Griots], alternately called "l'École des Griots" (Duvalier 1969, 141–42). The same year, they founded the journal *Les Griots*, a "scientific and literary organ," to advance their project (Duvalier 1969, 295). "Continuer l'œuvre de la Revue indigène et . . . bannir systématiquement la politique de nos activités scientifico-littéraires" [to continue the work of the Revue indigène and . . . systematically banish politics from our scientific-literary activities] were among the guiding principles that Duvalier and his fellow Griots enumerated in the founding "Déclaration" of their journal (reproduced in Duvalier 1969, 295).[15] Evocative of Price-Mars and the *Revue indigène* group, "The Essentials of The Griots' Doctrine" stipulated that "the search for our African origins . . . does not at all signify a return to Africa, even less the rejection of French culture, which, in terms of our historical formation, represents for us the other pole of our spiritual formation" (Duvalier 1969, 298). However, the Griots, still invoking Price-Mars's thought, increasingly saw "Haiti's African cultural origins" through a fundamentalist racial lens (Meehan and Léticée 2000, 1378), while their intellectual engagement took on a definite political dimension premised on color.

Duvalier and the other Griots intellectuals read their class identity in the cultures of the peasantry from the start of their movement. The late 1930s saw a political shift in the register of their black nationalism. Wary of the "moral disequilibrium" in the elite's predilection for "Gallo-Latin" values, they now sought to ground their nationalism in "the Haitian's biopsychological elements" (Duvalier 1969, 296, 297). Griots intellectuals, positing the elite as essentially mulatto and envisioning an empowered black *class*, operationalized the cultural postulates of their movement into the political project of noirisme. As politicians, they posited the racial, political, and economic conditions of the peasant as site of the national project. They situated the national interest in the interest of the *black* Haitian, and their nationalist strain was radically skeptical on mulatto political intent on the nation (cf. Piquion 1966, 176–77). They ultimately constructed a schema of two distinct classes, one *mulatto*, one *black*. In political practice, that entailed "a triangular class struggle" between the "masses" and an elite split between a mulatto faction and a black faction pretending "to be one with [the masses] under [the] mystifying term THE class" (Gaillard 1998, xxii).[16] In the final decade of his ninety-three years of life, Price-Mars felt compelled to remind the preeminent noiriste intellectual René Piquion that it was in "the conduct of an honest man" that he refused to see *the* social question in Haiti as a question of color rather than a question of politics and economy (Price-Mars 1967, 44).

President Elie Lescot (1941–1946), the last of four successive mulatto heads of state since the beginning of the US Occupation of 1915–1934, undertook an unprecedented mulattoization of the state by systematically excluding educated middle-class blacks from all significant levels of the public service. Up until then mulatto regimes had their black officers, and vice versa. Lescot's exclusionary practices were such a departure from Haiti's political tradition, it seemed like, politically and culturally, Haiti's very future was at stake (Trouillot 1990a, 128). He was forced out of office by a protest movement uniting blacks and mulattoes from the political center leftward. Lescot's black successor, Dumarsais Estimé (1946–1950), had been president of the Chamber of Deputies and a cabinet minister during (mulatto) Sténio Vincent's presidency (1930–1941). His term in office became the political concretization of noirisme. Estimé marginalized the left wing of the coalition that toppled Lescot (Nicholls 1974a), while socialists and communists formed a plethora of political parties defined in color (Smith 2009). Noiristes, generally a center-right political bloc, saw Estimé's election as the "1946 revolution," and François Duvalier claimed his legacy.

Expressly noiriste intellectuals have continued to think and write prominently in Haiti since the fall of the Duvalier dictatorship in 1986, but noiriste thought weighs considerably less in contemporary Haitian intellectual life than it did in the 1960s and 1970s. As the political scientist François Pierre-Louis notes (private communication), "noirisme is spent" as an intellectual framework in which to engage with the Haitian condition. Today, it is relatively common to find black nationalists as well as mulattoes who summarily reject noiriste proprietary claims on the nation. This rejection speaks to the political and economic violence of the Duvalier dictatorship across color and class lines. However, mulattoes and black nationalists reject noirisme differently. Black nationalists, including those who unequivocally reject noirisme as such, tend to view the privileged mulatto as a *social subject* "hostile to the interest of the people" (Gaillard 1998, xxiii). A black of Haiti's political left can thus reject noiriste color determinism in principle only to arrive in effect at a quasi-noiriste presumption on mulatto political agency.

In rejecting blacks' proprietary claim on the nation, mulattoes generally also contest the Black Republic trope, if only by sidestepping it in speaking of the country. In the absence of a publicly active mulatto nationalism, the more or less wholesale rejection of black nationalism is in fact the sole distinctively mulatto statement on the nation that I found in the field. In two unrelated conversations months apart, I asked two members of the economic elite who did not know each other—a wealthy fair-complexioned executive and a trader of Arab descent—whether they felt marginalized by the notion of Haiti as a Black Republic. They each began their answer with the same assertive exclamation, verbatim: "Tout sa k pou t a di se peyi yo pa la ankò" [All those who might say it's their country are no longer around], alluding to the native populations exterminated by the Spaniards within a few generations after Columbus's arrival on the island.[17] The trader of Arab descent, who is squarely in the mulatto formation by his wealth, light-skinned Latin American wife and quasi-white children, went on to wax poetic about Haitian Creole (in Creole): "Papa m te pale sèt lang men l te toujou di se Kreyòl ki pi bèl lang ki egziste. Kreyòl se lang mwen" [My father spoke seven languages, but he always said Creole is the most beautiful language that exists. Creole is my language]. He staked his claim of belonging to the nation in his identification with the nation's sole native language.

The linguistic nationalism of the trader of Arab descent obtained its phenomenal resonance in the social history of Haitian privilege since the 1920s, when Indigéniste authors began insisting on the validity of the nation's vernaculars as cultures of *all* Haitians. The ethnological movement sparked by Price-Mars in the 1930s and nurtured by the Griots into the second half of the century produced the systematic rehabilitation of the African heritage, and Duvalier's noiriste state initiated the ultimate validation of Haitian Creole as a bona fide language. On the one hand, this history created the space for a mulatto privileged Haitian to find his national identity in the Haitian Creole language. On the other, the trader's claim of belonging ultimately found its resonance in the persistent denigration of the language in the country's middle and upper classes, together with the persistent hold of French on the imaginary of the privileged or aspirational Haitian.

About the time the trader of Arab descent told me what Creole meant to him, a twenty-nine-year-old black man told me about a televised debate between candidates of the 2010 presidential elections. A former principal of a modest private school in Carrefour, a working-class municipality southwest of Port-au-Prince, he described with great enthusiasm what he considered Michel Martelly's winning performance in the debate. Urging me—in Creole—to review the debate on an internet website, the former principal concluded with a series of exclamations: "Micky pale fransè tout deba a! Pa yon grenn mo kreyòl! Moun sezi!" [Micky spoke French the entire debate! Not one single word of Creole! People were stunned!]. Martelly's stage antics as a pop musician were well documented, from wearing diapers to mooning audiences to soliciting oral sex from President Jean-Bertrand Aristide. Thus, in the former principal's telling of the solemn debate, Martelly's accomplished use of a transcendent symbol of "civilization" gave his debate performance the quality of staggering revelation. The former principal was still awed by his memory of the performance as he told me the internet address where I could see a video of the debate. The address was actually a Creole phrase, avannvote.org.[18] The irony was lost on the former principal. More ironic yet was the website itself, which was maintained by a civil society organization. On the entire site, among vast amounts of information about the candidates, the debates, the electoral process, and the host group, other than an occasional visitor's comment, I counted a total of four Creole words in a small-print slogan.

The Constitution of 1843 said that Haitians could speak whatever language struck their fancy and the law would specify the language of state affairs. That was the first time the Haitian state showed an official interest in what languages Haitians spoke, and the provision reappeared in all the Constitutions that followed in the nineteenth century. That changed with the Constitution of 1918, which flatly states: "Le français est la langue officielle. Son emploi est obligatoire dans les Services Publics" [French is the official language. Its use is mandatory in the public service]. This remained unchanged in the seven other (original and amended) Constitutions that followed through 1957. To those two sentences, the Constitution ratified in December of that year, three months after Duvalier's election, added one more: "The law will determine

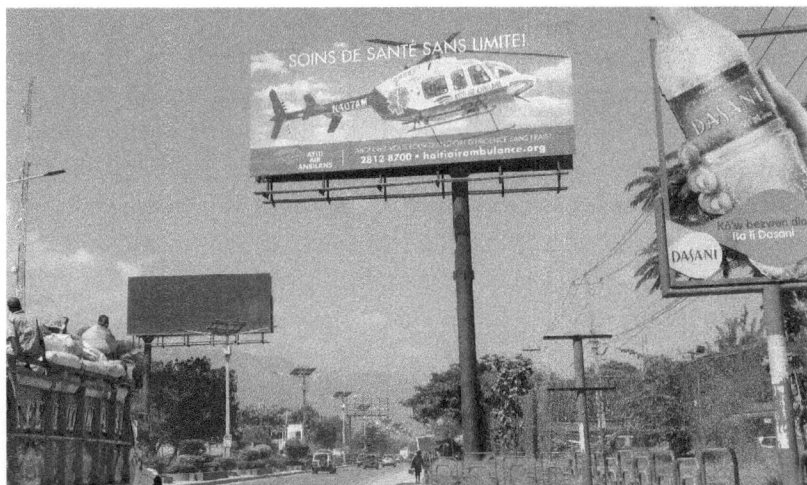

Figure 1.3. Two billboards and a *kamyon*, language and class in Haiti. The air ambulance service promises in French "Health Care Without Limits!" with an invitation to "Subscribe for Urgent Transport Without Cost!" One can reasonably presume that both taglines would be incomprehensible to the laborers riding on top of the sacks of charcoal in the cargo bed of the truck. By their socioeconomic position, it is eminently sensible to assume that the French language is totally foreign to them. Not incidentally, subscription costs range from US$25 for fourteen days to US$75 a year, effectively making the service a product for middle-class Haitians. The statement of the name of the organization (Ayiti Air Anbilans) nonetheless affirms the legitimacy of Haitian Creole, although "air"—with generally similar meanings in English and French—is not translated. This performative recognition of Creole makes salient the populist quality of the fully Creole text of the ad for the locally bottled Dasani water, which, at 23 gourdes (HTG) a bottle, approximately $0.30, is accessible to monolingual working-class Haitians. Photo by the author.

cases and conditions under which the use of Creole will be permitted and even recommended to safeguard the material and moral interests of those who do not sufficiently know the French language." The provision remained in Duvalier's Constitution of 1964, which made him president for life, and in the amended text of 1971, which paved the way for his son, Jean-Claude, to succeed him.

The Constitution of 1987, ratified fourteen months after the fall of the dictatorship, asserts that "all Haitians are united in a common language: Creole," and it makes "Creole and French [the] official languages of the Republic." This time, it would seem, the country's Constitution unambiguously legitimated the language of Haiti's monolingual Creole-speaking majority population. It did no such thing. For example, a monolingual Haitian Creole speaker who can read and write would not generally understand the information on the website of the Haitian Parliament. At the time of my fieldwork, the site was a domain of exclusive French expression, and it remains so as I revise this book's manuscript in the winter of 2018. Similarly, Haitian birth and death certificates are still issued solely in French. In practice, the 1987 Constitution merely legitimated the contextual use of Creole by privileged bilingual Haitians, while the Creole *speech* of the monolingual lower classes remained a powerful vector of sociopolitical marginalization (fig. 1.3).

Altogether, the formal legitimation of Creole initiated by the Duvalier regime ultimately created another terrain, in addition to the fiction of the Blackness of the Republic, in which performative discourses and practices could mystify both the vast sociopolitical chasm between bilingual and monolingual Haitians and the fallacy of some existential unity among the nation's dark-skinned subjects. In this historical conjuncture, noiriste effects permeate the sociopolitical terrain and amplify the mystifying capacities of the orthodoxy of Blackness decades after the end of the noiriste dictatorship. I took my time in the field to be within a post-Duvalier moment.

CHAPTER TWO

SNAPSHOT OF A WESTERN PLACE
Modern and Racialized, Unequal and Moral

The wife of one of my drivers in the field operated a beauty salon in a house in the Delmas district. A small room on the ground floor barely contained a few chairs and the more substantial equipment, forcing much of the work (manicure, pedicure, etc.) to be done in the courtyard. I periodically spent time there speaking with the beautician and her clients to apprehend viewpoints on the nation from the working class and the monolingual poor. An unemployed mother of two in her early thirties stopped by to say hello to her one day in late October 2012. The woman was on her way to her modest apartment a few blocks away after picking up her six-year-old daughter from school. I had once spoken with her at length after the beautician introduced us to each other on my previous trip several months before. Our brief exchange in the courtyard that afternoon showed her to be an aspirational Haitian Western subject far outside Haiti's privileged classes, revealing to me how deeply her country is a place of the West. That was one of the key moments in the field that helped me grasp that privilege and inequality in Haiti are most lucidly understood not through this or that trope of color but through locally adapted practices and ideologies of societal stratification in the West.

In the first part of this chapter, I link the experience of the unemployed mother of two to that of an upper-middle-class black couple to reveal across class lines Haitians' aspirational turn to Western ways of being social. I later tease out a political liberalism that circulates among privileged blacks and among privileged mulattoes, while the sociopolitics of color preempt linkages between liberals across the boundaries of their respective formations. Affirming the Haitian bourgeois liberal experience, I end the chapter with a critique of Susan Buck-Morss's ahistorical reading of the Saint-Domingue Revolution through Hegel's "universal." I see her exercise in dehistoricization as the epitome of a global imagining of Haiti as site of some absolute liberation derailed by global forces.

That afternoon of October 2012, as the unemployed mother of two remains standing while chatting with the owner of the salon and holding her daughter by the hand, I tell her that she is making "yon vizit doktè" [a doctor's visit], a phrase Haitians use to describe a short visit. She agrees, and she tells me that her weekdays are particularly busy. Enumerating morning chores that she does before walking her daughter to school, she says: "M fè bwat li" [I do her box]. I ask whether she is talking about preparing and packing her daughter's lunch. She is. After she tells me that, certain details of her life come to mind as we continue to talk. Both she and her husband were born in the capital of peasant parents who had migrated to the city's slums, and both are high school graduates. She lost her secretarial job two years ago. Her husband migrated to the USA before the birth of their eighteen-month-old son and now lives and works at a factory in the mid-Atlantic region in the east of the country. He supports her and the children with monthly remittances. She has never traveled outside Haiti. Before she leaves the courtyard, she suggests that in the early evening, after she finishes taking care of the children, we could meet at the nearby Epi d'Or. "Si w vle pale de peyi a ankò" [If you want to talk about the country again], she adds. I have seen a few Epi d'Or outlets around town but have never gone inside one. I ask whether it's a restaurant. It is. I ask what kind. "Kòm si m t a di w tankou yon Makdonal konsa" [I'd say, like a McDonald's, for instance] (fig. 2.1), she answers.

I did not see the woman again before I left Haiti over a week later, but I spent that afternoon thinking over her choice of tropes to describe her subjective experience and objective environment in Haiti. It was remarkable enough that she reflexively invoked McDonald's to describe a local restaurant, since she had never set foot outside Haiti and the US-based fast-food restaurant chain did not have an outlet in the country. Yet more striking to me was her use of an Anglo-Saxon idiom in translation to speak of ritually preparing her daughter's lunch and packing it in her lunchbox. She appropriated from

Figure 2.1. Epi D'or French menu, October 2012. Where it features variations on the ham-and-cheese theme on a baguette, its English counterpart features variations on the hamburger, and chicken nuggets. The branch on Delmas Road is generally frequented by a working-class and lower-middle-class clientele. Photo by the author.

the global North not simply a vocabulary but, more tellingly, a technique of motherhood to define her local experience. Although she was socially rooted in the Port-au-Prince proletariat, our brief exchange complemented my critical experience of a posh, upper-middle-class birthday party that I had attended some days earlier.

The party was at Le Villate, a versatile entertainment venue in Pétion-Ville variously used as a nightclub-restaurant or as a performance space. Tonight, the place is in its club-restaurant configuration. Dining tables and chairs line the dancing area in front of a permanent stage. Beyond them is a lounge of plush armchairs, benches, ottomans, and cocktail tables. Further beyond is a row of sliding doors made of glass panels framed in blond wood spanning nearly the width of the space. Behind the doors is an alcove, where a buffet dinner will be served. The festivities celebrate the fiftieth birth anniversary of a thriving black entrepreneur who owns an engineering contracting service with his wife. Trained as an architect, the wife is a teacher of mathematics at an iconic parochial school in Port-au-Prince that remains a destination for privileged girls. As collaborators in the field, I have come to refer to him as the engineering contractor, or the contractor, and to her as the math teacher. Their "well-bred" children, a daughter in her late teens and a son in his early twenties, receive arriving guests, from whom they collect presents that they arrange at the front of the stage.

The contractor is also an occasional entertainer of some note on the local scene. As the party progresses, from time to time he joins a small combo playing covers of pop and folk standards on stage. When the band stops playing, recorded music plays on the loudspeakers. Waiters serve soda, wine, beer, scotch, and other types of drinks from the open bar. The contractor and the math teacher are gracious hosts, constantly moving around and engaging with their guests, alone or together. Guests, dressed in "casual chic," dance, mingle, laugh together. About ten bottles of Moët & Chandon Nectar Imperial rosé champagne are deposited on the larger tables and waiters pour another four or so in glasses of guests in smaller clusters.

After a brief speech (in French), the math teacher wishes her husband a happy birthday. She concludes with "*ad multos anos*" as she raises her glass. However, the birthday toast is somewhat bungled. At a few tables, waiters are still pouring champagne in glasses or guests are still uncorking bottles. Eventually, the champagne flows for all who want of it. It is through and through an evening of worldly bonhomie. Yet, although to a European or a North American the guests would seem to be all *black*, except perhaps for a few Arab-Haitians, an attentive observer of the problematic of color in Haiti would notice a distinct pattern. At most tables, skin complexions of the given cluster of guests fall within a definite range. There are tables of clairs; there are tables of *blacks*. Notwithstanding guests' convivial table-hopping, fewer than a quarter of the tables seems to have a distribution of guests that does not fall in the pattern.

After a voice on the loudspeakers announces that *la table est servie* [dinner is ready], I join other guests filing to the wide alcove at the back of the room. We serve ourselves from a buffet that is as sumptuous as it is plentiful. Buckets, tilted forward, overflow with baguettes cut into pieces. There are trays of shrimp, griyo (fried pork), and beef; of avocado and olives; and of rice and various other "sides." I find an arrangement of prosciutto and strawberries particularly attractive and, I joke to myself, a relief from the prosciutto-and-melon cliché that I am familiar with in New York. A black woman greets guests as they enter the alcove. She oversees the room with a watchful eye and a warm smile. She is dressed in a slick black gown that hugs the contours of her slim body. The dress stops just above equally elegant metallic silver wedges, and her hair is swept upward at the back in a smart chignon. When the party ends, she will invite the house crew—about six or seven individuals—to the food. After they serve themselves, there will still be plenty of almost everything left.

As other guests and I return to our tables to eat, the contractor is on stage roasting several of his friends. He calls a man's name to make him the butt of a joke. The man—a clair—is a former schoolmate of mine, and when he stands up to shout a humorous retort back at the contractor, he still looks familiar more than three decades after I last saw him. I intend to go say hello to him sometime after I finish eating. Meanwhile, some inchoate thoughts become a more or less coherent reflection as I eat.

The contractor and the math teacher travel and shop in the USA. They occasionally order merchandise online from such purveyors of goods and aspirations to the American middle class as the department store Macy's and the clothing company Banana Republic. They have the purchases delivered to addresses of friends and kin living in North America, who may travel to Haiti in a relatively near future. Their son, who is home specifically for the party, will soon fly back to the southern United States, where he attends college. They have begun planning taking their daughter to France after the end of the academic year to begin her postsecondary studies. The party is certainly a statement of their social situation in Haiti to friends, family, and business acquaintances. It is also a statement of their belonging to the middle class of global Western prosperity. Michel Martelly, who has been president of the Republic for about a year and a half, also went to school with the man being roasted and me, and the two have remained close friends. Martelly might very well have been a guest at the party, and a future president of the Republic might very well be among the guests here tonight. The powers of Haiti's president over the nation's resources are practically as immense as the president's lack of public accountability. If a guest here tonight were to attain that office, how likely would she or he be—or Martelly and his entourage, for that matter—*not* to misuse the public wealth to realize aspirations to higher echelons of the global elite, and to state their arrival with commensurate sumptuousness?

After the party ends, I wait for the contractor, who will drive me home. As I lean against a railing, a black man of meticulously manicured nails and his somewhat less dark-skinned wife stop on their way out to chat with the contractor's daughter nearby. The latter tells them of her excitement as she anticipates studying architecture in France the following year. The man tells her that a degree in architecture sounds impressive but is of questionable practical value. He and his wife nonetheless wax poetic about architecture as a field of beauty, urging the contractor's daughter to travel to Spain, Italy, and Mexico and soak up architectural histories there in addition to her studies in France. The man eventually spins a few tall tales as he teasingly imagines her career. He tells her that she will settle in the USA, where the real money is: she will start her first job at $150,000 a year and eventually earn $250,000. He then closes the narrative (in French): "Dans dix ans, si je suis encore en vie tu me diras, Monsieur [nom], j'ai huit cent quatre-vingts, pas encore un million parce que j'ai trop acheté" [In ten years, if I'm still alive, you'll tell me, Mister [surname], I have eight hundred and eighty, not a million, because I spent too much].

When the man says his last name, I recall the time I incidentally heard of him in a casual conversation, during which I was also told that his wife was a mulatto. I make note of his wife's complexion as she stands several feet away from me. I register specifically that she is somewhat darker than I am, and I am not particularly light in the Haitian scheme of things, at least so I think. As the young woman chats with the man and his wife, her mother, the math teacher, approaches. She stands by them and looks on for a few moments with an appreciative smile. She eventually thanks the couple for coming to the party, embraces them good-bye, and they leave.

I had heard of the man who gave architecture advice to the math teacher's daughter about a year and a half before the birthday party. I was gossiping on the phone with one of my earliest collaborators on this project, a cousin of the math teacher who was not at the party. As we joked about the "parvenu" type, she invoked the man by name. Mimicking the man's voice with benign humor, she recalled that he once bragged about his tableware from Christofle, a French-owned brand under which a table setting for six might minimally cost five to six thousand US dollars at the time I was in the field. During the same telephone conversation, my collaborator told me that the man's wife was a mulatto. The day after the party, I called her. I told her that I had incidentally come across the man at her cousin's birthday party the night before. I said I was surprised that the man's wife was a bit darker than I since she had told me the wife was a mulatto. She answered (in Creole), "Bon, tout moun konsidere l mulat. Moun lakay li te gen . . ." [Well, everybody considers her a mulatto. Her folks had . . .], going on to talk about the trading business that the woman's family owned. The significance of the family's wealth supplanted the significance of her actual skin color in her situation in the mulatto formation. The finer nuances of colorization in Haiti could still throw me off, I thought as my collaborator spoke. In the early morning, I had categorized the man as "black" in my field notes. Now, for all I knew, he might prefer to be taken for a mulatto, too.

As my collaborator and I continued to speak, I alluded to the comments she had made about a year and a half earlier about the man's wealth and asked her about his professional occupation. "Musyeu se te patnè Jean-Claude Duvalier" [He was Jean-Claude Duvalier's buddy], she answered me in full. She was implicitly alluding to the period when François Duvalier's son, Jean-Claude, presided over the dictatorship before the collapse of the regime in 1986. In telling me of the man's friendship with Duvalier as the actual answer to my question about his professional occupation, my collaborator did not have any trace of irony in her voice. In Haiti, I gathered, access to high-level state power in and of itself can in fact be the profession that provides the economic underpinning of one's social existence. I humorously thought of the man who gave architecture advice to the math teacher's daughter as a professional Duvalier buddy, and the thought eventually became a contextual device through which I viewed the math teacher as a Western person.

The math teacher was an ardent *Lavalassienne* since the earliest days of the Lavalas movement, which generated unprecedented democratic political participation by Haiti's vast dispossessed majority and carried Jean-Bertrand Aristide to the presidency in the elections of 1990. She remains a steadfast Aristide loyalist, Aristide remains a formidable political force in the country, and she has routine access to him today, as she did during his presidencies. She nonetheless never became a "professional" Aristide buddy, and I have never found any suggestion that she, her husband, or their company ever sought extralegal access to state resources. To a generation of politically engaged Haitians, including the math teacher, "Lavalas" resoundingly refuted the Duvalierist past of outlandish corruption and arbitrary political violence. However, the math teacher does embrace noirisme, the signature political ideology of François Duvalier's dictatorship. She is a radical noiriste who does not take kindly to mulattoes, whom she routinely sees as an encumbrance on the national project. For all that, she remains old friends with the man who became wealthy as a professional Duvalier buddy, is married to a mulatto, and gave architecture advice to her daughter.

Figure 2.2. Coca-Cola Ak Kafe. A populist pitch in Creole for an icon of Western modernist mass consumption near the downtrodden *makèt Delma trannde*, a market along a stretch of the street Delmas 32: Drink New Coffee-Flavored Coca-Cola. The Li'l Coffee Taste Will Re-energize You. At 50 HTG a bottle at the time (2019), about US$0.65, it was relatively accessible far down the socioeconomic ladder. Photo by the author.

Eventually, I came to appreciate the making of the math teacher's *modern* subjectivity in shifting conjugations of streams of practical engagements and ideological positions. Her close friendship with the professional Duvalier buddy reveals that, notwithstanding the periodic relapse of Haiti's rough-and-tumble politics into spasms of bewildering violence, privileged Haitians can transcend ideological differences to realize their privilege within the norms of bourgeois "civility."

Where the contractor and the math teacher are well-traveled children of urban and provincial middle classes, the unemployed mother of two has never left Haiti. She will nonetheless enact her person through discourses and practices appropriated from the West during our brief exchange in the Delmas courtyard a few days after the party at Le Vilatte. She presumably appropriated ideologies and techniques of the self via the planetary *mediascape* that disseminates the planetary Enlightenment *ideoscape* of the modern West (Appadurai 1990). A daughter of landless peasants turned urbanized proletarians, she can certainly be counted among the "Conscripts of Western Civilization" (Asad 1991), people who inexorably arrive in the orbit of the global West (fig. 2.2).[1] This is not to suggest a reductive reading of contemporary Haitians as being overdetermined by external globalizing forces. This is rather to suggest that the contractor's birthday party and the unemployed mother's appropriated technique of motherhood make for a practical critique of the romantic longing for the anticolonial/anti-imperial revolution (Scott 2004), which permeates much of the scholarship on Haiti's social conditions. Together, the two events support skepticism of "the continued critical salience of" mythic anticolonial narratives (Scott 2004, 8), among which the tale of the Black Republic is an alluring epic. To paraphrase Scott (2004), aspirational Haitians will go about making themselves as Western subjects from whatever their nation has made of itself out of whatever past it has drawn since the Saint-Domingue Revolution.

❧   ❧   ❧

To use a phrase in which learned people began to conflate Haiti's upper classes in the 1990s, early on in the field, I met subjects who might be from a "morally repugnant elite," or middle class for that matter. Before I left New York on my first trip to Port-au-Prince in 2011, one of my collaborators, a man in his late thirties living overseas, gleefully predicted the election of Michel Martelly and the return of the Duvalierist old order. The son of a general in Duvalier's army, whose power persisted for a few years after the fall of the dictatorship in 1986, he anticipated his own return to Port-au-Prince, and the "disappearance" of the Lavalas movement.[2] He served on a death squad of the Front pour l'avancement et le progrès haïtien (FRAPH), a paramilitary group that preyed on Lavalas supporters after President Jean-Bertrand Aristide was ousted in a coup and exiled in September 1991.

I had contacted the man to ask for the telephone numbers of two mutual friends—potential collaborators in the field—who were on the FRAPH death squad with him. All three left in self-exile shortly after a US occupation force returned Aristide to power in October 1994. The other two had since gone back home. In a matter of months, both would have influential jobs in the Martelly government, and, a year after that, I would receive credible accounts of one of them stealing $150,000 from a poverty-alleviation program in the jurisdiction of his official position.

Shortly after I spoke with the former FRAPH death squad member, I found myself chatting with a businessman of Arab descent one evening on the sidewalk outside O'Brasileiro, another fashionable restaurant in Pétion-Ville. I had met him in the restaurant. When I arrived to have a drink with one of my collaborators, the two of them had just finished discussing a potential business deal over dinner, and I joined them at the table. The three of us left together an hour or so later. My collaborator said good-bye and walked to his car as the Arab-Haitian and I lingered on the sidewalk. He was telling me about the business he lost in the earthquake of January 12, 2010, a little more than a year earlier. After telling me he had not had insurance coverage for the catastrophic loss, he spent the final minute or two of our chat telling me about (in his view) the abundant assistance lavished on the poor by the international community. His concluding remark, his voice dripping with disdain, was that vast numbers of "those people" still lived in squalid camps all over the Port-au-Prince metropolitan area more than a year after the earthquake, because they simply did not want to move. They remained in the camps on purpose, he told me, solely to benefit from the largesse of aid organizations. At the time, poor Haitians displaced by the earthquake were reporting "'that aid distribution was arbitrary, chaotic, and insufficient'" (Joseph and Shah 2012, 140), and there were 640 *documented* cases of rape in camps of internally displaced persons during the year following the quake (MADRE et al. 2012, 158–59).[3]

By the time of that conversation outside O'Brasiliero, I had nonetheless also found ample suggestion that Haiti's elites, as elites go, were not undifferentiated in moral callousness. In the middle classes, too, I had routinely met subjects seeking a morally correct engagement with Haiti's everyday realities.

None of my collaborators in the field would be taken for "radicals" imagining or—as far as I could ever tell—acting for a "revolution" that would abolish political economic oppression in Haiti. Some nonetheless interpreted Haitian historical conditions squarely in the Marxist-materialist tradition. Any number of them engaged earnestly with varying degree of empathy and civic-mindedness on the condition of the nation, in particular on the poverty of the nation's majority population. They often wished for much greater state intervention toward the alleviation of popular hardships and for the public good in general. They also often couched this vision in a damning critique of public servants' systematic misappropriation of state resources toward personal enrichment. All could routinely be motivated to spontaneous acts of charity at the sight of personal economic suffering, and several were engaged in various forms of sustained philanthropy. Some supported the radically inclusionary socioeconomic vision of the Lavalas movement in the 1990s. Others, including social-justice activists of the left, never did. Some found Fidel Castro's Communist regime in Cuba inspiring; others abhorred Communism as a matter of bedrock principle. All took for granted defining markers of their class situations, from where they live to what (and where) they eat to social capital that expresses and reproduces their variously privileged positions. Those characteristics defined their experience of a bourgeois modernity, not their belonging to a color formation. However, the experience of color preceded their commonality in the bourgeois experience.

The day after I arrived in the field, the black physician, with whom I went to Kay Atizan, spent part of the afternoon at my house. He spoke of voting as "yon obligasyon" [a duty] and of his political views being "adwat" (on the right). An embodiment of the black-nationalist tradition, he had unsurprisingly voted for Mirlande Manigat in both rounds of the recent elections. Manigat's candidacy was rooted in the noiriste political elite. Her late husband, Leslie Manigat, was himself a former president and a strident theoretician of noirisme.[4] The physician supported the Lavalas platform in the 1990 elections. However, he said to me, shortly after the inauguration of Jean-Bertrand Aristide as President in February of 1991, he lost his illusions in what he saw as Aristide's populism without a programmatic agenda. He remarked that the urgency to lift the majority of the population out of a deepening impoverishment was such that distinctions between left and right in Haitian politics were now practically meaningless. He spoke warily of Michel Martelly apparently winning the run-off elections held five days earlier. He did not fret over behind-the-scenes illegitimacies that might explain Manigat's loss. She had once been the leading candidate, but, he said, it was clear that Martelly was preferred by the majority of the voting electorate. To him, that was that. His concern, arguably prescient, was that Martelly appeared not to be beholden to the political class, while, in fact, he was. Martelly's organization, "in its human dimension," as he put it, referring to Martelly's operative entourage, was not a departure from Haiti's political tradition.[5]

That afternoon at my house, I asked the physician about his civic engagement in general. He lamented not having time for that. Three days later, the following Monday, as we sat in his office between patients, a young man came by to see him. After they exchanged greetings, the man sat down next to me in front of the desk; he seemed to be in his late twenties or thereabout and from the lower middle class. After the physician began writing a check from his business account that he would hand to the young man, he invited him to tell me about his organization. He was an artist who led an after-school art program for poor children. The program, he told me, kept the kids engaged and offered them an alternative to loitering on the street and potential delinquency. The physician regularly donated to the program. After the artist left, I told him that I considered his support to be civic engagement. He told me that he had not remembered his involvement with the after-school program when we were speaking at my house a few days earlier. He added that he had thought of my question in the context of political activism.

The physician then described his membership in an organization of Haitian professionals, where his principal focus was in arranging health care for poor children with special needs. There was nothing transformative in these innocuous acts of private philanthropy. However, together with his casual remarks about Haitian politics, they held my ethnographic interest for two reasons. On the one hand, as an embodiment of Haitian political participation, the physician stood in sharp contrast to global discourses in which Haiti's politics appear as a relentlessly dystopic field. On the other, his embodiment of Western "liberalism," it seemed to me, was a critical challenge to the strain of scholarship on Haiti epitomized by Trouillot (1990a) that is wholly dismissive of the liberal tradition in Haitian political history.

Later in the week, when the physician and I were at Kay Atizan, I talked about the central themes of the project that had brought me to Haiti. He listened intently, sitting casually askew at the table, sipping a beer. When I made a passing remark about my interest in "social inequality," he turned to face me. Looking at me directly with furrowed brow, he interjected a succinct question that spoke volumes of skepticism: "Egalite sosyal w ap pale?" [Social equality, that's what you're talking about?]. It was the first time in the field—and not the last—an ethnographic subject was talking back to me from within anthropology's epistemic universe. Before I arrived in Port-au-Prince, I knew not to expect in this study the asymmetry of power between ethnographer and subject usually found in anthropological studies, in which subjects are traditionally from variously marginalized populations.[6] Still, the moment was mildly unsettling. Responding reflexively, I simply switched rhetorical gears and assured him that I meant to speak of social inequity, not of egalitarianism. Although he clearly was not interested in any questioning of his class privileges, from that point forward, he did not flinch from a critically constructive conversation on the failure and possibility of an equitable Haitian society.

The day before that conversation at Kay Atizan, I visited the wealthy fair-complexioned executive at her office not far from the National Library in downtown Port-au-Prince. While she worked, we spent the afternoon speaking of everything and of nothing, as French-speaking people say. Her paternal grandfather immigrated to Haiti from north-central Europe in the early decades of the twentieth century. In a pattern typical amongst immigrants from Scandinavia (and other parts of Europe), he married a local light-skinned woman; so did his son, the fair-complexioned executive's father. She told me that her mother's family established itself in the region of Cap-Haïtien so far back in the nineteenth century that she could not estimate when it might have also arrived from Europe. Neither she nor I knew then— and I later found and told her—that one of her direct maternal ancestors was born in Saint-Domingue in the second half of the eighteenth century.

The business founded by the fair-complexioned executive's father in the second half of the twentieth century grew into a conglomerate. As we chatted at the firm's headquarters, I asked her whether she felt there was a problem of socioeconomic inequality in Haiti. She responded in Haitian Creole, "Gen neuf milyon pwoblèm e gen ti sa a lan nou. Si m pa kwè gen w pwoblèm m t a suisidè" [There are nine million problems and there's this little of us. If I don't believe there's a problem, I'd be suicidal], showing me the tip of her forefinger to illustrate the relative size of "nou" (us) within Haiti's generally estimated population at the time.[7] She spoke of making more or less regular donations in person to L'Hopital général, the teaching hospital of the State University of Haiti and the principal public health care facility of the city. She did so, she told me, because her business includes a fleet of delivery trucks, and she wanted to ensure preferential treatment of any of her drivers who might ever be in an accident.[8]

The fair-complexioned executive's husband is as blond of hair and as light of complexion as she. The paternal and maternal sides of his family established themselves in the country sometime around the middle of the nineteenth century from Europe and North America, respectively. As we killed time over a beer on a December afternoon in 2011, he seemed vague, apparently reaching in some murky memory, when he told me that he dated dark-skinned girls in his youth. He was quite the opposite, passionate and precise, in angrily vilifying the US financial elites. He was as adamant in expressing agreement with Occupy Wall Street, the street protest movement against economic inequality that had begun the previous September in the financial district of New York City. Alluding to the "morally repugnant elite" discourse, he vehemently asserted that Americans had no standing to lecture Haitians on inequality. His expression similarly dripped of existential angst in denouncing what he considered Aristide's populist suggestion to Haiti's poor that violence against the rich was the solution to their problems.

At a business meeting later the same afternoon, the voice of the fair-complexioned executive's husband spiked up in a different register, when a Brazilian consultant made passing mention of a low-cost portable water-filtering system. The consultant had barely finished describing the device, when he exclaimed excitedly (in English), "That's what I'm giving my employees for Christmas!" He went on to estimate with earnest enthusiasm how much the machine could save low-income households, because poor Haitians, like the rich, have been buying treated water to drink, avoiding tap water out of fear for their health, since the quality of the municipal water supply began to deteriorate sharply around the turn of the 1990s. In a more sedate tone, another day several months later, he would remark that Haiti's taxation level relative to its economy was below some international index, suggesting an unused possibility of state agency toward the allevia-tion of poverty. Incidentally, a few years earlier he and the fair-complexioned executive were involved in an initiative to expose tax evasion in the business sector. The project produced and submitted to the Haitian state an analysis of tax payments by enterprises big and small, expressly calling attention to payments to the state that appeared particularly low relative to revenues.

The fair-complexioned executive told me more than once that her opin-ions on Haiti's political and economic dilemmas were her own and not to take her as representative of any group. However, a group of elite civil society actors was evidently involved in the production of the corporate-tax study. I had already received a copy of the report from another daughter of mulatto dynastic wealth, whom I had met independently of the fair-complexioned executive. She also was involved in the process of researching and preparing the study and delivering it to the state.

I was introduced to the fair-complexioned executive by the engineering contractor. The afternoon she told me of Haiti's "nine million problems," she also told me of her engagement in the social lives of her employees. She used language that was nearly identical to that used by the engineering contractor, who had brought up the same subject with me earlier the same week. They both support their employees with cash gifts and salary advances for life events like weddings, christenings, and funerals, and occasionally for seasonal household expenses like school fees. The engineering contractor deliberately schedules the workday to allow his technicians to get off early enough to pursue freelance job opportunities of their own; for the same reason, they are off on weekends. He frames this scheduling practice as a strategic move to help keep the technicians' wages lower than they might otherwise be. The practice is arguably a neoliberal tactic of wage depression, but, to him, the employees' schedule affords them the possibility of augmenting their total income.

Both the engineering contractor and the math teacher—his wife—are nonetheless passionate in their respective views of Haiti's social ills. She sees in René Préval, Martelly's predecessor as president of the Republic, a cretin who co-opted and botched both Aristide's legacy and the radical promise of the Lavalas movement. He sees public-policy successes—particularly in infrastructure—which Préval himself failed to make salient due to his public detachment. Her fiery political rhetoric draws deeply on noiriste ideology; in the most casual chitchat with close friends and family about the state of the country, she almost inevitably frames the national condition as a "question of color." By contrast, color is generally absent from the contractor's sociopolitical vocabulary in any context. In any case, for all the difference in their ideological dispositions, the politics of both can most meaningfully be thought of as a pragmatic politics of middle-class people.

Like the fair-complexioned executive, the mulatto woman who first told me about the tax study is a leading executive of the family conglomerate. Unlike the fair-complexioned executive, in Europe or North America, she could not be taken for white. Of skin complexion more or less the same shade as US President Barack Obama's, she would be cogently black. I refer to her as the clair executive. Her paternal lineage reaches back to the colonial mulatto population and has operated in the economic elite since at least the nineteenth century. The family gained public visibility in key functions of national politics after the turn of the twentieth century, about the time her maternal grandfather arrived in the country as a European immigrant. Beyond its commercial enterprises, in recent decades, the family has been a key player in education and cultural production. Uncharacteristically for an upper-class mulatto woman, she married a middle-class black man. The same day she told me of the corporate tax study, she made a point of telling me assertively about her family: "Nous n'avons pas d'appartements à l'étranger. Nous sommes ici" [We do not have apartments overseas. We are here].

I met the clair executive through a son of the mulatto elite, a respected fair-skinned Marxist intellectual of supple blond hair. In the North-Atlantic country where he lives, he could not racially be distinguished from a "white." He and the clair executive are childhood friends. He first talked to me about her while we were having lunch at an international intellectual event outside Haiti. As we ate, I mentioned my initial findings of a political liberalism circulating within the Haitian business elite and middle classes. He was summarily dismissive of elite liberals' political significance. I pressed the point that, in the history of the modern West, it seemed liberal elite segments had been instrumental in interclass alliances that variously advanced social justice to some degree. I further posited that radical activists and intellectuals from the global North tended to dismiss bourgeois liberalism in Haiti reflexively, while at home they assiduously defended what was left of the welfare state in the neoliberal moment. I wondered what might justify the ideological dichotomy, but we did not debate the question.

The fair-skinned Marxist intellectual eventually came to talk of the clair executive's personal involvement in community development outside the family business. He spoke in earnest tones of her long and anonymous engagement in development projects in poor communities and recommended that I reach out to her as a possible collaborator. The clair executive herself never brought up her community-development work with me. She spoke about it, and sparingly at that, only when I brought it up on a few occasions. She simply did it, she seemed to suggest, because it was valuable and she could do it. She also told me of being called a communist by acquaintances in the elite, because of her interest in socioeconomic issues, after she returned to the country in the mid-1980s following a fifteen-year absence. She has since been raising the problematic of extreme poverty among her peers, she told me, telling them, "If we don't do something about it, they'll eat us." She spoke of those in the elite "who want a better Haiti," if only out of a concern for the country's global image, and those who don't and "only want to get rich."

❧   ❧   ❧

For all the commonality of views on the political economy of the nation that light-skinned and dark-skinned privileged Haitian liberals might share, it is generally negated in the sociopolitics of color. The fair-complexioned executive and the engineering contractor have a warm and easygoing business relationship. She is generally friendly and considerate, and can be affectionate, with her black peers. As far as I could tell in my time at the headquarters of the family firm, color does not determine employee hierarchical ranking there, notwithstanding positions held by family members. She nonetheless embodies the color prejudice that can provoke fulminating anger in black educated Haitians. After breakfast at her house one morning more than a year after I visited her at her office for the first time, she candidly discussed her prejudice in choosing the man she married. She further told me as a banal matter of fact that she could not countenance the thought of any of her children marrying a dark-skinned Haitian.

The fair-complexioned executive distinctly values her lightness of complexion and her blond hair. From family lore she shared with me, it would seem that her prejudice came for a good part through her grandmother, and she actively passed it on to her children. We talked about all of that during a jovial conversation, when we also cracked jokes and "fè zen" (gossiped) about another elite mulatto family, a member of which had recently been arrested on charges of leading a kidnapping ring. She had hugged me when I arrived for breakfast a few hours earlier, and she would kiss me good-bye when I left about an hour later. Throughout the morning, she occasionally squeezed my hand or tapped my forearm for conversational emphasis as she spoke. She was assuredly prejudiced in her children's affairs of romance (as she had been in hers), which might be a prelude to marriage, however far that horizon might be. Yet her amply illustrated prejudice in no way preempted her affection for me, or, I must admit, mine for her. Her banal frankness in telling me about her prejudice ultimately underscored rather than trivialized for me the deep complexity of the question of color in Haitian social relations.

I occasionally spoke about the fair-complexioned executive and her family with a well-read black man in his mid-fifties. He is an engineer by profession and is deeply rooted in the petite bourgeoisie of Port-au-Prince. He paints and writes poetry as a hobby. Of my collaborators, he is the poet-engineer. In a transnational marriage, he lives and works in Haiti, but also spends extended periods at home in Mexico, where his Mexican wife lives with their daughter.[9] His late parents moved in each other's social orbit as adolescents in a middle-class neighborhood of the capital but met as university students in Germany in the early 1950s. His father was from a black family of considerable land-holdings, and he owns significant inherited real estate in the Port-au-Prince metropolitan area. His maternal grandfather was a physician from a family with roots in the Plaine du Cul-de-Sac region northeast of the capital. His light-skinned mother did not think of herself as a mulatto. As he told me, "She saw the color question as an anachronism." He has worked extensively with grassroots groups both in the countryside and in the city, both in develop-ment projects and in cultural production, particularly on circuits where the grassroots and the intelligentsia intersect. He is friends with any number of mulattoes, and he rejects noirisme's color determinism as political parochial-ism, invoking the Duvalier regime's deployment of color ideologies despite its violence on the poor. He is nonetheless a black nationalist.

The poet-engineer and the fair-complexioned executive grew up and still live about eight blocks apart in a genteel neighborhood. The first time her name came up in conversation between us, I told him of her speaking to me of the urgency to alleviate poverty in the country. I then asked him whether he might envision a common political action with her on the national condi-tion. His answer was laconic but assured: "M pa wè sa non" [I don't see that]. The fair-complexioned executive is wealthy, and lightness of complexion is uniform in her family. She would not need to tell a black Haitian that she is prejudiced; she would be presumed to be. Thus, her mulattoness precedes her politics in the poet-engineer's black-nationalist imaginary, even though he is someone who tends to roll his eyes or shake his head at noiriste arguments.

In spite of the clair executive's marriage to a black man, and in spite of her family's support of the nation's higher-education infrastructure and cultural history, her color also precedes her politics in the black-nationalist imaginary. One evening at an academic conference in the Caribbean some months after she gave me a copy of the corporate-tax study, I found myself chitchatting at the bar of the conference hotel with a Haitian noiriste intellectual based in Haiti and two US academics based in the USA. After one of the Americans—an African American historian—held forth on Haiti's mulattoes in the "morally repugnant elite" rhetoric, and the other listened intently, I spoke the family name of the clair executive. I was beginning what I intended to be general remarks about the family's involvement in education and community development in the country. I did not get far. A few words after I said the surname, I had to stop talking. The noiriste intellectual had turned to me chuckling with glee. He was evidently anticipating my own amusement by the story he had excitedly begun to superimpose over my words. He turned to the Americans to tell them the broad lines of the story first in halted English. He then turned toward me again to tell it to me more elaborately in Haitian Creole.

In summary, a daughter of the family had married a black man (the clair executive, I surmised) and the husband (invoked by his first name) had squandered their fortune. The point of the story in general and of the humor in particular, it seemed to me, was not the husband's spendthrift ways but rather that a black man had made fools of a mulatto family. With my own interrupted remarks, I had wanted ultimately to arrive at a discussion around the sociopolitical significance of the clair executive's activist engagement with the problematic of poverty in Haiti. However, as I picked peanuts from a bowl on the cocktail table, it—correctly or not—seemed unlikely that I could do so without somehow or other debating the question of color with a noiriste intellectual. I was in no mood for the potential challenge.

I did not resume my intended remarks as I continued to chat with the three others around the cocktail table. Several months later in Port-au-Prince, while waiting to start a meeting with the general manager at one of the family's businesses, I told the clair executive of being told that her husband had squandered her inheritance. I asked her whether there was any truth to the story. She shrugged with amused resignation, as if the notion was a kind of absurdity which she had heard before. She proceeded to describe various instances of friction that did exist in the family among siblings and in-laws, making the point that color and money did not figure in them. In an unrelated conversation over a year earlier, her husband, whom by his literary engagements I came to think of as the moneyed black intellectual among my collaborators, had told me about "in-law issues" along the same lines.

※   ※   ※

Besides the black nationalist's skepticism of the possibility of a progressive mulatto, among thinkers and activists of the left, there is a tendential resistance to imagining or legitimating the elite liberal Haitian. This is so even within the elite, as with the fair-skinned Marxist intellectual who introduced me to the clair executive. During and after my fieldwork, in myriad conversations with Haitian black-nationalists, and with many a foreign academic, I began telling about the clair executive's work in community development or the thoughts that the fair-complexioned executive and her husband shared with me on poverty. Generally, attention was too lax or too incredulous, or both, for me to finish the stories. I suggest that the underlying logic of this resistance to a Haitian liberalism on the left relates to Susan Buck-Morss's conclusion that "Haiti's political imaginary . . . was too grand for statist politics" (2009, 147). For Buck-Morss, the Saint-Domingue Revolution would have defined transcendent liberty in universal history, had the Revolutionaries not made it a vector of entry to the presently existing world, or had the Haitian people not made it a fulcrum of its identity. The argument aligns with a widespread view among thinkers and activists on the left, including Haitians across the boundary of color, which holds that state powers of the Atlantic prevented the Revolution from fulfilling its promises of popular liberation. In either perspective, bourgeois [statist] liberal politics could not possibly be an appreciable substitute for the Revolutionary vision.

In the field, I also spent time talking with a black political activist of the left in his fifties. He ran an influential and widely respected advocacy NGO. His work in Haiti's social and political economies is informed by a Marxist understanding of the country's inequalities. He holds a nationalist vision of a cohesive civil society, viable institutions of substantial democracy, and a foregrounding of the problems of the urban poor and the peasantry. He supported Aristide through his first election to the presidency in December 1990. He continued to support Aristide and defended the Constitutional order in general after the coup d'état the following September and was tortured by the de facto government during Aristide's exile. Aristide won the presidency again in 2000, and again he would not finish his term. However, this time the political activist publicly supported his removal from office in the weeks leading to, and in the aftermath of, the second coup against him in February 2004.[10]

The father of the Marxist political activist, a black man of great political power in the heyday of the Duvalier dictatorship, amassed a fortune in his time working for the regime. After the death of the father, the man disclaimed his inheritance. He nonetheless offered a modulated assessment of his father's morals and politics. He is still grateful that his father maintained a copious home library, with books one might not expect to find on the shelves of a prominent agent of the dictatorship. They shaped his political consciousness in his formative years. He cites the work of Arthur Koestler, one of the leading European intellectuals engaged with the Western condition in the half-century before his suicide in 1983. The political activist names particularly Koestler's novel *Darkness at Noon*, a biting indictment of Stalinism, as a catalyst of his precocious opposition to the Duvalier dictatorship. For all that, he thought his father's sister, who lived in the family home, was his mother and called her "mom" until he was ten years old. That is when he learned of and got to meet his biological mother. She was an illiterate peasant woman. She had never been and was never to be in the father's household.

The subjectivities of Haiti's Founding Fathers were formed in the crucible of European Enlightenment ideological legacies that have historically shaped dominant politics and economies of the Atlantic. In Haiti, as elsewhere in the global West, competencies in dominant Western cultural modes have remained a pivotal instrument in the contestation of privilege in the upper and middle classes. As the Haitian sociopolitical tradition has radically marginalized the nation's rural universe in its African cultural heritage (Barthélémy 1989), it has also radically distanced the peasantry—along with the urban proletariat—from access to those pivotal Western cultural competencies. In Haiti, the political activist's mother, an illiterate peasant, could thus not have become the woman of the house in a family of the educated elite, even in the household of a cosmopolitan dark-skinned black-nationalist statesman at the service of a noiriste dictatorship. How thoroughly the importance of class trumps that of color in the articulation of privilege transpires even more clearly in the fact that the Marxist political activist's father and his biological mother had three children together, not one, and the man's two younger siblings had a similar history with their mother.

Without his father's fortune, the political activist nonetheless remains a worldly person of advanced education and privilege. He went to high school at Lycée français, then and now perhaps the country's most elitist institution for children of expatriates and the upper crust of Haitian society. He spoke wistfully of his experience with a mulatto classmate at the Lycée, when they were both fifteen years old and in thrall of Karl Marx's ideas. Using access facilitated by his father's power, he and the classmate once snuck in the offices of a religious order after hours to use its mimeograph to make copies of a protest leaflet. They then went to distribute the flyers around the light-assembly factory zone near the Port-au-Prince airport. The classmate became a key player in one of the most powerful industries in the country, and by various indications he seemed to be part of a cadre of mulattoes from the economic elite who remained pro-Aristide.

At the time I met the Marxist political activist, he and the classmate had not spoken in decades. I asked him whether he had ever considered reaching out to the classmate to see what common ground they might share in their respective visions of the country. He dismissed the idea with humorous flair in a mixture of Haitian Creole and French: "Kounye a, musyeu, c'est un bolchévique du capital" [Now, the guy, he is a Bolshevik of capital]. After we both laughed, I found the quip evocative of momentary squabbles that can pop up among "radical" learned urbanites in the global North around the limits, if not pointlessness, of liberal politics. Yet in his professional work as an activist, the man relied significantly on the world of—hardly *revolutionary*—governmental and nongovernmental agencies of the North that fund global human development projects. His work is very much in the realm of statist politics.

The youthful radical political engagement that the black Marxist political activist shared with his mulatto high school classmate, and their subsequent variegated life trajectories as children of elite subjects who themselves remained elite subjects, are not imaginable in the Haiti routinely reduced to this or that trope at the service of so many Western modernist thinkers. Rare is the Western student of the Saint-Domingue Revolution who is not seduced by its sweep and its irrefutable genius into conflating slavery with political economic oppression, and thence apprehends its world-historical significance.

Buck-Morss argues that the Saint-Domingue Revolution was the inspiration of Hegel's theorization of "universal humanity," in which "master" and "slave" live in balance through a dialectical articulation of their respective agencies as mutually constitutive subjects of a shared world. Writing a few years after Napoleon's army left Saint-Domingue in defeat and the former slaves made themselves a nation-state, Hegel might very well have found the source of his thought in the Revolution. However, with what Buck-Morss now knows of its aftermath, she evidently cannot situate Hegel's master-slave dialectic in it. She nonetheless continues to pine for a mystical universality as she objects that by defining Haiti vis-à-vis the enemy and arguing within the context of European civilization that "the blacks, like the whites," [are] capable of founding "a civilized nation according to European standards"—complete [with] (export-oriented) commerce, (plantation) agriculture, and a monumental, royal palace (built by forced, "free" labor)—[Haitians] allowed the contribution to the cause of universal humanity that emerged in this [Revolution] to slip from view. (Buck-Morss 2009, 146–47)

The slave here, it would seem, appropriated rather than negated the master's modalities of power. In the process, the slave becomes a new master who redeploys the newly acquired instrumentalities of social domination in a sovereign domain, and Saint-Domingue/Haiti can no longer be where Hegel begins to theorize his balanced, humanistic universe.

Buck-Morss proposes to resolve the theoretical inconvenience presented by the Revolution's actual outcomes by delegitimating the Revolutionaries' appropriation of Europeans' reproductive structures of power for their own sovereign project of domination and exploitation in the Atlantic. Her argument is but a particularly outlandish Romanticism that fits with a cottage industry of scholarship that gazes at Haiti in deep longing for a renewal of the Saint-Domingue Revolution. In this strain of scholarship, the Revolution was arrested in the realization of a Black nation-state by Atlantic powers that would not countenance such temerity, and its renewal would arrive at the definitive anti-imperial revolution. In Buck-Morss's variation on this theme, the Revolution had just about instantiated universal freedom, but the Revolutionaries and their descendants marred the achievement by unfortunately making of it an actually historical, *particular* world of their *own*.

Notwithstanding Buck-Morss's Romantic—and ultimately racist—objection, the victorious Revolutionaries of Saint-Domingue, with the founding of their nation-state, did assertively *intend* to inscribe their achievement in the dialectical history of the existing Atlantic world. Every single day, the political activist and the poet-engineer, the fair-complexioned executive and her husband, the engineering contractor and the math teacher, blacks and mulattoes of the privileged formations, the Delmas beautician and the unemployed mother of two, Haitians in general, embody the inscription as they enact the historicity of their nation.

CHAPTER THREE

NOIRISME AND THE POLITICAL
INSTRUMENTALITY OF BLACKNESS

At the American Anthropological Association (AAA) conference of 2011 in Montreal, Canada, a panelist informally prefaced his presentation by noting that the day, November 18, was the anniversary of the *Bataille de Vertières*, the decisive battle of the Haitian War of Independence in the northern town of Vertières. The "Haitian Revolution," the scholar reminded us, triumphed on this day in 1803 over Napoleon Bonaparte's expeditionary forces. The former slaves declared Independence on January 1, creating the "first black republic"; and Western powers had ever since made the country pay dearly for the accomplishment. The remarks were unmistakably extemporaneous musing and clearly not intended as scholarship. They indeed turned out to be wholly unrelated to the research findings presented by the scholar. Their very banality nonetheless reinforced the taken-for-granted quality of widely circulated postulates in the dominant narrative of Haiti as a nation-state, including—albeit unsaid by the AAA panelist—the exceptionality of a black people defeating a white army to assert its national sovereignty.

The scholar's remarks at the 2011 "Triple-A" conference were effectively an overarching framework of *whatever* a forthcoming presentation on Haiti or Haitians might contain. They should give pause to scholars engaged with Haiti as a land of actually existing people, because the invoked Blackness of the Haitian Republic that the global intelligentsia reproduced in that moment ultimately remains a political instrument in the reproduction of privilege and inequality. In François Duvalier's hands—through *noirisme*—the political instrumentality of that globally essentialized Blackness was spectacular and its effects profound, lingering in Haitian life into the twenty-first century.

I describe below moments in the field in which I capture the differentiated resonance of the dominant nationalist narrative of Haiti in the privileged classes and in the poor majority. I initially do that by way of a reconstruction of François Duvalier's ritualized Oath of Fidelity to The Flag, one of the fiery statements of his noiriste nationalism. In the middle section of the chapter, I critically read the production of the internationally famous sculpture *Le marron inconnu* [The Unknown Maroon], an homage by Duvalier and the mulatto architect Albert Mangonès to the colonial maroons. I reveal their mutual accommodation of the nationalist traditions of their respective color formations, while Duvalier does blunt discursive violence to the memory of the colonial bossale to celebrate the founding of the nation and its current condition. I then similarly read a reportage in Le Nouvelliste from the time when I was in the field. It insistently delegitimates the views of poor Haitians who fail to see any historic significance in The Unknown Maroon. In the final part of the chapter, I further map patterns of significance and insignificance of the Black Republic narrative between, respectively, privileged and poor Haitians.

About a month after the AAA meeting in Montreal, and seven into the presidency of Michel Martelly, a fleeting moment of a morning radio show gave me a succinct glimpse of the current state of Haiti's Blackness as both historical process and political instrument. It is early December, and I am in the passenger seat of a car made available to me through family relations, headed toward downtown Port-au-Prince. The driver, a soft-spoken man in his mid-twenties, is the brother of the beautician who operates the salon in a Delmas courtyard. Today, he is off-duty from his regular job operating a "tap-tap," a colorful communal taxi that shuttles passengers between outlying neighborhoods and the center of the capital. He is one of a handful of drivers of similar socioeconomic standing, whom I informally employ based on their respective availability. He wears "pèpè," recycled garments from overseas sold in street-side bins and market kiosks. Born and raised in a village in southern Haiti, where his mother still lives, he is now thoroughly urbanized. He dresses neatly and with understated taste: this morning, casual loafers, khaki shorts, and polo shirt. The car radio is tuned to a program of local and international pop music interspersed with the host's smart banter.

Traffic on Delmas Road is crawling. A throng of vendors and the occasional pile of garbage push pedestrians onto the roadway from either side of the thoroughfare, where they dart between the slow-moving vehicles. I am on my way to an academic conference on Anténor Firmin, the nineteenth-century Haitian statesman and intellectual. This will soon be poetic irony, given the depth of noiriste scorn for Firmin's Parti libéral. The final notes of a local pop song fade out on the radio, and the disc jockey intones solemnly in French: "Eight o'clock, the hour of the flag in the entire expanse of the national territory." When the DJ says the words, the unbridled vitality of the street appears to me as an expression of political rights reclaimed at tremendous human costs since the fall of the Duvalier dictatorship, and I have the proverbial sinking feeling in my gut. The announcement is a relic from the Duvalierist past; it portends surrealist political violence, or so I feel in an instant of panic.

Jean-Claude Duvalier returned to the country the previous January, but his presence has settled into banality rather than political significance. Martelly, since his election in April, has been said to restore respectability to Duvalier's cronies, but I have not seen much political effect of that, either, on the ground. However, I feel definite distress at a Duvalierist catchphrase on a rush-hour program of a major radio station. Fortunately, to my great relief and amusement, it is a false alarm. No sooner has the DJ finished that rhetorical ritual of yesteryear, he announces the day's weather forecast without further ado. There are no contextualizing comments about his seeming nostalgia for the Duvalierist past, nor any explicit sarcasm, but as he switches rhetorical register to announce the weather, the scorn in his tone is unmistakable.

I ask the driver whether he grasps what the disc jockey has just done. He does not. While I am at it, I try to engage him on Duvalier's legacy. When I ask him what he knows about life under Duvalier, he shrugs with a bashful smile, not knowing much. "There were the macoute guys," is his only answer. I tell him the broad lines of what would have come after the marking of "eight o'clock" on radio stations during the Duvalier regime, and we chat about other things as he continues to drive me to Université Quisqueya, which is hosting the symposium to commemorate the centenary of Firmin's death.

"Eight o'clock, the hour of the flag in the entire expanse of the national territory" was the prelude to a piece of formidable political theater. From the 1960s well into the 1970s, on practically all radio stations across the land, a rendition of the national anthem would have followed the announcer's voice.

On the grounds of the national palace in the Champs de Mars area of Port-au-Prince, a live brass band would have played an instrumental arrangement of the anthem to the raising of the flag. Drivers on nearby streets would have stopped their cars in whatever spots they happened to be at the onset of the ceremony. Lest they risk considerable harm to themselves by (legal and extra-legal) police agents of the state, drivers and passengers alike would have stepped out of the vehicles with deference. Along with pedestrians who had similarly stopped in their tracks, they would stand at attention facing in the direction of the palace until the band played the last note and the flag reached the top of the pole. Meanwhile, on public and private school grounds, pupils would have been singing a stanza from the national anthem as a pair of schoolmates raised the flag.

On the radio, the closing note of the anthem was not yet the end of the ritual. Duvalier's nasal drawl would follow in triumphalist cadence as he renewed his *Serment de fidélité au Drapeau*, his personal Oath of Fidelity to the Flag of the nation, which he first took in a speech introducing the Constitution that proclaimed him president for life in 1964. The Oath was a paean to the heroic forebears of the Haitian *nègre* (negro). Each verse spoken by Duvalier would be re-affirmed in echo by another male voice of neutral tone and matter-of-fact cadence. Meanwhile, at the "écoles nationales," as public schools were known, children of the urban poor would similarly follow the anthem with a live recitation of Duvalier's Oath:

Je jure devant Dieu et devant la Nation d'en être le gardien intraitable et farouche. Qu'il flotte désormais dans l'azur pour rappeler à tous les Haïtiens les prouesses de nos sublimes martyrs de la Crête à Pierrot, de la Butte Charrier et de Vertières qui se sont immortalisés sous les boulets et la mitraille pour nous créer une Patrie où le nègre Haïtien se sent réellement souverain et libre.[1]

Duvalier complemented the sort of ideological spectacle that he produced around the raising of the flag with spectacular populism. On national holidays marking historic moments of the Saint-Domingue Revolution, he brought peasants by the busload to Port-au-Prince to cheer on his public speeches. He encouraged his association with vodou practices in the public imagination. Through the Volontaires de la sécurité nationale—the VSN, more commonly known as the Tontons Macoutes—a militia that vastly outnumbered the formal Armed Forces of Haiti (FAd'H), he empowered thugs in the rural interior as well as in the urban proletariat and middle classes to wreak havoc on the general population with impunity. On New Year's Day, a motorcade paraded through both popular and ritzy neighborhoods of Port-au-Prince and Duvalier (first François, then his successor son, Jean-Claude) tossed coins and banknotes from the back seat of the presidential limousine. Throngs of the poor on the side of the road, who had cheered enthusiastically with anticipation, now scrambled for the money on the ground.

Duvalier's populist gestures were readily legible to the Haitian poor and intended to induce popular allegiance. They were also legible to privileged Haitians, to whom Duvalier posited himself as the embodiment of a Revolutionary promise to defend the interests of Haiti's poor black majority, particularly the peasantry. However, the verbal theatrics such as those around the raising of the flag were not comprehensible to the "masses." Both the national anthem and the Oath to the Flag were French texts. As such, their publics could not possibly have included Haiti's "ordinary people" (Fass 2004, xxvii), those who do not matter in the political process: the poor monolingual Creole-speaking majority of Haitians. Such texts were ideological spectacle rather than ideological populism. Although they were public ideological grandstanding, they were not addressed to the "people." They were texts intended for French-speaking Haitians of the privileged classes.

Less than a year after the Firmin symposium, I returned to the theme of Duvalier with the driver who took me to Université Quisqueya. I was on another errand in a different car. It was then that I found an ethnographic significance in the DJ's passing remark that December morning of 2011. In the latter conversation, in October of 2012, I asked my driver more specifically about his impression of what Duvalier did for the "black people of Haiti." This time there is no shrug or smile, just a look of incomprehension. He glances at me quizzically. Rather than keeping the focus on Duvalier, about whom and about whose regime he genuinely seems to have very little clue, I switch the conversation toward the Black Republic thesis in general.

I ask my driver: "Do you understand that Haiti is a black country? Y'know, sometimes people call it a black republic." His answer again is the shrug and the bashful smile as he mutters: "I don't know." Significantly, he says this without irony. He really has no idea about what I am saying. I ask him whether he ever studied about that in school; he shakes his head, and then summarizes his educational history for me. After he finished the "certificate," the sixth year of instruction that marked the end of primary school, his mother took him from their native village to live with a sister in the capital, hoping for him to continue his schooling. He was fifteen years old. The mother and the sister—then in her late twenties—continually struggled to find money for school fees, uniforms, and other related expenses. Two years after he arrived in the capital, bowing to economic realities, he quit school; his scholastic education was over. As a twenty-six-year-old driving me on my errand today, he has no living memory of Duvalier's spectacular populism; Duvalier's ideological constructs do not inform his lived experience; and his socioeconomic history has precluded the formal education that articulates the national past of the *Black Republic*. It is little wonder that the narrative of the nation's presumptive Blackness is hardly meaningful to him.

The radio announcer's sleight of rhetoric that December morning of 2011 ridiculed a pivotal ritual of the noiriste ideological underpinnings of the Duvalier dictatorship's fantastical violence. In François Duvalier's historical context, his choice of the word nègre in the Oath to the Flag was of political significance. He could have used "noir" to denote the black Haitian. In 1801, Toussaint Louverture spoke of himself as "Le premier des noirs" (The First of the Blacks). This "noir" is descriptive, providing for the objective identification of a certain subject among others, and the term has remained in common usage. Colonial practices created the *nègre*, a being of African origins who was made to seem of a lesser humanity. In the late eighteenth century, the use of "noir" or "nègre" might situate the speaker politically or geographically. In Paris, a prominent abolitionist group would call itself "La Société des amis des Noirs" (The Society of the Friends of the Blacks), not "des amis des Nègres." In the colony, a physician played on the two terms sarcastically to castigate its members: "Et vous osez, Amis des Noirs, parler des Nègres" [And you dare, Friends of the Blacks, talk about the Negroes]. He continued: "Amis des Noirs, si les Nègres pouvoient se faire entendre, ils vous demanderoient au nom de l'humanité, de les enlever des contrées barbares qui les ont vus naître" [Friends of the Blacks, if the Negroes could make themselves heard, they would ask you in the name of humanity to remove them from the barbaric lands that saw them born].

Three months into the slaves' insurrection in Saint-Domingue in 1791, a similar pattern transpires in Nantes, a major port of the Atlantic slave trade in western France, as a group of locals tried to forward a colonist's letter to the King. Where the *Nantais* spoke of the rebellion of the "Noirs à

Saint-Domingue," the colonist wrote that "les Nègres, armés de poignards aiguisés . . . ont égorgé leurs maîtres" [the Negroes, armed with sharp daggers . . . have slit their masters' throats].

The transliteration of "nègre" in Haitian Creole is "nèg." However, "nèg" means neither "black man" nor "negro" in Creole. It means "man"; only in determinate context might it specifically denote a black man. Although the extant literature does not provide for a history of the present meaning, it seems implausible that it also applied in Saint-Domingue. A word of the lingua franca that would be "nègre" in French is unlikely to have denoted the universal social being "man" in the colonial context, applied without differentiation to whites, mulattoes, and blacks. This signification perhaps points to the making of a post-Independence vernacular identity that transcends the relentless colonial racialization of the human experience. The meaning of the word possibly evolved post-Independence to mean "man" as Africans and descendants of Africans reclaimed the universality of their humanity from the colonial past.

When Duvalier spoke of the nègre to bilingual privileged Haitians, he did not speak a French transliteration of nèg. The Haitian nèg on the street is not what he had in mind. The *nègre* of the colonial imagination was a barbarian. That was not Duvalier's nègre, either. Through the turn of the twentieth century, Haitian authors similarly did not in general use the term "nègre" to denote a social subject of African ancestry. The word began to enter the routine vocabulary of black writers of the French Atlantic in the 1930s with the authors of the négritude movement. Then, it denoted not so much a political subject as a cultural subject, a native or diasporic African who embraced Africanity.[2] Beginning in the 1950s, more aggressively polemical authors like Cheikh Anta Diop and Frantz Fanon made the nègre a definite political subject with a grievance specifically against colonial powers. By the 1960s, the historical trajectory of the French word "nègre" had arrived where the US "nigger" would also be by the end of the twentieth century in the vocabulary of US blacks: a derogatory term appropriated and redeployed with defiance by those whom colonial and postcolonial powers intended it to degrade. The nègre Duvalier invoked in his Oath to the Flag as he declared himself president for life would bear memory of colonial violence as he defiantly stared down postcolonial powers. As national avatar, the figure was a logical end point of noirisme, of a piece with the ideological shenanigans that legitimated Duvalier's dictatorial powers.

❧   ❧   ❧

The internationally known bronze sculpture *Le marron inconnu* (The Unknown Maroon), one of Duvalier's most spectacular ideological productions, has fared better in public esteem than his more vacuous ideological undertakings. It is nonetheless, perhaps counterintuitively, very much a site of black-nationalist symbolic violence against the populations of Haiti's rural universe, as Barthélémy (1989) calls the existential world constructed by Haitian rural folks in retentions of the African past. The sculpture is generally associated with its acclaimed author, the mulatto architect Albert Mangonès. It was installed across the street from the National Palace in the *Place du Marron inconnu* (Square of the Unknown Maroon), which Mangonès also designed, imagining the whole as *Le Monument au marron inconnu*, a monument memorializing the maroons of Saint-Domingue. Although Mangonès initiated and executed the project in the context of his body of work as an artist, it was a signature production of Duvalier's dictatorship.[3] Deploying the statue across the street from his palace was no less an act of political theater than his orchestration of the raising of the flag. At the time he decided to patronize Mangonès's memorial, he had been for years an international icon of political turpitude and his extreme political violence had ceased to be a novelty. Prior to Mangonès's redesign of the space, it had in fact been known as "la place du Marron de Saint-Domingue" (Duvalier 1969, 132), and in 1967 Duvalier issued a commemorative 200-gourde gold coin representing the maroon figure under that name (fig. 3.1).

The groundbreaking of Le Monument au Marron inconnu was on September 22, 1967.[4] It was one of several events marking the tenth anniversary of Duvalier's coming to power.[5] It did not have more editorial prominence than any of the others in the day's issue of *Le Nouvelliste*, none of which was a grand gesture to the world. *Le Nouvelliste* presented the project alternately as an "Hommage au Nègre marron inconnu" [Homage to the Unknown Maroon Negro] or a memorial to the "Nègre marron de St. Domingue" [Maroon Negro of Saint-Domingue] to be built on the "Place du Nègre Marron de St. Domingue." The newspaper's short announcement used "Le marron inconnu" neither for the statue nor for the square where it would be located. Similarly, although Duvalier's Minister of Information invoked the "Nègre Marron inconnu" six times in a speech—and "Nègre marron" twice—not once did he use the specific phrase "Le marron inconnu."[6] The regime was speaking to internal publics at that time, not to the world.

Figure 3.1. Marron de Saint Domingue commemorative gold coin issued by François Duvalier's state. © CGB Numismatique Paris.

On December 6, 1968, under a headline spanning six of the eight columns on the front page, *Le Nouvelliste*—an evening paper—reported on the unveiling of the memorial that morning to "an immense crowd comprising personalities from the political, social [and] *diplomatic* [world]" (emphasis added).[7] The headline announced that President Duvalier had inaugurated Le Monument au *Marron inconnu* (emphasis added). Duvalier referred to the statue or to the whole monument a total of five times in his speech that day, and each time he spoke of the "Marron Inconnu." The three times he spoke of "Nègre marron," he referred specifically to the colonial figure, not to the memorial.

At the unveiling of Le Marron inconnu (fig. 3.2), Duvalier was not speaking only to national publics as at the groundbreaking the year before. He was now speaking on the global stage; the name of the memorial had changed accordingly. "Le marron inconnu," evoking the French "Soldat inconnu" and the Anglo-Saxon "Unknown Soldier," carries a derivative luster in the global

Figure 3.2. Le Marron inconnu in April 2018. A metal plate on the side of the base to the right bore Duvalier's words that effectively framed him as author of the memorial. However, the statue was sculpted and the square in which it lies was designed by Albert Mangonès. The plate disappeared from the base sometime later that year. Photo by Bdx.

symbolic economy of the modern West that "Nègre marron" does not. "Le Marron inconnu" situated the sculpture in a global Western field of righteous armed resistance. The year after the unveiling, the National Presses of Haiti published a volume of speeches by various personalities at the event. It is now in library collections of major academic research centers on both sides of the North Atlantic. Meanwhile, Duvalier's ideological voice (in French) remained firmly attached to the base of the statue in an epigram:

> Le monument érigé à la mémoire du Marron inconnu de St-Domingue est
> un rêve caressé par moi longtemps avant d'accéder à la présidence de la

République parce qu'aucun chef d'Etat ne pensa à faire sortir de l'ombre le sublime inconnu dont la lutte pendant trois siècles demeure la plus vivante préfiguration qui devait nous créer dans la vaillance et la gloire cette patrie éternelle qui ne sera remise à personne.[8]

Duvalier's view of the maroon's "struggle over three centuries" as prefigurative of the Revolution resonates particularly with black nationalists (Geggus 1992, 23), but his memorial is a noiriste ideological cooptation of *marronnage*. Geggus (1992) finds no documentation to date that can reasonably place marronage in the direct genealogy of the slaves' 1791 insurrection.[9] Marronage was "an alternative to rebellion, a safety-valve" (Geggus 1992, 27), which removed the threat of revolt from the plantation. A diminished space for maroons' refuge, due to the widespread expansion of coffee estates in mountainous regions, may in fact have directly motivated rebellion on the plantations in 1791 (Dubois 2004, 54). However, Haiti's elites' ritualized remembrance of the maroons of Saint-Domingue as precursors of national sovereignty may yet be historically logical.

At the base of Le Marron inconnu, Duvalier insistently speaks French to the memory of slaves who escaped French colonial violence into the mountains of Saint-Domingue. Moreover, there is no Haitian Creole translation of his text anywhere around the statue. For his part, in a section of the monument (a wall representing the colonial mountains), Mangonès uses an architectonic vocabulary that invokes (in his words) "pages from the collection of ancient wisdom that is the Bible, [to] exalt the dignity of the man who fights for his liberty."[10] Nonetheless, this all would not be as unseemly as it might seem. Like the Revolutionary victors who founded the nation, the maroons were mostly colonial natives and as such bore embryonic traces of Latinity, root of the cultural requirements of a privileged class situation in contemporary Haiti. The Maniel, the most enduring maroon community, were practicing Christians and, for the most part, born in the colony (Geggus 1992). They left the mountains after negotiating a treaty with colonial administrators, in which they committed to "capture and return [runaway] slaves" (Geggus 1992, 25).

Thus, in a Haiti of a small French-speaking privileged minority variously dominating a vast, disenfranchised, monolingual majority of no competence in elite Western cultures, a memorial to the maroons of Saint-Domingue by privileged people does make sense. However, the blackness of the Unknown Maroon has been so mystifyingly reified, its imagined significance so thoroughly universalized, that the sculpture's global audience can actually find in its "aesthetics and symbolism [a] primary marker of freedom [in] Haiti" (Roberts 2015, 12). Or it can yet more grandly be found to convey "Édouard Glissant's notion of 'a prophetic vision of the past' [utilizing] past ideals for imagined trans-historical politics" (Roberts 2015, 12).

Against the backdrop of the historiographic record, Duvalier's memorial to the maroons of Saint-Domingue underscores the chimera of reading social, political, and economic conditions in Haiti through the blackness of Dessalines and the other Founding Fathers, or through the contradistinction of the mulatto. At the unveiling of the monument to the world, Duvalier was remarkably explicit in the symbolic violence done to the memory of the vanquished bossales by Haiti's dominant black nationalism, and by those who reproduce globally the prevalent meanings of Mangonès's sculpture. In his speech at the unveiling lauding the maroons, Duvalier named two native Africans in asserting: "Among them, there were always the unruly ones, such as Petit-Noël Prieur and Lamour Dérance, whom Dessalines [had] to kill so as not to disturb the destiny of the future Fatherland and of the Race."[11] Dérance and his troops were in fact the last bossale army that Dessalines's creole alliance defeated before defeating the French in the second half of 1803. The bossale leaders' "goals, cultural values, and [worldview]" had been different from the vision of *national* sovereignty (Fick 1990, 231), and they are the values and worldviews that would create the cultural system that places Haitian rural folks *andeyò*, practically outside the national polity (Barthélemy 1989). Moreover, the rural cultural universe—the cultures of the bossales' sociopolitical descendants—remains "a global retort to the values of the North" (Barthélemy 1996, 8), which to a considerable extent are at the core of the cultural experience of Haiti's privileged bilingual minority population.[12] Le Marron inconnu could not possibly be speaking to the history of Haiti's monolingual Creole speakers.

In the midst of the noiriste ideological spectacle that introduced Haiti's Unknown Maroon to the world, like Nord Alexis in his speech commemorating the nation's centennial in 1904, Duvalier decolorized the "Race" of the Haitian people as he normalized the murder of the dissenting bossale by the Revolutionary creole (effectively, because of the Africanness of the bossale's vision). This is not surprising as the monument originated with an

Figure 3.3. Albert Mangonès at the unveiling of Le Marron inconnu. The section of the monument in the background represents the colonial mountains. Photo courtesy of ISPAN.

elite mulatto, mulattoes do not speak the nation through color, and Mangonès and Duvalier were introducing it together to the global bourgeois world as united representatives of the nation. Noiristes accommodated mulatto nationalism for the occasion. In his own speech at the unveiling (fig. 3.3), Mangonès indeed did not present the monument in any ideology of color, thereby upholding mulatto nationalist tradition on his side of Duvalier's spectacle. Thus, while deploying a lasting moment of symbolic violence on the monolingual Creole-speaking "masses" of Haiti, a mulatto nationalist and a noiriste jointly managed the ideology of blackness from within the respective nationalisms of their color formations.

When the Monument au Marron inconnu was unveiled, as historical text, it was not addressed to the "people," and it is not now. Its Haitian Creole name, *Nèg mawon* (Maroon Negro), resonates across class lines on the streets of Port-au-Prince, but strictly as reference to a landmark of the cityscape and its surrounding neighborhood. "Nèg mawon"—and I refer specifically to the Creole phrase—does not evoke a moment of historical memory to monolingual Creole-speaking Haitians. The sheer meaninglessness of the sculpture as national symbol to nonprivileged Haitians transpires in an article that appeared in the August 12, 2011, edition of *Le Nouvelliste*. The piece is a heartfelt exposé on conditions in IDP camps that sprouted on the Place du Marron inconnu and elsewhere on the Champ de Mars after the 2010 earthquake. The reporter bemoans that the statues of The Heroes of The Independence spread over the area

> are encircled since 12 January 2010 by a desperate population. Nèg mawon, an islet of tents. The Place du Marron inconnu is an islet of tents not far from the National Palace . . . Nègre marron, symbol of liberty. Very practical for the homeless, the conch shell [in] his hands holds [electricity] cables "[allowing] us [to] watch TV and listen to the radio," says Jean [who] has taken refuge in the shade of the Nègre marron . . . Marie-Lourdes Louis, a laundress, [is] Nèg mawon's neighbor and she doesn't really know what this statue represents. She sees it with its conch shell, she says innocently [and] finds that this object retains a lot of heat and dries quickly the clothes [of] her clients . . . This symbol of liberty, these refugees do not care much for it; it is [for] Bernadette . . . an object of witchcraft . . . Justine protests "since 12 January 2010, a lot of whites have taken pictures of Nèg mawon. They photographed me with him . . . Nèg mawon . . . allowed the world to know that I'm there," [said] the old woman.

The article bears witness to a "geography of despair" among the twenty thousand people living in tents around a statuary representing leaders of the Revolutionary past. However, as it enumerates the ignominies encircling each statue, it also reaffirms the privileged Haitian's authority to determine what the national past is, and to write the present meaning of that past. In lamenting "Nègre marron, symbol of liberty . . . these refugees do not care much for," this authority is clearly exercised against the agency of Haiti's poor to imagine the past from *their* subjective experience of national conditions. While noting "the misery of the people is without mercy," the report reasserts (mulatto) Alexandre Pétion as "the father of Panamericanism" and (black) Henri Christophe as "the builder king." The reporter shows no interest at all in how and where his poor interviewees might situate Christophe, Dessalines, Pétion, and Louverture in the national past (fig. 3.4). The passage on the Mangonès sculpture is particularly significant as the rare text in the literature on Haiti that captures a spontaneous popular interpretation of a

Figure 3.4. Founding Father Toussaint Louverture in the Champ de Mars IDP Camp. The people going about their business around the base of the statue in January 2012 would be part of the population of the Champ de Mars "tent city" that the *Le Nouvelliste* reportage generally found lacking in reverence for the heroes of the national past. Photo courtesy of IOM Haiti.

symbol of the national past constructed by the elites. It is deeply revealing of the alienation of the dispossessed Haitian from the Black Republic narrative.

It is analytically helpful to know that a literate Haitian would need neither an editor's note nor an in-text indication that the interviewees originally spoke in Haitian Creole the words attributed to them in perfect French in quotation marks. The interviewees are poor people living on the street; the *Nouvelliste* readership would presume that they are not speakers of French. With this in mind, one can better appreciate a conspicuous exception in their translated remarks: the reporter quotes everything they said in French, except what they called the sculpture. The Creole phrase "Nèg mawon" is effectively a neologism, a transliteration of the French "Nègre marron." The two phrases are nonetheless not equivalent in signification, precisely because "nèg" does not have the historical-political resonance of "nègre." In contemporary Creole, "mawon" also does not carry the political dimension that the French "marron" and the English "maroon" carry in a certain Western political imaginary. "Mawon" does indicate flight from social or state authority, but without any suggestion of guerilla resistance. A thief, for instance, can

Figure 3.5. Nèg Mawon surrounded by IDP tents in January 2012. Residents of the camp found practical utility, and not much else, in this symbolic object of historic reverence by privileged bilingual Haitians. Photo courtesy of IOM Haiti.

interchangeably be said to be "nan mawon" or "nan kache," both phrases meaning "in hiding."[13] It is little wonder that the monolingual "people" could not read in Mangonès's work the history lesson that both he and Duvalier wished the sculpture to bear (fig. 3.5).

At the time of the *Nouvelliste* article, Creole has been an official language of the nation for nearly a quarter of a century, and it is routinely—if sparingly—used in respectable media. Yet the reporter consistently uses the French "Nègre marron" to refer to *his* subjective experience of the sculpture. In not translating the name in his interviewees' otherwise translated remarks, he emphatically reserves the Creole name Nèg mawon for the *squatters'* subjective experience of the statue. These expressive choices are significant. The linguistically differentiated reference to the sculpture helps keep clear to the *Nouvelliste* readership who is saying what about the work. In general, "Nèg mawon" no more evokes a grand historical past to privileged Haitians educated in French than it does to the monolingual poor. To the privileged, also, the phrase only refers to a place of the city, or to the statue as object. Privileged Haitians would not say "Nèg mawon" to refer to the "symbol of liberty." Matters of august import to people who matter in Haiti are not expressed in Creole by people who matter. Such things remain rigidly in the sphere of French expression.

That the reporter systematically switches to the (French) "Nègre marron" to reaffirm the symbolic significance of the sculpture is hardly the end of the sociopolitical calculus underlying his vocabulary. Although he does refer to the square in which the statue is located as "La Place du Marron inconnu," he always uses "Nègre marron" rather than "Le marron inconnu" to refer to the sculpture itself. This is no less significant than the rhetorical *pas de deux* that he choreographs between "Nègre marron" and "Nèg mawon" to differentiate *his* understanding of the work from the understanding of the squatters. "Nègre marron" and "Le marron inconnu" are both French, but they resonate in different registers. "Nègre marron" is in fact a pleonasm. As Jean Casimir points out, there could not have been a white maroon in Saint-Domingue any more than there could have been a white slave (Casimir 2000). As a rhetorical construct, the phrase has its logic in Duvalier's noiriste populist spectacles.

To the learned classes of Haiti, who articulate the Black Republic narrative, Mangonès's memorial to the maroons very much remains a symbolic instrument in the telling of their story to themselves and to the world. "Le marron inconnu" remains the work's quasi-official name. It is the name by which it continues to be invoked in official ceremonies, and ceremonial commentaries around its symbolic significance are still generally made in French. However, writing on the post-quake IDP camp, the reporter of *Le Nouvelliste* is turned inward, not to the world, addressing national—and more or less nationalist—publics. While noting past glories—presumably yet to be recovered— he endeavors to record ignominious failures of the nation toward its poor subjects. With his use of the phrase "Nègre marron" rather than "Le marron inconnu," "nègre" makes him explicitly "black" in a way the "marron" trope does not. Furthermore, the assonance of the French "nègre" and the Creole "nèg" suggests he is one with the *people* of Haiti. Thus, in effect, as he indicts the nation for a distressing postcolonial condition, "Nègre marron" allows him to manage the protocol of French usage for evoking the solemnity of the memorial, while simultaneously managing the shadow of the French colonial heritage that he embodies. With the appellation "Nègre marron," privileged Haitians reassert Mangonès's history lesson, and with it their construction of the broader national past, while, in effect, imbuing themselves with an illusory proximity to the "people," the poor monolingual Creole-speaking nèg on the street. Indeed, in the article of April 2011, the *Nouvelliste* reporter uses the national avatar fashioned by Duvalier to achieve quite a remarkable feat. The article excludes dark-skinned, dispossessed Haitians from a narration of the Black Republic and, at the very same time, reproduces the trope of blackness as pivot of national unity.

❧   ❧   ❧

I also talked on the theme of the Black Republic with the math teacher, who owns the engineering contracting firm with her husband, the contractor. A woman in her late forties, she steadfastly holds on to substantial ancestral land in the rural southeast of the country. Her father and his siblings were the first generation of the family to migrate to Port-au-Prince to complete their studies; they had successful careers in the liberal professions and established families in tasteful homes in fashionable neighborhoods. I asked her, "What do you think that means, when we say Haiti is a black republic?" Her spontaneous response was baffled hesitation. However, it was not my twenty-six-year-old driver's hesitation about what exactly I might be talking about, when I asked him a similar question. On the contrary, the woman's reaction was that of someone asked to explain a taken-for-granted that is so manifest that one no longer thinks about its underlying rationality. She finally answered, "Our ancestors, the slaves, revolted, and they gained their freedom." We were speaking on the telephone, and she wondered what her seventeen-year-old daughter might think. The girl was nearby, and she eventually passed her the telephone.

I repeated the question to the daughter, a student at the school where her mother teaches. The daughter also hesitated, sounding demure. She was not generally shy around me: I had known the family for a few years and had visited their home on numerous occasions during my fieldwork. After I assured her that I was not putting her on, she let go of her answer: "That means, the slaves, they were black, and we became independent." She could not elaborate further on the theme as she intermittently paused and muttered a few inconsequential words. She seemed as baffled as her mother at being asked to explain an irreducible proposition. Her mother returned to the telephone and reframed the issue to assert that "our ancestors gave us a country, but others make it difficult." I asked her what "others." "Those who don't care," she said. She and I had had enough conversations about *la question de couleur* for me to know that, in her view, "those" would be the mulattoes. I asked her anyway whether she was alluding to the color question. She chuckled, sounding as if she would rather drift off the subject. I did not press it.

I also asked the poet-engineer what the notion of Haiti as a black republic meant to him. He is a well-read black-nationalist activist engaged with issues of social inequality and development. He, too, was baffled that such a question was being asked of him. Knowing that he reflected on issues of nationalism on a regular basis, I prodded him: "Is it for you a taken-for-granted?" He answered: "It is first a taken-for-granted, if one must think about it. It is a historical reality. You could take it as a working hypothesis. But it's a project that stopped with the death of Dessalines."[14] I asked him how the reality, or hypothesis, of the Black Republic might have been inflected by national subjects whose ancestors arrived from Europe and the Levant over the course of the nineteenth century. He answered, "Well, the project was not later developed to redefine 'black independent republic' as a human grouping." He did not provide any suggestion on how the project might be revived. He nevertheless made it clear that however the Black Republic might be redefined, the new definition would be predicated on Dessalines as pivotal axis of nationalist expression. In that, like the math teacher, he ultimately held onto a historical memory of Saint-Domingue's enslaved people, later a people in rebellion, as a social formation undifferentiated in historical situations and material conditions.

Although the math teacher's answer to my question about the meaning of the Black Republic was not intellectually as agile as that of the poet-engineer, their respective answers had something in common: they were both the precipitate of intellectually mediated encounters with the archive. Neither answer was the sum of concrete experiences lived day-to-day. This was brought home to me by answers to my questions on the Black Republic theme from the urban proletariat.

After I asked the twenty-six-year-old driver about the meaning of the Black Republic, I also explored the theme with other poor Haitians. In early December 2011, I discussed the cost of living with a sexagenarian, who earned approximately US$150 a month working as a messenger at the Ministry of the Environment. After enumerating comparatively the costs then and now of various staples of the Haitian diet, he remarked, "Duvalier was mean, but he always wanted the people to eat. It's the big shots who pushed people down." He explained that, in the Duvalier years, a vendor who raised prices above official rates was at risk of violence at the hand of a "tonton makout."[15]

Unlike the math teacher, who clearly alluded to mulattoes in saying "others make it difficult" in the country, the sexagenarian man did not seem to see "the big shots" through color. Because he did not frame the situation in a colorized context, I thought of bringing up Haiti as a "repiblik nwa" (Black Republic).[16] He could neither read nor write, but he answered me with aplomb. He told me that to say Haiti was the first black republic meant "it was the first country black people established." When I asked him what he meant by that, he added: "We were free. But we're not free anymore. It's the Republicans over there and the big shots over here who control everything." He continued seamlessly in a train of thought grounded in concrete experience, explaining that "*Magazen leta* [the State Store] used to sell to the people, making life affordable. Now if a president wants to reopen Magazen leta, foreigners and the big shots get rid of you. That's what we pay for our freedom. When Aristide asked France to repay the price we were forced to pay for our freedom, they came to take him away in the night. Under Duvalier you could eat, but you couldn't talk. Now you can talk."

While in the Black Republic narrative, "educated" people generally subsume the nation's existential realities in an ideational blackness as identity, the illiterate sexagenarian defined a national blackness grounded in his lived experience of local and global realities. He told me that he did not vote in the presidential elections of 2010 because it was clear to him that "his" candidate, Mirlande Manigat, would not win. "M te gen moun nan Maniga. M pa t gen pèsonn nan Mateli" [I had people in Manigat. I had nobody in Martelly], he told me before adding, "the mass of the people moved behind Martelly, so I didn't vote." I realized then that his understanding of the Republic's Blackness was informed by his practical experience of the Duvalierist state rather than by the cultivation of historical memory.

Haitians often give primordial importance to having "moun nan" [people in] an actual or potential agency or process, particularly within the state. If a significant linkage to the state apparatus is actually realized, the "moun nan" becomes a prized asset. Before his current job at the ministry, the sexagenarian had worked at some point as a custodian at L'hopital général, the public teaching hospital in downtown Port-au-Prince. He befriended a physician there, and the two kept in touch over the years. The doctor eventually became involved with the Manigat campaign, thus becoming his "people in" a potential Manigat government. This potential connection to a significant state agency came in a pattern that was central to the man's urbanized experience.

The sexagenarian was born and grew up in the landless peasantry deep in the rural south. He migrated to Port-au-Prince in the middle of the 1970s. His first job in the capital was as the groundkeeper in the home of a family with an authoritative presence in middle- and upper-level state offices since at least the second half of the nineteenth century. The head of the household, an erudite black man with influential friendships in Duvalierist circles, found him his next (and better-paying) job on the ground crew of a fuel depot. In the late 1980s, the superintendent of the depot lost his job in a power struggle; he had hired the sexagenarian, and the sexagenarian was loyal to him. Shortly after a new superintendent took charge of the fuel depot, the sexagenarian also lost his job. He was then hired as a delivery man by a floral designer, a cousin of the erudite black man. In the early 1990s, to pressure the de facto government that succeeded deposed President Jean-Bertrand Aristide, the United Nations imposed a trade embargo on the country. The floral designer lost her last corporate client—the local Citibank—in the resulting recession. The florist then helped the man get the job at the hospital. About ten years later, she was an advisor in the administration of President René Préval—Aristide's former protégé—and got the man his current messenger job in the Ministry of the Environment.

Thus, throughout the trajectory of his life in Port-au-Prince, the sexagenarian had earned a living linked to state power through subjects embodying the black-nationalist tradition. During the entire time, he would have been reading the practical populism that Duvalier articulated with the Black Republic narrative, from the power of violence with impunity vested in the tontons macoutes to the tossing of money from the back seat of the presidential limousine on New Year's Day. At no point would he have been able to read the French texts through which the black-nationalist tradition posits a teleology of color in the nation's political history.[17]

I spoke of the nation being black with another man who could neither read nor write. He and the sexagenarian are from the same village in the South department and know each other well. In the early 1980s, when he was around eleven years old, an aunt of the sexagenarian brought him to the capital to live with an elderly woman as a *restavèk*, practically an open-ended form of indentured domestic servitude. In his case, that lasted less than a month. He was summarily sent to live as a servant in the clergy house of a Catholic parish of the capital three weeks after his arrival, without notice or explanation. He only recalled, "Pè yo te vin chache m" [The priests came to pick me up]. He remained there for eleven years. The parish priest, whom he recalls with deep respect and gratitude and who was a close ally of Jean-Bertrand Aristide, was assassinated during the latter's first exile (1991–1994). The man left the clergy house after the assassination and has since scraped a living in the informal economy. I met him in the Delmas courtyard, where the beauty salon operated (and where I met the unemployed mother of two). For over a decade, he has been a factotum for the absentee owner of the house, who lives overseas, his duties ranging from maintaining the owner's apartment to overseeing minor repairs to paying utility bills.

When I asked the former restavèk whether he knew that Haiti was called a black republic, his answer pointed to the vast gap between the meanings of the nation to its sociopolitically privileged people and its meanings to its dispossessed population. As he answered affirmatively, I asked him more specifically what it meant to him that Haiti was a black republic. He told me: "Sa vle di Desalin te ban n depandans nou" [That means Dessalines gave us our dependence]. I said: "Ou di li te ba nou depandans?" [Did you say he gave us dependence?]. He said, yes. I clarified for him: "M mande w sa paske mo a se endepandans. Yo di Dessalines ba nou endepandans" [I asked you that because the word is independence. They say Dessalines gave us independence]. "An," he said, stretching the syllable the way a French or English speaker might stretch "Ah" or "Oh" to acknowledge an error. I nonetheless asked him whether he knew "endepandans" was the correct word and said "depandans" anyway for his own reason. He said, no. I asked him whether he knew the difference between the two words; he did not.

I explained the difference between "depandans" and "endepandans" to the former restavèk in the context of political sovereignty, and then asked him how he had learned that Dessalines gave us our "dependence." He told me that he had once worked as a field hand for an engineer on some construction projects, and the engineer used to tell him about the history of Dessalines "ak lòt nèg nan tan lontan yo" [and the other men from the old times]. I asked him whether the engineer used the word "depandans." He shook his head, adding: "Sa w di a fòk se sa l te di. Li te konn tout listwa sa yo" [What you said must be what he said. He knew all those stories]. Thus, his response to my inquiry on a national blackness was ultimately similar in a certain way to the response of the sexagenarian who worked at the Ministry of the Environment. In both cases, the understanding of Haiti's presumptive blackness was derivative of encounters with embodiments of the black nationalism that circulates in the privileged classes.

The twenty-six-year-old "tap-tap" driver who drove me to the Firmin symposium and his sister, the owner of the beauty salon in the Delmas courtyard, are cousins of the sexagenarian. The owner of the beauty salon is married to the driver of a minibus transporting passengers between Port-au-Prince and Saint-Marc, a city in the Artibonite region north of the capital. The minibus driver's answer to the question of what it means to call Haiti a Black Republic was a telling non-answer: "Black Republic, I know about it, I hear people say it, but I don't really understand it. There are people in the country who are not black. There's a place called Kazal. People you see in that area, they are light. They look different. They're descendants of Germans. You also find people who look like that in another place, a place called Fondènèg." I mentioned to him that the folks of Kazal, also an Artibonite town, are descendants of Poles, and that perhaps it is folks from Fondènèg, a southern town, who may be of German descent. He answered: "Oh, OK. They look alike, but the difference between them, Kazal people are tall. Fondènèg people are shorties. Maybe that's in a difference between Poland and Germany."

Texts by educated people for educated people in Haiti generally invoke the populations of Casale and Fond-des-Blancs as exceptions that make salient the fact of a *black* republic.[18] In such texts, these light-skinned groups in the rural interior become localized specificities in the broader history of the (black) peasantry. However, the minibus driver invoked them to problematize rather than to reaffirm the Blackness of the Republic. He is obviously aware of his world at both local and global levels, but he is not aware of what it is that people are talking about when they speak of Haiti as the Black Republic. Unlike the sexagenarian ministry messenger, he can read and write. He is a high school graduate. "I don't really recall learning about the Black Republic in school," he said to me. I asked him whether none of his Haitian history teachers ever mentioned the phrase. After hesitating a moment, reviewing his memory, he added: "That would be in the lower grades, fifth, fourth grade of secondary school. I don't remember. I wasn't interested in those classes. They were boring. The teachers didn't make these classes interesting. They made me sleepy." I asked him whether he might have been exposed to discussions based on Haiti as a black republic in the higher grades.[19] He answered assertively: "In the higher grades, second to philo, we didn't talk about a black republic."[20] I asked him, "How about later on in life?" He answered: "After school I never was in discussions or to be thinking about the subject 'black republic.' When I got onto the question with you, that was the first time I had somebody bring up this conversation with me."

The minibus driver did not go to college, because his father could not continue to send money home from Florida to support him through school. He began to scratch out a living in the informal economy and eventually started driving on the minibus circuit several years ago. His penmanship and the level of his fluency in written and spoken French do indicate a level of formal schooling at which the Black Republic thesis would presumably transpire in the history curriculum. If it, in fact, did in his case, he obviously has no firm recollection. What is significant here is not so much his relative lack of familiarity with the thesis as his utter lack of reverence toward it. It is also significant that the thesis evokes neither irony nor disdain in him— that would yet be affective engagement informed by ideology. My questions about the Black Republic to him elicited only a matter-of-fact consideration of an objective proposition. As he is now in his late thirties, much like the twenty-six-year-old "tap tap" driver, and unlike the sexagenarian Ministry of the Environment messenger, in his formative years he would have had no significant exposure to Duvalier's practical populist gestures. If he indeed ever had any scholastic education in the Black Republic narrative, and now has no recollection of it, the underlying ideological positions of the narrative must not have cohered with his concrete experiences in the more than two decades since his formal education stopped. Yet to privileged adults and adolescents of post-Duvalier Haiti, although they are generally at a loss to explicate it, the Blackness of the Republic continues to be a taken-for-granted. The chasm between the ideology of Blackness and the fact of class is glaring.

The general incomprehensibility of the Black Republic narrative to Haitians outside the privileged formations of color lends credence to the argument that any Haitian exceptionalism—whether deployed to idealize or to denigrate Haiti—will inevitably fail to account for the human dimension of the Haitian experience (Dayan 2010). In constructing the exceptional world-historical glory of the founding of Haiti, that narrative remains a romantic mythology of the blackness of the Saint-Domingue slave (cf. Scott 2004), which has mystifyingly dominated the imagination of generations of students of Haiti. It is a national narrative that *logically* precludes a space either as author or as audience for the dispossessed Haitian actually existing in the nation's tragic postcolonial present (cf. Scott 2004), because it is fundamentally an instrument of class formation at the service of the privileged.

CHAPTER FOUR

CLASS AND BLACK-NATIONALIST SOCIALITY

"La Dessalinienne," adopted as Haiti's national anthem in 1904, advanced the Black Republic thesis in its reference to Dessalines, but it did not reduce the national subject to an ethnotype. The reference is in fact limited to the title, and the lyrics are thoroughly devoid of any evocation of an identitarian subjectivity. Thus, the hymn and François Duvalier's Oath of Fidelity to the Flag arguably express contradictory nationalist visions. Duvalier nonetheless produced deep nationalist affect by collapsing them into the singular statement of the ritualized raising of the flag every morning at eight o'clock throughout most of the duration of the dictatorship. The spectacle was part of a deft ideological program that ultimately infused "noirisme" with the appearance of irrefutable historical coherence. At the time I was in the field, as ideology and political project, noirisme had long been in pronounced retreat. However, its historic force was still central to the praxis of black identity in Haiti's elites and middle classes. Mythically embodying African cultural retentions borne by the peasantry, affectively alluring and historically coherent, Duvalier's *nègre* has in fact remained the essential Haitian in the privileged black-nationalist imaginary since the 1960s.

Below, I first situate the figure of the nègre as the pivot of a black-nationalist sociality of the privileged, where it preempts mulatto participation. I then show (black) constituents of this sociality crossing class boundaries into a space of popular expression—an art fair—where their markers of class none-theless remain operative as they socialize with lower-class "blacks." They then seamlessly move into a transcendent sociality—at a trendy bistro—where mulattoes and blacks together realize and reproduce their class situations. I am with them again yet later at another space of privilege—another restau-rant—where the black-nationalist sociality reproduces itself in contradistinc-tion to the mulatto, who becomes the *other* Haitian. I end the chapter with an empirical illustration of the inability of the black-nationalist sociality of privilege to contain or deny the class tensions that inhere in social relations between privileged and nonprivileged blacks of the nation.

From the 1930s into the second decade of the twenty-first century, for Hai-tian black nationalists, the nègre was to define the "proper [form] of being" in everyday life (Bruun, Jakobsen, and Krøijer 2011, 2), a distinct sociality which—in ideological habitus and everyday praxis—reproduces the Black Republic narrative as lived experience. In the post-Duvalier moment, the fig-ure—always a *nègre*, never the feminine *négrèsse*—has receded from political discourse, but, among privileged black-nationalist Haitians, he nonetheless continues to be the default form of being properly Haitian. As it was during the dictatorship, black-nationalist sociality in the post-Duvalier moment is a black qua black sociality. It is so not because it requires a specified degree of dark complexion of its constitutive subjects but rather because it effectively reaffirms Duvalier's nègre—unambiguously a *black*—as the ideal type of Haitian. In this colorized mode of being social, educated black-nationalist Haitians construct between themselves and "blacks" in the "masses" an ide-ational "equality as sameness" (2).

In determinate forms of being together, organic constituent subjects generally produce a hierarchy of abilities of properly being social (Bruun, Jakobsen, and Krøijer 2011). In Haiti, a minimal reverence for the nègre is a minimum prerequisite to enter spaces of social practice that the figure undergirds. Since the early nineteenth century, when mulattoes represented themselves as the éclairé segment of the national population by virtue of their education in French cultures, their formation has ritually reproduced a defin-ing distance from the nation's African heritage. In general, contemporary mulattoes could not display in their habitus that minimum reverence for the nègre required to partake of the black-nationalist sociality. Since the repro-duction of the black and mulatto formations within the privileged classes nonetheless requires some positive articulations between the two formations, the proper form of being together among black nationalists is as permeated by ideological contradictions today as it was during Duvalier's dictatorship.

The poet-engineer devotes enthusiastic energies to art and cultural events at the socioeconomic margins, often in spaces generally perceived in privileged circles as dens of violence and insecurity. A black friend often joins him in these events. The friend, a cultural impresario, is assertively dismissive of not only noirisme but also of the Black Republic thesis itself. To the impresario, as he put it to me once, "the idea of Haiti as a 'black' Republic diminishes the achievement and does not place the Haitian Revolution with the French Revolution and the American Revolution in the history of modernity." He nevertheless adamantly values the African heritage in Haitian life and its representation in both the mainstream and at the margins. To him, it is the sine qua non of national identity.

The cultural impresario and the poet-engineer took me at an advanced hour of a December night to the opening of the 2011 edition of Ghetto Biennale, an art fair hosted by Atis Rezistans [Resistance Artists]. The latter is a collective of half a dozen artists on Boulevard Jean-Jacques Dessalines, popularly known as Grand-Rue, an artery that runs through several slums in downtown Port-au-Prince. They produce works sculpted or otherwise created from the refuse of urban life. The two founding sculptors and the other members of the group grew up and still live in the surrounding slum. The open-air base of the collective, a lot set back from Grand-Rue, reflects their life experience. In addition to their work and exhibition spaces, the site also contains some precarious living quarters (Vanneschi 2013). The work of the two principal members has been exhibited in the USA and in Europe. However, by their social location, they are outside the respectable sociality of privileged black nationalists. The math teacher, a noiriste Aristide loyalist and steadfast supporter of the populist Lavalas movement, considered it reckless adventurism that the cultural impresario, a close friend of hers, and the poet-engineer took me to Grand-Rue at all, let alone at night, for the Ghetto Biennale.

The Ghetto Biennale, a celebration of art at the margins, is actually one of the places where I feel most secure in the field. It is curated by the two founders of Atis Rezistans and a British artist. In addition to the members of the collective, participants include several foreign guest artists, who created their works locally over the preceding weeks. The art on display in this year's edition of the fair range from the intimate to the monumental, shown in, on, and around shacks spread about the unpaved lot of the collective.

Notwithstanding the particulars of the location, the scene—around 10 p.m. about two weeks before Christmas—is reminiscent of trendy art-show openings at the margins of global art centers.

The artists and some early-career curators mingle with visitors that include local and foreign cognoscenti and neighborhood residents. The foreigners, as far as I can tell, are all whites (mostly Europeans, it seems), except for a smattering of Asians. A small group of Americans apparently affiliated with an NGO operating in Port-au-Prince come by for a brief visit with their Haitian guides. The local cognoscenti—during the time I am here tonight, at least—are a handful of blacks from the intellectual elite. Haitian Creole is de rigueur here as language of conversation among them. The poet-engineer and the impresario introduce me to a Haitian scholar who has founded a socialist political party and taught at Haitian and French universities. All three seem to have personal acquaintances in the community.

The local cognoscenti's visit to the Biennale realizes a black qua black sociality not by the fact that visitors and artists are "blacks." Rather, it is the visitors' operative presumption of their existential unity—as national subjects—with the artists, if not with the broader neighborhood. The presumption is there, when the cultural impresario leads me to the shack of a young artist who works with discarded tires and the two of them discuss a pending visit by a foreign collector arranged by the impresario. It is there, when I later join the poet-engineer on the sidewalk on Grand-Rue, while he chats with one of the leaders of Atis Rezistans about the state of things—political and social—in the neighborhood. The privileged blacks' assumption of sociopolitical unity with their artist hosts is in the tone of genuine familiarity of their conversations. It is in the absence of false modesty as they partake of the camaraderie of equals that underlies the encounters.

Neither the poet-engineer nor the cultural impresario is concerned about my safety as I stroll alone around the darkest recesses of the grounds and over to an adjacent lot, where an NGO is showing a movie on a giant screen. It is not that any of the middle-class blacks here holds any illusion about the state of insecurity in Port-au-Prince. Rather, it is taken for granted that we are in a respectable community organized and maintained by subjects of legitimate and viable civic agency. While, in privileged national life, vodou is routinely made out to be a questionable exceptionality, to the poet-engineer, the cultural impresario, and the other educated blacks at the Biennale, the vodou cosmology underlying nearly all of the art on display has nothing of the exotic and is instead an everyday dimension of the national experience. The privileged blacks present effectively presume that they share a political project with neighborhood residents over against the powers that be. In their presence here, they embody the common cause with the dispossessed Haitian that is pivotal to the black-nationalist imaginary. Yet class differentiation of national belonging remains, ever so subtly, even if it remains subsumed in the ideology of Haiti's Blackness.

The poet-engineer, the cultural impresario and a few others briefly debate what they might find to drink around here at this time. By my experience dining and drinking with him, the poet-engineer drinks no other alcohol but Prestige, the locally produced beer.[1] The cultural impresario's taste in alcohol is very versatile, ranging from red wine to Barbancourt rhum to cognac and many things in between. The consensus is that at this hour there would not be a place open nearby to buy liquor. One of the leaders of Atis Rezistans is part of the discussion. I detect the smell of "kleren" on his breath, which I also detected on the breath of other artists as I walked around the grounds. Potent and inexpensive, "kleren," distilled from sugarcane, is the default spirit of the lower classes. A sidewalk vendor in the vicinity is still "open," someone surmises; we are likely to find beer there. But it is likely to be warm, someone else adds. Kleren is probably yet more likely to be available, but it is not a consideration of what we may find to drink at the vendor's stand. The poet-engineer sends for beer, and we are indeed all soon having lukewarm Prestige, including the leader of the collective. Eventually, the cultural impresario and I are hungry; the poet-engineer—who has already had dinner—proposes to find us a place to eat.

After we get back to the poet-engineer's SUV, we begin to consider the options for food. As he pulls away from the curb, he steers the vehicle as a matter of course toward the "residential" areas east of downtown Port-au-Prince. I ask him, "Kote n prale?" [Where are we going?] He answers, "Nou pa di m nou grangou? Nou pral chache jwenn yon kote pou n manje" [Didn't you say you were hungry? We're going to try to find a place for you to eat]. The poet-engineer is heading away from downtown Port-au-Prince by default, although he is not sure exactly where he is going to take us to eat. It just would not have occurred to him to think of looking for a place to eat in the neighborhoods surrounding the Ghetto Biennale, and I realize it would not have occurred to me either, now or in the years when I was a regular on the nightlife scene of Port-au-Prince as an adolescent and as a young adult.

We first drive to an open-air café kept by a French expatriate in the Pacot neighborhood. Haitians of all shades are mingling with an international clientele in a jovial atmosphere of bourgeois good living. The bar is open, but the kitchen is closed; we leave. We end up at Presse Café, a trendy nightclub-restaurant in Pétion-Ville not very far from the hills where the poet-engineer and the fair-complexioned executive live.

A few stock phrases from the North American urban vocabulary lend themselves to describe Presse Café: a "cool" place of "casual chic" with a vaguely "bohemian vibe." When we arrive tonight, a band is playing, led by a mulatto musician who has been entertaining the bourgeoisie and the middle classes since the 1970s. Photographs of American jazz legends hang on the walls. A distinctly ideological artifact hangs in the interior dining room: a framed poster of the front page of the February 6, 2004, issue of the daily *Le Matin*. The blown-up page features the onset of an armed rebellion the day before, which led to the ouster of President Jean-Bertrand Aristide about three weeks later. As it happens, both the poet-engineer and the cultural impresario welcomed Aristide's ouster, though they abhor the neo-Duvalierist rebels who were the catalyst of the coup. The three of us take a table on the enclosed terrace. The place is not ostentatious; its prices are moderate for a restaurant in Pétion-Ville that caters to the middle classes. When we are done eating two dinners with four or five bottles of beer (Prestige) and three glasses of wine (the cultural impresario and I having had the same dish of fried pork, rice and beans, fried plantains and salad), the check will add to US$87, excluding tip. At breakfast, omelets are around US$9.

At the table behind me, three women, an older one with perhaps her daughters or nieces, will converse mostly in French throughout the hour and a half or so that we are here. Not long after we sit down, the host of the restaurant leads a couple to the table across the aisle to my left. The man, a clair, was my classmate in elementary school. Like myself, he went to the USA for college after high school, and our paths have crossed intermittently over the intervening years. He introduces me to the woman. As it turns out, the woman's older sister is a friend from my adolescence who teaches at a prestigious art college in the New England region of the USA. After I exchange pleasantries with them, they turn their attention to each other. They seem to be on a "date," and their conversation is in French. That reminds me of my own date with the woman's older sister several years ago in New York City, before she took her current position in New England. She and I attended a prominent museum exhibit on postcolonial modernity in sub-Saharan Africa and had dinner at an Italian restaurant afterward. During the four or five hours of our date, discussing, among other subjects, colonialism and its legacy and our high school days (same institution, she one year ahead of me), my early attempts at using Creole did not seem welcome, and we spoke French and English alternately throughout the evening.

Tonight, at Presse Café, my old classmate and his date—my friend's younger sister—do not use Creole either. Their conversation remains in French. Haitian Creole is not the language of courtship in places of privilege in Haiti. For either of the potential partners, fluency in the French language signals to the other not only a minimal assurance of belonging in the privileged classes but also the minimum capacity required to reproduce the class situation. Throughout an ensuing marriage, French usage within the household would remain a ritual reassertion of that belonging.

A mulatto man approaches the three women at the table behind me to say hello. He chats with them in French. He wears a pink wristband symbolizing his personal allegiance to President Michel Martelly. Constant demonstration of fealty to the person of Duvalier and to his regime in some fashion or other was a requirement for access to the largesse of his state, and not an unreasonable precaution for routine personal safety. Wearing the pink wristband under Martelly is a growing practice, and those—including the poet-engineer and the cultural impresario—who would rather be rid of Duvalier's ghost once and for all view it warily as a proto-Duvalierist affectation. The man's face looks somewhat familiar; I think he is an acquaintance, the son of a Duvalier-era Port-au-Prince mayor. He, too, may be thinking that we know each other, because after speaking with the women he steps up to my table. He shakes my hands, asking (in French) how I am doing. He also shakes hands cordially with my tablemates. The poet-engineer seems nonplussed; the cultural impresario does not seem to care one way or the other. By now, I am sure the light-skinned man is not who I first thought he was, although I cannot tell who he is. After he walks away, I remain uncertain about his identity, but he never stopped seeming as if he knew me.

The poet-engineer still seems mildly annoyed that the man with the pink wristband stopped at our table and—worse, it seems—shook his hand. To both him and the cultural impresario, the Duvalier dictatorship was a degeneracy of the national project, Michel Martelly is a Duvalier political heir, and that man broadcast his fealty to Martelly with his pink wristband. The poet-engineer remains nonplussed as the cultural impresario and I chitchat. I try to make amends with the poet-engineer. I say I thought the man was the son of that former Port-au-Prince mayor. I want to suggest that I had merely been interested in situating my memory, not that I particularly cared to speak with the man. I realize too late that invoking a prominent Duvalier-ist from the actual Duvalier regime cannot possibly help the poet-engineer's mood. I follow this minor blunder by simply asking him and the cultural impresario whether they know the light-skinned man. They do not, but they agree he is not that mayor's son as I first thought. I will never have any idea who the man in fact was.

The evening moves on. Inside, the music plays, and fashionable couples dance. The big and small things that the poet-engineer, the cultural impresa-rio, and I talk about at our table are not qualitatively different from what we spoke about earlier in the evening at the Ghetto Biennale. The poet-engineer updates the cultural impresario and me on the state of things at Noailles, another community of sculptors in Croix-des-Bouquets, a municipality just outside the city limits northeast of Port-au-Prince. Noailles sculptors work with cut metal and, like the Atis Rezistans collective, in a tradition steeped in vodou symbolism. The poet-engineer's and the cultural impresario's remarks, invoking the artmaking in both places, tread on the theme of artists at the margins asserting a national voice that is neglected, if not disdained, by the elites. This is to say that black nationalists do not suspend circulation of the Black Republic thesis, when they enter a place like Presse Café. However, all in all, the sociality here at Presse Café is not the stuff of which the Black Republic narrative is made.

Not long after the Martelly supporter walks away from our table, a black man and two women are brought to sit at the table behind the poet-engineer. The man seems to be a senator I saw discussing fiscal policy on television a few nights ago; the poet-engineer confirms that the man is indeed the senator. He is a principal architect of the country's fiscal priorities. I ask the poet-engineer and the impresario whether one of them knows the senator or knows someone who can introduce me to him. I would like to interview him for my project. The poet-engineer matter-of-factly recommends that I simply walk to the senator's table and introduce myself. This is not an unreasonable proposition, and it is the suggestion of someone accustomed to the routine articulation of sociopolitical privilege. I did recruit a number of collaborators whom I had not known before by approaching them "cold."

However, on my current trip, two prospective collaborators—two wealthy mulatto businessmen, one of whom I was friends with in adolescence, the other a complete stranger—withdrew their respective promises of collaboration. With that in mind, I rather wish for a personal introduction to the senator, and I serendipitously recognize one of the women with him. She is a Haitian-born scholar who directs a research program at one of the most prestigious American universities. I met her earlier in the year at a conference abroad and discussed my research with her; she eventually facilitates a brief conversation between the senator and me at their table.[2]

By somatic appearance and social situation, the scholar who introduced me to the senator might be a mulatto. She, the other woman at the table, and the senator might nonetheless very well chitchat about the politics and history of their country from the premise—stated or unstated—that it is a black nation, much as the poet-engineer, the cultural impresario, and I have in fact done intermittently at our table. The three of us, much as the senator and the two women at their table, are actually having a swell time at a place of bourgeois conviviality, capping off, in our case, a night that we started at the Ghetto Biennale in a slum of downtown Port-au-Prince. At the Ghetto Biennale, we—*blacks*—lived the Blackness of the nation. Here, as will be the case every time I return, there may be any number of black nationalists present, quite possibly the majority of those present, but the disparate social relations that animate the place find their coherence in a commonality of privilege, not in the nation's Blackness. Presse Café would not become a site where black nationalists realize their ideological convictions about the Blackness of the Republic. It is a place where privileged Haitians realize their privilege and reproduce its underlying social relations across the boundaries of color.

❧   ❧   ❧

On my final trip to the field in October 2012, I lived a moment of befuddling political ideological incoherence within the sociality of privileged black nationalists, incidentally at another moderately-priced bistro that is neither ostentatious nor pretentious. It was a Saturday evening, and I was again with the poet-engineer and the cultural impresario. We were at Vert Galant for drinks and snacks. An earlier plan had been to meet up with a friend whom the poet-engineer and I had known since childhood. However, he and the cultural impresario eventually lost their interest. Our friend expected us to

meet him at an upscale restaurant in Pétion-Ville, where he was having dinner with his wife as he did every Saturday. Tonight, we found out belatedly,
the couple would also be eating with a high-ranking officer of Jean-Bertrand
Aristide's political organization. Both the poet-engineer and the cultural
impresario found the thought of breaking bread with one of Aristide's top
political advisors insufferable. The cultural impresario remarked that the restaurant was in any case overly pretentious and overrated, compounding the
poet-engineer's general distaste for the "bourgeois" manners of our friend's
clair wife. They elected to take me to Le Vert galant instead.

Le Vert galant is in a classic gingerbread house in the Bois-Verna section
of Port-au-Prince, an area that long ago lost its high-end sheen from the early
decades of the twentieth century. The place sometimes presents music and
other cultural programs versed in Haiti's African-influenced vernaculars or
the African diaspora. It is run by a slim, white French expatriate, apparently in
his thirties. As his dog gleefully darts around the bar area sniffing patrons, then
darts back to him, the animal's lustrous black hair accented by sheer white
spots at the belly makes it as much pet as fashion accessory. A few blocks up
the street is the "Institut français d'Haiti" [French Institute of Haiti], a prestigious instrument of French diplomacy on the cultural scene of the capital
for several decades. Patrons often repair here for drinks following events
there. The smart set, the literati, and the artsy who want a fashionable setting
without the elitism of Pétion-Ville would find it here. When the poet-engineer,
the cultural impresario, and I arrived, access to the wraparound porch was
barred. A sign at the threshold of the porch, off of the entrance to the dining
room, announced that it was closed to the public for a private reception. The
sign gave no indication of who was giving the party or for whom it was being
given, and it did not at all impress the cultural impresario or the poet-engineer.

The poet-engineer and the cultural impresario strode through the interior of the restaurant with the bearing of the entitled, and I followed them.
Through a door in the dining room, we reappeared on the other side of the
terrace in the middle of the reception. The poet-engineer and the cultural
impresario quickly realized that the host of the party was Fokal, a Haitian
NGO funded by the Open Society Foundations of the Hungarian-US financier George Soros.[3] Without further ado, they effectively made themselves
bona fide guests at the party.

The poet-engineer walks over to greet three black women—Fokal officers—holding court on a sofa. The majority of the other guests are youthful

white foreigners working on projects variously affiliated with the organization. As the women acknowledge the goodwill of their guests with light-hearted conviviality, the moment distinctly strikes me as a realization of the Black Republic's promise—educated, worldly, black Haitians leaving no doubt about their self-confidence and their self-esteem as sovereign national subjects of the modern West.

At least by superficial indications—by the presentation on its website, by its architecturally impressive headquarters in Port-au-Prince (fig. 4.1), by my collaborators' casual reference to it in conversation—Fokal seems to be the most important local patron of cultural production and educational initiatives in the country. Although it is not usually written in capital letters, "Fokal" is in fact an acronym. The widely known full name of the organization is Fondasyon konesans ak libète [Foundation for Knowledge and Freedom]. The phrase is Haitian Creole, the lingua franca that unites the nation's subjects across class and color boundaries. If Creole is the nation's co-official language with French, it is the sole national language. Borne by such a prominent agency as its nominal identification, Fokal's formal name is of considerable symbolic significance in the black-nationalist imaginary. However, other than in the name, Haitian Creole is completely absent from the organization's website, and it will still be at the time I write this more than five years later. Fokal's internet home is yet a bilingual site, of French and English expression. As the poet-engineer chats with them, the cultural impresario and I walk over to the serving station, where waiters help us to savory hors-d'œuvres, wine, and rum punch. While the three Fokal black officers hold court now on the restaurant's terrace, the organization's nominal appropriation of the Haitian Creole language might mystify their vast existential distance from the country's (generally dark-skinned) monolingual Creole-speaking majority population.

The poet-engineer, the cultural impresario, and I reconvene at a table in the garden of the restaurant and order more drinks and food from the menu. A trio is covering standards from the folk and pop repertoire. Eventually, Haiti's arguably best-known noiriste intellectual arrives at the party on the terrace. One of my collaborators in the mulatto elite knows him and told me about him a few days earlier. From the little of the intellectual's writing that I have read and critical commentaries that I have heard about his work, I gather that he engages earnestly with the national condition. The poet-engineer and the cultural impresario have told me as much, while remaining dismissive of what they considered the noiriste framing of his concerns.

Figure 4.1. Facade of Fokal's Headquarters on Avenue Christophe in Port-au-Prince. Photo by the author.

Meanwhile, three other individuals have joined us. When we came to the garden, a German woman was sitting by herself at a nearby table. The impresario, ever the promoter, in short order struck up a conversation with her, introduced himself, and had her come to our table. A little later, he noticed an acquaintance, an older black woman, with a much younger female companion at another table on the other side of the garden. The two soon also joined our table at the invitation of the cultural impresario. The younger woman is a student in her early twenties at a nearby private university. The cultural impresario will later tell me that she serves the older woman as a "tchoul" [lackey], a social-climbing strategy for access to social spaces that might otherwise be closed to her.

At the moment, in a voice of imperious elocution that matches her erect torso and graceful hand gestures as she speaks, the older woman is regaling us—in French—with a tale of her career trajectory before she retired. She started out as a secretary. After detours in various fields, the high point of her professional life came as a consultant hired by failing companies to restore their viability. With evident pride, she tells us of her skills and lack

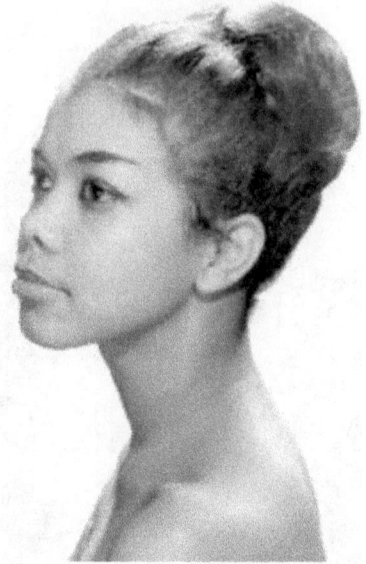

Figure 4.2. A daughter of the black state bourgeoisie, Toto Bissainthe was born in 1934 in Cap-Haïtien and left Haiti in 1950 to study in France. She had her start in the theater in the context of the "négritude" movement. She returned to Haiti in 1986. Photo courtesy of Gérard Bissainthe.

of sentimentality in firing workers and cutting costs to bring her clients' enterprises back to profitability. In at least a few of the instances she enumerates as illustration, she is evidently firing working-class people, who, in Haiti, would almost inevitably be "black" Haitians. Laughter and bonhomie continue unabated at the table. The poet-engineer, a community organizer, is highly critical of capitalist exploitation; as a Haitian in Haiti, and an anthropologist in the world, I am, too. The two of us are very much in the woman's audience. I glance at the poet-engineer, but I cannot tell whether he finds the moment incongruous. I, the ethnographer, perceive the incongruity in what I, the Haitian, organically *know* to be the unity of the Haitians here in blackness.

At some point, the trio starts to play an instrumental cover of "Pòs Machan," a ballad created by the black Haitian actress and singer Toto Bissainthe (fig. 4.2). The retired woman spontaneously leaves the table after the trio plays a few bars of music. She walks over to the musicians and claims their microphone in time to begin singing on cue. The first part of the song tells of a woman who leaves the popular neighborhood of Pòs Machan and arrives on the Champs-de-Mars. When the narrator, a man, first catches sight of her, he "is standing by [the statue of] Dessalines, feeling like chatting." The girl smiles at him, he smiles at her. He eventually follows her past the statue of Alexandre Pétion to the back of a reviewing stand. Night has just fallen;

they "bite" and "squeeze" each other. "Girl, what a party!" exclaims the narrator, leaving the rest of the story to the imagination.

The second part of the song begins with the narrator at a café in the area, having a drink with "moun debyen" [people of good society]. The girl is passing by again. She approaches to talk; all of the narrator's friends flee, fearing contamination of their social standing by the girl's lower-class appearance. "Girl, what's going on?" the narrator asks. He smiles; she cries. She then tells him that she is pregnant. His answer is succinct: "Leu pitit la va fèt, si se yon ti milat, w a remèt li Babyòl" [When the baby's born, if it's a li'l mulatto, you'll drop him off at Babiole], a hillside residential neighborhood that is geographically and socially clear across the city from Pòs Machan, the woman's neighborhood. After the song ends, as the retired black woman rejoins our table, the poet-engineer, the cultural impresario, and the two other women at the table applaud her impromptu performance, with warm applause also emanating from the terrace where the noiriste intellectual is hanging out at the Fokal party.

Although the trio that backed the retired woman played folk songs in addition to pop classics, it was not a *folkloric* combo. The trio that greeted me two weeks earlier, when I arrived at Toussaint Louverture Airport, was. That group wore colorful costumes that any Haitian was highly unlikely to wear on the streets of everyday Port-au-Prince. I lack the critical vocabulary of a musicologist or a melomane to make transparent in text the sonic distinctions between the band at the airport and the band at Vert Galant, but I certainly *heard* them. What I saw and heard of the trio at the airport greeted arriving Haitian and foreign tourists with folklore, a "romantic primitivism [that] 'enslaves' its objects" (Middleton 1990, 169), idealizing Haiti in sight and sound that are imaginatively *not* of the present moment. The trio at Vert Galant was very much of the present moment, in the musicians' clothes as much as in their harmonic arrangements, even as songs they played from the folk repertoire remained imaginatively "authentic expression of a way of life now past" (Middleton 1990, 127).

The pop classics covered by the trio at Vert Galant, in their durability in the national imaginary, were no less an authentic creative expression of the presently existing nation than the folk songs that they played. The "authenticity" of the music as a salient dimension of the black qua black sociality of privilege was punctuated by the rendition of "Pòs Machan." The song is a lilting ballad from beginning to end, and throughout the lyrics remain innocuous behind the melody. Nonetheless, in the fictional narration of a privileged mulatto man making a slut of a young (black) woman from the lower classes, the retired black woman reprised the trope of the mulatto as bogeyman of the nation, incidentally just after telling my tablemates and me her very real story of firing workers to enhance business profits. Moreover, in this momentary instantiation of black-nationalist sociality, with not one mulatto in sight, the poet-engineer, the cultural impresario, and I were at a social distance from Atis Rezistans that was no less vast than when we were at Presse Café after visiting the Ghetto Biennale. We were also almost certainly at a considerable ideological distance from the retired black woman on the politics of the human condition in slums such as those surrounding Atis Rezistans. In effect, our political liberalism—our political-economic ideological opposition to the retired woman—was subsumed in the ideology of Haiti's Blackness.

❀   ❀   ❀

In the middle of the week after the Saturday I crashed the Fokal party at Vert Galant, I am at Presse Café for the first time on this trip. The poet-engineer has arranged for a small group of friends to get together to celebrate the return of a local artist who migrated to Canada about a decade ago. A fashionably slim middle-aged black woman sits next to me. Her hair is styled in lush dreadlocks and her outfit of jeans and chiffon blouse is meticulously accessorized. She studied architecture in the USA and runs a design firm with her sister, a fellow architect. Her two other siblings are physicians, as was her father. The cultural impresario is also here. Together with the artist, who has an upcoming exhibit at a local gallery, we are the core occupants of the table. Several others will join us temporarily as the afternoon turns into evening, much as we will also individually table-hop. The German woman will come and go, again at the invitation of the cultural impresario.

At some point, another black woman sits across the table from me. Her close-cropped hair seems free of chemical treatment. Today, as it happens, she worked her last day at Fokal. We strike up a conversation and within a few minutes she tells me about her "withdrawal symptoms" from not having been to Paris in a relatively long time, not since she returned home from her university studies. She muses wistfully (in French), "The air in Paris, the atmosphere. Oh! I just miss it."

Like his colleagues at the Atis Rezistans collective, the artist at the table today does reclamation art, creating original works from discarded objects of urban life. The poet-engineer, the cultural impresario, and the woman with the lush dreadlocks have known him for a long time, since well before he left for Canada. Like the rest of us at the table, the poet-engineer excepted, he routinely alternates between French and Creole as we chat, eat, and drink. The poet-engineer speaks strictly Creole in a setting like this, among friends. I have seen him speak French with Haitians on relatively limited occasions, for example, in formal work-related conversations or speaking with an elder who would rather not speak Creole. Incidentally, language is the site where Haiti's drama of class trumping color begins to transpire at the table.

When the reclamation artist speaks French, his closed "e" (as in "je" [I]) sounds closer to "é" and his open "e" (as in "heure" [hour, time]) tends toward "è." His "u" similarly tends to sound like "i." In Haiti, such diction marks origins in the lower classes, and privileged Haitians use merciless humor to delegitimize as interlopers Haitians of such French speech in spaces of privilege. Such speakers of French are said to have "bouch su" [sour mouth]. The artist is now speaking with aggrieved intensity. He is holding forth about the insignificance of worldly concerns relative to spiritual power, which, he implies, he is now acquainted with and the rest of us at the table is not. He wears a pendant with a Buddhist motif on a necklace and—as much as I can tell—his remarks reveal an inchoate spirituality with a vaguely Buddhist bent. As he speaks, the woman with lush dreadlocks, the poet-engineer, and the cultural impresario do not physically pull away from him, but they certainly disengage from the conversation. All three look at him in suspended animation. When I notice their reaction, I, the native anthropologist, reframe my Haitian's objective observation (Narayan 1993).

As the artist speaks, his upper lips and brows are scrunched just so in something of a scowl. The "sour mouth" is in his French phrases. It now occurs to me that his facial gestures as much as his diction (both French and Creole) are a *distinction* of the Haitian at the table without an organic education in Haiti's bourgeois ways of body management (Bourdieu 1979). It occurs to me, the ethnographer, that the poet-engineer, the cultural impresario, the woman with lush dreadlocks, or I, the Haitian, would not generally express some variation of being upset by scrunching our brows or lips the way the artist has done.

Later, it will also occur to me that our Creole pronunciation at the table fundamentally reflected our French diction rather than the academically correct orthography of Creole, while the spoken expression of that orthography underlay the artist's French speech to produce his sour mouth. Now, at the table, the woman with lush dreadlocks is turned toward the artist with a half-smile of thinly veiled embarrassment. The cultural impresario and the poet-engineer do not seem to have a better idea of how to react. I hypothetically read in their reaction a polite rejection of the artist's spirituality as mysticism at the margins, or, to put it differently, a polite resistance to a transgression of class boundaries. The artist stops talking. He stares in his drink before taking a sip, then looks straight ahead, seemingly holding to his position defiantly. The poet-engineer intervenes with "Eben" [Oh, well] to break the tension, then deliberately changes the subject.

A few months later, as I tried to understand the moment in the broader scope of my research, I returned to it in a conversation with the poet-engineer. He acknowledged that class distinctions did mediate the artist's sullen intensity and the reaction of conversational paralysis at the table. He persuaded me that my hypothesis was otherwise wrong. He, the cultural impresario, and the woman of lush dreadlocks had not at all meant to marginalize the man's spirituality. The three of them had in fact subsequently discussed the moment in independent conversations with one another. For a while now, the artist had been showing an "inner aggressivity" after a few drinks in "certain environments," the poet-engineer told me. I asked, "In an environment like Presse Café?" The poet-engineer answered, "Wi, nan yon anviwonnman ti boujwa" [Yes, in a petit-bourgeois environment]. He continued in Haitian Creole: "In other places, too, but much more in a bourgeois place. We attribute it to the experience of his accident." The accident in question, in Canada, severed the artist's hand, which was surgically reattached to the forearm. He had since lost use of it. The head of an international art organization told the artist's friends in Haiti that the accident happened while he worked at a bakery. The artist was incensed; he suggested that the accident had to do with his printmaking machinery. To him, the person who informed the Port-au-Prince art community of the accident had bad-mouthed him.

The poet-engineer believed that the artist felt diminished by the suggestion that he had been a manual laborer in a bakery. His "inner aggressivity" dates to that time, and when it resurfaced at Presse Café, his friends were taken aback. The artist's "inner aggressivity" among his tablemates disrupted the ideational unity of "black" Haitians in their nation's Blackness. In that moment, black nationalism could not contain a tension that inhered in class differentiation.

CHAPTER FIVE

MULATTO, PREJUDICE, AND OTHER WHITE TIDEMARKS OF THE NATION

Colonial encounters contingently produced bodily traces of whiteness in eventual authors of Haitian Independence and in post-Independence generations. Moreover, by the logic of a sovereignty articulating with Atlantic global exchanges, notwithstanding Dessalines's massacre of whites remaining on the national territory after Independence, whiteness began to enter the nation afresh relatively soon after the French defeat and continued to reenter beyond the nineteenth century. Its systematic reentry in the national space—culturally and somatically—reinforced the significance of its residual presence in native national subjects. However, a radical externality of whiteness has remained deeply ingrained in the Haitian schema of national belonging. Mulattoes nonetheless in general fetishize the *appearance* of whiteness in the body, and the color prejudice that reproduces that somatic trace in the mulatto formation is itself another tidemark of whiteness in Haitian society.

The mulatto elite does not mince its vigilance in measuring a constituent's mulattoness, valuing discernible traces of whiteness on the body in direct proportion to their visibility. Privileged light-skinned Haitians are generally grouped broadly as "*mulâtres*" (mulattoes), alternately "clairs" (lights), by Haitian thinkers and in popular discourse. However, among elite mulattoes, an elaborate terminology marks various intermediate types before the *mulâtre* proper, who might seem indistinguishable from a *white* (cf. Labelle 1987).[1]

This is not a movement away from a *Haitian* identity but a claim on the value of global whiteness within an alternate (of the black) national imaginary. Fair-complexioned Haitians in Haiti with relatively deep roots in the nation do not generally *become* a white people. Mulatto Haitians, as products of dialectical histories of the nation, are in fact organic Haitian national subjects.

In this chapter, I explore the complexity of relations among mulattoness, blackness, whiteness, and national belonging in Haiti, with a particular emphasis on mulattoness relative to the other phenomena. I first tease out the peculiar place of whiteness in the privileged Haitian imaginary, which, in both color formations, vehemently denies it any agency to distinguish the Haitian subject. Yet racialist tidemarks of whiteness bequeathed by the colonial experience remain historically operative in the nation, particularly color prejudice favoring lightness of complexion, which I eventually apprehend in its material logic. Drawing on the work of Andrew Hacker (1992) and Melanie Bush (2004) on the material valuation of whiteness in the USA, I delineate the practice of color prejudice as a pivot of the mulatto endogamy, which seeks to preserve the derivative valuation of relatively light complexion in a privileged formation of a nonwhite people. Drawing on Trouillot (1990a), I then show that color prejudice is but one modality among others that black as well as mulatto Haitians operationalize toward the reproduction of a privileged-class situation. In the final section of the chapter, the ethnographic moment captures the rupture of liberal politics in Haitian civil society by the politics of color.

When the engineering contractor—the husband of the math teacher—introduced me to the fair-complexioned executive at a real estate development that her family owns, I took her for a foreigner. In that moment, I *knew* that she was white. That lasted a short while, perhaps the five minutes after we were introduced to each other. I ceased *seeing* her whiteness when I realized that she was a native Haitian. As she shows somatic traits that are practically near the mulatto elite's ideal, she could in fact be white *elsewhere*. Two days later, I went to visit her in downtown Port-au-Prince at the headquarters of the family enterprise founded by her late father. As I made my way to her office after I arrived, I noticed several commemorative portraits of her father throughout the complex. His somatic features, like his daughter's, are markers of whiteness as it is generally known in the West. I had seen him in person once as an adolescent, when he and my father stopped to greet each other in a setting that I no longer recalled. I presume that he was a mulatto to me at the time, as he was now. Classmates of similar somatic appearance throughout my primary and secondary school years in Haiti were and had since remained mulattoes to me.

The erasure of whiteness in national identity fits in Haiti's social and intellectual traditions. Jean Price-Mars, the founder of modern Haitian social science in the 1920s, wrote on Haiti's politics of color well into the 1960s. Nowhere in his work does he speak of an existing or potential white Haitian identity. Contemporary authors and cultural commentators do not speak of white Haitians either. A recent popular history series sketching the "settlements" of Italians, Germans, Jews, and Arabs in Haiti quite remarkably not once uses the word "white" even in reference to the *original* immigrants, let alone to their Haitian descendants (Bernard 2010, 2011a, 2011b). Yet again, I had arrived in the field after living nearly twice as long in the USA as I had lived in Haiti. My inability to read whiteness in the person of the fair-complexioned executive and in her father might very well have been owing as much to Haitian praxis as to my reading in the Western academic literature on Haitian social organization.

Michel-Rolph Trouillot (1990a), for example, essential reading for a social science of modern Haiti, does not think of or allude to "white" in reviewing the taxonomy of Haitian social color.[2] A wide breadth of scholarship by foreign authors engages directly or incidentally with Haiti's *question de couleur*. I found none that speaks of white Haitians either. Labelle (1987) reports that in her survey 3 percent of mulatto "bourgeois" and 2 percent of black "petit-bourgeois" used "blanc" ("white") in their repertory of color descriptions (111–12). However, her subjects described sketched human faces, not actually living persons engaged in the nation's social life. In any event, she herself does not use the term as a mode of Haitian identity. Where she finds Haitians using "blanc" to describe the person of other Haitians, the usage is for the most part in the peasantry and is inevitably metaphorical, connoting outsider wealth and privilege (cf. Labelle 1987, 152).

As the fair-complexioned executive and I spoke about national belonging in her office, she made an exceedingly exceptional reference to herself as white, and her remark became a point of entry for my investigation of the relation between the phenomenon of whiteness and the phenomenon of being Haitian. I had asked her whether she felt marginalized, when Haitians spoke of Haiti as a *Black* republic. Her assertive answer was, "No. It was abroad that I was first treated differently because I am white." As she continued talking while sitting at her desk, I mulled over the thought that she had effectively staked a claim on whiteness. The moment was somewhat discombobulating as I sat on a sofa across from her, because she was *being* utterly Haitian. "White Haitian" is not a phrase generally uttered by Haitians. I had in fact never heard it spoken or implied by anyone, in Haiti or abroad. That was the first time the very notion had ever entered my imagination. I became conscious then of my relation to the woman's somatic features. I had been talking to a *mulatto*, because she had been a *Haitian* all along. A practicing Roman Catholic, she has an iconographic poster of "Notre Dame du Perpétuel Secours" (Our Lady of Perpetual Help) pinned to her office door, to the side of her desk. "Notre Dame" is the patron saint of Haiti. Like religious icons in homes and businesses throughout the country, the poster seems integral to the place that holds it.

In the half-hour after the fair-complexioned executive evokes her whiteness, her maid calls. Results of the second round of the presidential elections are expected to be announced in the days ahead. In November, there were arsons and violent demonstrations in the capital, when the Conseil électoral provisoire (CEP), the decisive electoral authority, declared that Michel Martelly finished third in the first round of balloting, thereby eliminating him from the runoff between the top two candidates. Calm returned after the CEP revised its findings and placed Martelly second, ahead of the governing party's candidate. At the moment, popular opinion holds that Martelly won the presidency. Rumors have it that the CEP will imminently announce the winner, and no one seems to know exactly when or who that will be. It will eventually be a few weeks before the winner is declared. Meanwhile, several Manigat supporters will have told me that they believed Martelly won the vote. However, in the Haitian political imagination, Martelly, a son of the respectable middle class, remains an anomalous candidate, Manigat is of the political elite through and through, and in Haiti's political history announced electoral results do not necessarily reflect the number of ballots cast for this or that candidate. Like others who pay attention to the "word on the street," the maid is aware that there is no certainty Martelly will be announced the winner of the runoff against Manigat.

The maid has called to alert the fair-complexioned executive of foodstuff that the household needs to stock up on in case there are civil disturbances after the CEP announces the election results. She called from the house in which the fair-complexioned executive grew up, and in which she and her husband later reared their own children, with her parents now living in a house on an adjacent property. The family assets include two vast warehouses in different cities of the country and extensive real estate holdings. Employees seeking her attention intermittently stream in her office. The family presumably would have contingency plans that speak to business practicalities should political violence shut the city down in coming days. Whatever those plans might be, she addresses the situation at home with the maid as a Haitian rooted in Haiti.

On the phone with the maid, the fair-complexioned executive carefully goes through an inventory of what there is and what there is not enough of in the house—from sugar to rice to cooking oil. The family has homes in the neighboring Dominican Republic and in Florida, but she does not seem to give any thought to going abroad as a precaution. After she hangs up the phone, our chat turns to the elections, and she genuinely does not have a better clue than I do as to what to expect from the CEP. One morning more than a year later, she will tell me that she travels on a Haitian passport and does not hold any other. Although she has held a US Alien Residency card for decades, she has no plan to seek US citizenship. She will not give up her Haitian citizenship because "mwen pa vle pou w leu mwen ta vle fè w bagay nan peyi a pou m pa kapab paskeu m pa sitwayen" [I don't want one day not to be able to do something I'd like to do in the country because I'm not a citizen].[3]

In the few days after the fair-complexioned executive alluded to her whiteness, I separately asked the poet-engineer, the cultural impresario and two other black friends in Haiti's cultural elite whether they knew any "white Haitians; not mulatto: white." They all without exception were baffled by the concept. The phrase made no more sense to mulattoes, whom I also asked. The responses from both color formations were consistent with the total absence of the phrase "white Haitian" in Haiti's public vocabulary. I continued to ask for nearly a year and a half, and I did not speak with a single Haitian of any color in Haiti to whom the notion of a white Haitian was not intuitively nonsensical. During that time, I also searched the Internet periodically for "blanc haïtien" [white Haitian] through Google. I practically found no document at all in French mentioning the phrase as a fact of Haitian life.[4] I similarly searched "white Haitian," and the results pointed to a relatively stable set of web pages. None were discussions or artifacts by Haitians in Haiti about actual or potential white nationals.[5]

The fair-complexioned executive's dual assertion of her whiteness and Haitianness eventually led me to grasp that the mulattoness of her Haitian identity was generated in my imagination by local and global discourses of educated privileged people across lines of race and color. Yet, while the reproduction of the mulatto identity keeps whiteness nominally at bay in Haiti, it also inherently cultivates the sociopolitical significance of lightness of complexion in Haitian social organization. It is thus analytically sensible *not* to view the *mulâtre* and *mulâtrisme*, including color prejudice, as incongruities of the nation. As social phenomena, they need to be understood in their relations with other reproductive modalities of privilege and other modes of being privileged in the nation.

❀   ❀   ❀

On my final trip to the field in the latter part of 2012, the response of a mulatto entrepreneur to the notion of Haitian whiteness was particularly illuminating. He grew up in the upper-middle class of the business sector and now owns a company that manufactures engineering components for various industries. His genealogy stretches back to the mulatto population of the colonial period. His skin is more or less as light as that of the fair-complexioned executive. As we drove around Port-au-Prince on various business errands one day, he talked about his color prejudice as candidly as the executive did. To him also, it was just another fact of life. He just as freely spoke of his grandfather being "black." He also spoke at some length about his light-skinned great-grandfather being a physician whose children traveled to Europe to finish their education and told me with a touch of family pride of his grandfather being the first black student admitted to his Paris high school. The grandfather went on to graduate from a polytechnic college in France and married a French Jewish woman. They briefly lived in South America before returning to Haiti and starting a family. Their children married fair-skinned Haitians.

As he steered his SUV in slow-moving traffic in downtown Port-au-Prince, the mulatto entrepreneur joked about putting his grandfather's color to tactical use when dealing with Haitians who taunt or tease him for his color ("wouj" [red]) or his presumed class. His grandfather was not simply "nwa" (black), he would say, but "nwè," an idiomatic Creole word that connotes a particularly dark shade of black. Although he was currently in a committed romantic relationship with a black woman, he freely told me that he would not have married a dark-skinned woman. He in fact had never dated a black woman before he met his current girlfriend.

The mulatto entrepreneur married a white European woman, whom he met when she vacationed in Haiti, and they had two children before divorcing. When I asked him whether, in retrospect, his prejudice made sense to him, his full answer was a flat "Non" [No]. He also maintained that his parents never told him or otherwise communicated to him not to "bring home" a black girl. When I pressed him to explain how he learned to be prejudiced, if not at home, he shrugged earnestly: "Stupidité. C'est le milieu" [Stupidity. It's the milieu]. He described his constant effort to minimize encounters between his girlfriend and his ex-wife and daughter—practically, a white French adolescent—because they disapprove of the relationship on the basis of color. When I asked him what he would do if one of his children were to date a black person, he shrugged without actually answering me.

It had been more than a year since the fair-complexioned executive alluded to her whiteness. As we drove near the slum of Bel Air, I asked the mulatto entrepreneur whether he considered himself white. He answered matter-of-factly, "No. I'm Haitian." He turned to me with a quizzical expression similar to that of my black friends, when I asked them whether they knew any white Haitians. His younger brother, who is more or less of the same somatic appearance and has lived overseas for decades, had also reacted similarly a month earlier. I had called the brother from the USA. As we chatted on the phone, I wondered whether he might have considered himself white when he was growing up in Haiti. With a chuckle of amused surprise at my question, he answered: "No. My education, the idea is absurd."

As we drove past the National Archives in Bel Air, the mulatto entrepreneur continued his own thoughts on the subject. Using "pè," the Haitian word for "pop," followed by the maiden name of the fair-complexioned executive, he invoked her father in a disparaging tone.[6] Pop so-and-so, he told me, was the only Haitian he knew who taught his children that they were white. His reference to the fair-complexioned executive's family caught me thoroughly off guard; only through deliberate self-control did I not look dumbfounded. No comment I had made in any of my conversations with him could have elicited this specific reference. Nor could I have known that he knew her, although in speaking of "Pop" so-and-so without further context, he seemed to presume that I was acquainted with the family.[7] Be that as it may, he did know the fair-complexioned executive as a young woman on the dating scene of their adolescence. In his recollection of those days, which was not necessarily reliable but nonetheless telling, he would never have had any romantic interest in her because of the centrality of *being* white in her father's vision of the family.

While the mulatto entrepreneur actively sought to reproduce a "white" phenotype in his family, and seemed like he might rather want his daughter do the same, he objected without hesitation to a Haitian's presumption of whiteness. He, his brother, and my black collaborators, in their reaction to the notion of a white Haitian, reveal that whiteness as such, notwithstanding its global value, shall not have transactional liquidity in the nation's social economies. Yet colorist practices in the nation are pegged to global whiteness as standard currency.

Another Marxist mulatto intellectual—not the Marxist academic who referred me to the clair executive—was to tell me a story of existential angst over the dissipation of lightness of complexion in a branch of his family. He has worked at a major pedagogic center outside Haiti for a few decades. Looking at photographs on the institution's website, one could not summarily distinguish him by race from his white colleagues. Throughout his career overseas, he has remained actively engaged with Haiti's national life privately and professionally. He told me of a cousin's despondency on the wedding day of the cousin's daughter. At some point, he found the father of the bride contemplating the social swirl at the site of the reception with what seemed like an expression of gloom not at all commensurate with the occasion. "The guy looked like he was at his child's funeral instead of her wedding," he related to me. When he asked his cousin what was the matter, the latter answered: "Bagay yo pa bon menm. Se yon ameriken nwa" [Things are not good at all. It's a black American].

The daughter of the intellectual's cousin was indeed marrying a black American. Yet the cousin was himself dark-skinned, the intellectual said, chuckling in disbelief at the memory and adding: "Leu m di w nwa, kòm si m t a di w ou senegalè" [When I tell you black, I mean like a Senegalese]. When I asked him about the rest of the man's family, he told me in a mixture of Haitian Creole and English that the man's siblings, like his daughter getting married, were "tankou m, yo mulatre, ou mèt di blan" [like me, they're mulatto, you can say white], "some like people from Sweden." When I asked whether the man was in any way marginalized in the family because of his skin shade, the intellectual told me that he was not at all. He further asserted that the shade of his cousin's skin did not practically interfere with his belonging to the mulatto elite.

It is indeed not particularly rare to find relatively darker-complexioned members in elite mulatto families. Yet, at the time of my conversation with the Marxist intellectual, I had also already found that mulatto parents who speak about the color of eventual spouses with their children almost inevitably also speak at the same time about the eventual color of the children's children. The anguish of the intellectual's cousin over his daughter's marriage to a black man was at bottom an anguish over the fact of a spouse with whom the daughter would have children more likely to be of relatively dark rather than relatively light complexion. That is, the anguish was over the forfeited possibility of a spouse who would more likely augment rather than diminish the store of lightness in the lineage. Although the anguish proceeded from a fetishism of skin complexion, to dismiss the cousin's concern as irrational is to remain oblivious to the social fact—and to lack lucidity in combatting the fact—of race as concrete value in social economies of the West.

As the intellectual and I spoke of color, class, and privilege in Haiti, I thought of asking him about the color of Claudinette Fouchard. At the time, Fouchard was a septuagenarian woman who had entered the nation's consciousness in 1960 after winning a beauty pageant in Columbia. She had since remained an icon of national beauty for living generations of Haitians across color lines. I had been thinking over how the politics of color inflected the moment in which she entered the public imagination; I asked the mulatto intellectual in what color category he thought she might fit. I posed the question because I was intrigued by the ambiguity of the one assigned to her in popular discourse. In public photographs, she is of a lighter complexion than that of the US entertainer Lena Horne. On cover pictures of the US magazines *Jet* (February 4, 1960) and particularly *Ebony* (July 1960), which catered principally to a middle-class black US readership, her skin is made emphatically light. Her father was the noted historian and diplomat Jean Fouchard, whom Haitians generally classify in the broad category of mulatto. Yet, in Haiti, contemporaneous media coverage of her crowning as an ideal of beauty describes her as a "brune" (brown), a description that is also routinely applied to noticeably darker skin tones.

The intellectual seemed personally familiar with the Fouchard family and answered me unequivocally about Claudinette's color, with no undue thought to the issue: "Oh, Claudinette is black." I told him that I found his assessment surprising, because her skin seems decidedly light in the Haitian context. He provided more contextual and descriptive details: "Cheveu l. Se pase l pase cheveu l. Ou konnen, lontan fi ki te konn pase cheveu yo" [Her hair. It's a hot iron she uses for her hair. Y'know, back then, the women who used a hot iron in their hair], "whatever product they use today." He also pointed out that she would in fact not be as light as she seemed in pictures, because she applied cosmetic products that made her facial skin tone appear lighter than its natural state. He then added: "Brune is probably a good way to describe her color. Edwidge [Claudinette's sister], she is black. She's darker than Claudinette. Her nose is flat. Their father, Jean, maybe you can say he was a mulatto. He had hair like mine. His nose is not. I have a flat nose. Jean's nose was straight."

I was later to think quite some more about the assessment of Claudinette Fouchard's color in contemporaneous media coverage of her crowning as a "beauty queen." The insight I gained in my conversation with the mulatto intellectual was much less about that than about the relationship of mulattoes to mulattoness. By his work, I consider him a progressive, engaged thinker on the Haitian condition. He did not find his cousin's bearing a dark skin in the mulatto elite to be a contradiction either at the level of family or at the level of class, and he derided the cousin's prejudice of color without reservation. However, in his assessment of color in the Fouchard family he adhered to the conventions of the mulatto colorist tradition identified by Labelle (1987).

Black privileged Haitians tend to elaborate ever more nuanced typological categories to differentiate "black," while generally lumping together subjects of relatively lighter complexion as "mulatto." In the mulatto formation, the tendency is reversed: gradations of relatively darker complexion are conflated to "black," while subjects of relatively lighter skin are filtered through ever more nuanced characteristics that create various subcategories before arriving at the "true" mulatto (Labelle 1987, 98). Thus, in speaking to the situation of the Fouchards in the scheme of social color among privileged Haitians, the Marxist mulatto intellectual became Gramsci's organic intellectual. He spoke to his community's social order from within its lived history, grappling with materialities that regulate its viability, not simply the color of the skin but the shape of the nose and the objective characteristics of the hair. The Haitian mulatto who would not condone color prejudice, and who a priori would not countenance *being* a national white, would nonetheless keep careful inventory of the material building blocks of whiteness. Haitian colorism effectively becomes a quasi-arithmetic accounting system: whiteness is meaningful as a measurable social weight, not as a state of social being.

The fair-complexioned executive initially clung to a pragmatic logic in describing her color prejudice to me. She first attributed to her grandmother the central and—from her point of view—highly practical argument for not marrying a black man: a marriage is difficult work; to marry someone of a different race or color is to stack the deck yet more against conjugal success. She told me the story of her sister's unhappy marriage to and bruising divorce from a philanderer. She then said in Haitian Creole with a touch of humor: "Imagine you've got to worry you're not marrying someone who's going to cheat on you, someone who's not going to treat you badly, and now for me to worry also about what kind of problems we're going to have about color."

Invoking her sister's experience, the fair-complexioned executive told me that she passed her grandmother's wisdom on to her daughter. She also spoke of her anxiety, when her son insisted on pursuing a "serious" relationship with a black woman. Remarkably, only in passing did she mention that the woman had a child from a previous relationship. That the woman had a child out of wedlock was relatively of little significance in her disapproval of her son's relationship with her. In fact, while the relationship remained an irremediably doomed proposition to her, she told me that the sole encouraging sign was the affection between the woman's toddler and her son. The color issue is what consumed her in telling me the history of the relationship. She had ultimately resigned herself to the prospect of the union, she said, "men heureusement, pitit, bagay yo pa mache" [but luckily, dear, things didn't work out]. The son and the woman had recently broken up over reasons not having to do with color.

As we continued talking, the fair-complexioned executive returned to her grandmother's wisdom on matters of marriage and color. She eventually revealed roots of her color prejudice in a conscious appreciation of what makes someone concretely white, imagining a tactile experience of the white body as she waxed poetic in Haitian Creole: "My grandmother used to tell me, 'Wouldn't you want a baby with blue eyes?' Beautiful li'l blue eyes! Oh! And blond hair, quite long. When you're brushing it, holding it in your hands, it's such a nice sensation." As the executive spoke of her imaginary child's blond hair, she wistfully cocked her head sideways and mimicked holding a strand of hair in front of her with one hand while brushing it with the other.

It is then that whiteness appeared to me most cogently as a definite social value. Her color prejudice was not after all solely about the anguish of living and managing a marriage across the color line in Haiti. She *appreciates* the bodily materialities of the social edifice of whiteness.

The fair-complexioned executive is not irrational in her appreciation of the white body. Whiteness was invented by European powers in the colonial antecedent of Western capitalism, and it remains now what it was then, a pivotal instrument in the regulation of forms of power and wealth in determinate regimes of political economy (cf. Dupuy 2015 on race and differential division of labor in the colony). Whiteness also remains a shifting ensemble of cultural practices and ideologies. The ideal European body, constructed as it is by white symbolic power, indicates a *potential* subject of whiteness and the forms of power and wealth that it indexes. That body would have some residual value in Western bourgeois economies as, in its somatic appearance, it is the earliest signal of the person who might be due privilege reserved for whites. When non-whites in the West have attained privileges that had been exclusively whites', what I am broadly calling the European body as a heuristic convenience would remain a value to whites, perhaps enhanced. This is so, because such a body remains the first phenomenally perceivable characteristic in a set of varying characteristics that *in toto* grant access to the privilege of whiteness. For the non-white privileged actor, not bearing the European body becomes *un manque à gagner*, a lack to be made up, among the remaining characteristics that will grant access to privileges similarly accessed by whites qua whites.

As the European body remains the fulcrum of instrumental racialism in the Western capitalist project of domination, in Haiti and elsewhere, its value must be confronted and destabilized, if the goal is an anti-imperial resistance, or merely a level playing field, so to speak, among contestants of privilege. It nonetheless remains that a subject of the modern West who might attain that bodily ideal, or some significant approximation thereof, would be acting as rationally in reaching for it as in reaching for other forms of socioeconomic value. Thus, mulatto prejudice, Haitian colorism in general, can best be understood when it is situated in the global context of whiteness.

In the USA, for example, Melanie Bush (2004) finds that, while whites do not see themselves constituting a "race," they do nevertheless expect an acknowledgment of their distinction in whiteness. Whites may not think much about their racial identity (Bush 2004, 60), but they do care about being visible as whites in everyday life for the benefits to be accrued from unacknowledged structures of institutional racism (15).[8] To put it differently, whiteness may not be indicative of a race to whites, but whites are very attentive to the concrete value they accrue in whiteness. This transpires cogently in Andrew Hacker's thought experiment, in which white US students wanted compensation of one million dollars per year if they were made to live as black, making being white akin to possessing a valuable "gift" (Hacker 1992, 32).

For the subjects of both Hacker's and Bush's respective studies, although their whiteness is concretely realized in social settings of everyday life, it is nonetheless not routinely experienced in the distinctive somatic dimension of their being. Whiteness is lived rather as an intrinsic, invisible feature of their social condition. This is not so for the fair-complexioned executive. Like the mulattoes who insist on not being white but actively want what makes whites white, and quite unlike Hacker's and Bush's subjects, her vision of the self is consciously grounded in the objective parts of the body whose phenomenal sum becomes the base on which whiteness is socially constructed.

Given the foundational imbrication of the nation of Haiti in the racialist order of the global West, privileged Haitians—constituents of the West's global elite and middle classes—could not possibly fail to apprehend the value that whites attain in whiteness in dominant Western economies. The mulatto privileged Haitian *logically* becomes vigilant in guarding what value might yet derive from an approximation of whiteness. It should come as no surprise that, in a nation that transcendently wishes to blacken them, relatively light-skinned Haitians, unlike their counterparts in the global North, are deeply conscious of their complexion and other somatic traits as objective bearers of a potential social value. Where the North American white subject might be stimulated to place a concrete value imaginatively on the edifice of whiteness, as in Hacker's thought experiment, the mulatto Haitian needs no such studied stimulation to grasp lightness of complexion as concrete value. The fair-complexioned executive values whiteness in its actuality, here and now, in her practical awareness of its tangibility.

In the 1979 film *Manhattan*, as the seventeen-year-old character Tracy, the actress Mariel Hemingway performs to sublime affect a variation of the act of whiteness that the fair-complexioned executive performed in brushing the hair of her imaginary child. As is often the case in the work of US filmmaker Woody Allen, whatever else the story is about, it is also about the cultivation of the self. Tracy is waiting for a taxi to go to the airport to fly off to London, where she will study acting. Standing in the lobby of her apartment building, she distractedly brushes hair that luminously cascades to her shoulders (Allen 1979). This is at the end of a tale substantively enacted entirely by white actors embodying existential afflictions of distinctly privileged modern subjects. The sheer visual lushness that supports Hemingway's performance turns the scene into a normative moment of the universal non-race. To Hacker's and Bush's subjects, such hair would simply inhere in an ideal North Atlantic self. One should have such hair not because one is *white* but because one simply *is*. The fair-complexioned executive would not be so complacent about the stakes of whiteness. To her, the hair is a primordial technique of the self, and it is a tactile materiality of whiteness.

Where the fair-complexioned executive is assertively aware that whiteness is something that one can literally hold and *possess*, the mulatto intellectual's cousin despairs at the forfeiture of lightness of complexion in his daughter's marriage to a black American. Between the two lies the discovery of lightness of the skin as an object of transactions in a determinate economy. By the logic of transactional relations, lightness of complexion in Haiti is thus a material value. No clubs, restaurants, and the like existed that blacks with the requisite socioeconomic capitals did not unexceptionally enter together with mulattoes. Yet privileged blacks and privileged mulattoes sharing enduring friendships can be found clustered by color at restaurant tables, for example. The phenomenon can be understood by way of the anguish experienced by the mulatto intellectual's cousin at his daughter's wedding, helplessly watching his child make—to him—a debilitating choice of spouse. His distress was most fundamentally the concrete outcome of the daughter's contingent encounter with a black man. From that encounter ensued the marriage, and from the marriage the increased possibility of a diminution of lightness of complexion down the family's lineage. Managing the risk of such an encounter is a preoccupation of mulatto sociality.

Notwithstanding the cultivation of approximations of the white body, the colorist gaze ultimately assesses somatic characteristics in the context of the bearer's total socioeconomic situation. Trouillot correctly argues that color is an "exchange value" (1990a, 122). The actively prejudiced light-skinned person manages the color-value in a cohesive field of various other socioeconomic exchange-values besides lightness of skin, from genealogical and personal prestige to wealth to social capital. In that field of exchange, which I call the economy of color, the privileged black who wishes to *mete krèm nan kafe a* [put cream in the coffee] or to *améliorer la race* [ameliorate the race] might arrive at a marriage with a relatively light-skinned person whose socio-economic situation could be strengthened.[9] Privileged Haitians can make something of a parlor game to imagine transactional rationalities—values exchanged for a light complexion, compromises made—when Jean-Claude Duvalier and Jean-Bertrand Aristide, two black men, married clair women while they were presidents of Haiti.

Mulatto prejudice and color ideologies in general do not fundamentally destabilize the societal unity of Haiti's elite and middle classes because they articulate with an exchange economy from which privileged people are not precluded on the basis of color. Over the course of my time in the field in Port-au-Prince, the poet-engineer and his younger brother periodically returned to stretches of the 1970s through the mid-1980s, when they and their friends in the neighborhood moved through their teenage years to young adulthood and university studies. Four doors up the street from their house lived a sister of François Duvalier's wife and her family, whom I collectively refer to as the Duvalier in-laws. Two houses up and across the street from them lived a mulatto family. It was hardly of the mulatto elite. It was a solidly middle-class family, whose three children remained distant from their peers on the street, in the recollection of the poet-engineer and his brother.[10]

A clair man in his late forties, who also lived on the street, similarly recalled in a separate conversation that the younger of the two daughters— the youngest sibling—of that mulatto family kept to herself relative to the other youth on the street. Both of the clair man's parents were from light-skinned families, and he married a clair woman and they had clair children. In his reminiscence as we spoke at his house near Pétion-Ville one evening, he, too, nonetheless alluded to the colorism of the mulatto family who lived across the street from the Duvalier in-laws. He effectively repeated what the poet-engineer and his brother had variously related to me. Through adolescence and young adulthood, the younger daughter of that mulatto family routinely walked down the street from her house to the house of another mulatto family living two doors past the poet-engineer's. She would not speak to anyone in her age group she might come across along the way. The clair man noted that she had no relationship to speak of with her peers of either gender on the three blocks between the two houses.

As it happened, the daughter of the mulatto family was actually friends with the older of the two daughters of the Duvalier in-laws, her neighbors across the street; the two were about the same age.[11] The Duvalier in-laws

relocated in a foreign country several years before the fall of the dictatorship. I visited them there in the fall of 2012, a month or so after I was in their
old neighborhood in Port-au-Prince. I was the family's guest at one of its
regular Sunday dinners at the home of the surviving parent. As usual, the
meal brought together children, grandchildren, and various cousins living in
the surrounding area. In my youth, I was as close to the children as I was to
the poet-engineer and his younger brother, and the surviving parent knew
me since my boyhood. The younger of the two daughters was not there that
day; the older arrived after me. I had not seen the latter since she left Haiti
for a college preparatory boarding school abroad about thirty years earlier.
Her brother and I engaged in a conversational whirlwind from the time he
opened the front door for me, when I arrived, until we sat down to eat. As
we ate, he and I were now both part of various streams of conversation at
the table.

The family knew that I was studying the intersection of class and color in
Haitian society, and that was an intermittent theme of the chatter during the
meal. I mentioned that their old neighborhood had wholly escaped the *bidon-
villisation* [slummification] that had encroached on so many upscale areas of
Port-au-Prince since I last was in Haiti (in 2002) prior to my current project.
The family's older daughter was pleasantly surprised at my choice of word.
In her opinion, "bidonvillisation" was not a word that a Haitian who had
been living in the USA as long as I had would routinely use in conversation.
She told me that she was pleased that I was still "à l'aise" [at ease] in French.

My comment about bidonvillisation eventually got the Duvalier in-laws'
older daughter to share her own memories of growing up in the neighborhood. She spoke of friends with whom, and homes in which, she played in her
youth. After she reminisced about the children of the family next door, which
produced a prime minister (and presidential candidate) in the post-Duvalier
era, she talked about playing with the younger daughter of the mulatto family
that lived diagonally across the street. She recalled with particular empathy
her visits to her friend's house: "When I went to her house, I felt sorry for
her, truthfully. I felt like she was in prison. She used to watch the kids play
in the yard across the street with envy." The girl's mulatto parents evidently
did not forbid her from leaving the house as a matter of principle, because
she routinely walked down the street to visit her mulatto girlfriend two
doors past the poet-engineer's home. Playing with the children in the house
across the street would have been a different proposition, because those

kids were black. By generally precluding her from socializing with her black peers, her parents narrowed the risk of the situation in which the mulatto intellectual's cousin found himself, looking on with anguish at the reality of a light-skinned daughter marrying a black *peer*.

As the Duvalier in-laws' daughter described her mulatto friend's loneliness, François Duvalier was looking at me from a small portrait on a console table several feet to my right, and one of his children was eating directly across the dining table from me. This dual reminder of Duvalier's power underlined for me the logic of the friendship between his in-laws' older daughter—his niece—and the younger daughter of the presumably prejudiced mulatto family who lived across the street. To the Duvalier in-laws' daughter, her mulatto girlfriend seemed imprisoned in her own home; to the girl's parents, her color was a value to be managed pragmatically in the context of her life possibilities. Children's fields of play being also fields of potential affective attachment, to allow her to play with the black children—blacks who were her socioeconomic peers—across the street was to risk a romantic attachment that might lead to a marriage in which her lightness was granted to a black without commensurate social and economic advancement. With the Duvalier in-laws' older daughter, the mulatto girl did not have just any dark-skinned girl over to her house. Her dark-skinned friend, the only one among her dark-skinned peers on the street with whom she routinely socialized, was the first cousin of President for Life Jean-Claude Duvalier. That friendship across the boundary of mulattoness occurred in her parents' tactical management of color and social status in the family through the policing of her body.

❄   ❄   ❄

The Sunday after the rains of Hurricane Sandy in October 2012, a wealthy erudite clair businessman picked me up at my house after he had gone to church, and we spent the morning at his. I had met him in 2011 at an academic event where he presented a paper. He had been engaged for years in poverty alleviation as an affiliate of an international NGO. As he drove back to his house near the approach to Laboule, another enclave of wealth further up the hills from Pétion-Ville, he came to speak about corruption in the Martelly government, a topic we had discussed earlier in the week. The previous Friday, about a day after the hurricane passed, the executive branch had requested and Parliament had authorized disbursement of emergency funds to assist affected populations. By then, the erudite clair businessman had learned that, in the rural area where he did his poverty alleviation work, the assistance would consist of "trois mille plats chauds" [three thousand hot meals]. He had by then also assessed that the considerable damage in the area was caused almost exclusively by a local river that overflowed its bed. He reached out to a few key decision makers on the hurricane relief effort in the Martelly administration.

The erudite clair businessman explained that merely distributing free meals to local residents would not address the root cause of the damage. He argued for a structural intervention. In a matter of days, he proposed, he would set up a project to employ local labor to shore up the banks of the local river with gabion walls. The project would cost no more than the meals, he assured his interlocutors in the Martelly government. He might even be able to pull it off with only a portion of the funds allocated for the meals, he told them. He summarized his argument for me in the Frenchified Creole of educated Haitians: "Au lieu w bay moun yo ou plat manje, embaucher yon gwoup pou yon mwa. W ap ba yo travay, y ap bay fanmi yo manje, e w ap enjekte menm kòb la nan ekonomi lokal la" [Instead of giving a meal to the people, hire a group for a month. You'll give them work, they'll feed their families, and you'll inject the same money in the local economy]. In the end he was rebuffed, because, he said, "Se youn ladan yo k ap bay pla cho yo. Korupsyon gen pluzyeu sans" [It's one of them providing the hot meals. Corruption means many things].

Later that morning, as the erudite clair businessman argued that Jean-Bertrand Aristide gave in to corruption and misspent the promise of the Lavalas movement, he got up from an armchair in his library, an airy room of the same understated elegance as the rest of the house, and looked up a volume on the shelves. As he found the quote that he was looking for to buttress his point, I saw him as a moneyed intellectual who wears his wealth lightly. I had also visited him at his office not far from Delmas Road earlier in the week, a day or so before Sandy bore down on the country. He told me then that not only did he consider himself black, "M se w nwaris" [I'm a noiriste].

The erudite clair businessman denounced mulatto color prejudice with disdainful anger, telling me in Haitian Creole: "It's so stupid. In the US, I'm a black man. And a whole lot of others, it's the same thing. This prejudice is a senseless thing. In the US, we'd all be suffering it as black people. You'd think that would make them think." Alluding to the US presidential elections less than a month away, he added: "For real, if Obama weren't black, there'd be no elections. If the best Republican is Romney, if Obama were white, nobody would bother. They'd just appoint him to a second term." Among the Founding Fathers, he admires Christophe as a visionary nation builder and creator of state institutions. To him, Dessalines is a murderer for his massacre of the whites who remained in the new country after Independence, and the mulatto icon Alexandre Pétion is no better: "Pou mwen l se w asasen pou wòl li nan asasinasyon Dessalines" [For me he's an assassin for his role in Dessalines's assassination].

Although the erudite clair businessman is prominently situated in the economic elite, in the presidential elections of 2010 he did not vote for Charles Henri Baker, a wealthy mulatto who would be a white man in any dominant Western country.[12] Over the few hours I was with him in his office, I raised the widely discussed issue of the Haitian oligarchy's clientelist relations with the state. In careful allusions, he deplored the persistent influence of specific families on the state, giving me examples of Martelly's own power being circumvented.

As illustration of the current state of oligarchic power, the erudite clair businessman sketched the broad lines of a case dating to the government of the previous president, René Préval. An enterprise with which he was substantially associated currently operated under contract with the Haitian government. Under the terms of the agreement, the enterprise was paid distinctly less than what was paid to a competitor similarly contracted to the state to deliver the same product. Moreover, the competitor was in fact a former state enterprise whose control and ownership had been summarily transferred to a family with a long history of deal-making with the state. As depicted by the erudite clair businessman, the situation was as farcical as it was consistent with persuasive accounts that I received from other sources during my fieldwork about the long history of that family's influence over decisive state authority.

That day in the office of the erudite clair businessman, I told him that I was increasingly noticing the lack of a transcendent space in Haiti's civil society, where blacks and mulattoes can together engage critically with the state and the national condition. As he mulled over what I had said, he was clearly resistant to the notion that such a space was lacking. Since he was well acquainted with the intellectual elite, I asked him whether he, personally, was in any sustained political conversation with *black* nationalist thinkers or activists, either at the private level or in civil society projects. He remained pensive for a brief moment and then he shook his head.

After acknowledging that he had not been in any meaningful political conversation with any black nationalist Haitian, the erudite clair businessman said the name of a prominent black noiriste intellectual, the one who, incidentally, would come to the Fokal party that the poet-engineer, the cultural impresario, and I crashed a few days later at Vert Galant. The erudite clair businessman asked me whether I knew the noiriste intellectual. I had not read his fiction, but I had a passing acquaintance with his thought from an essay and a newspaper column of his that I had read over the past few years. He seemed to me broadly interested in the failures of Haiti's state and civil society and in what I would call—from the way he framed the issue—the discounted citizenship of Haiti's poor. These were also reasonably the broad themes of my conversation with the erudite clair businessman that morning in his office.

After I answered the erudite clair businessman that I knew the noiriste black intellectual by reputation, not personally, he told me that the two of them were acquaintances. He then related to me an unsuccessful attempt to engage the intellectual in a common project. The latter had become an expert in a cultural form endemic to a region of the country's rural interior. The erudite clair businessman and several business associates were interested in that cultural practice. He proposed to hire the intellectual to hold a series of workshops to educate them in the tradition. The intellectual refused and suggested instead that the erudite clair businessman go to the region himself and learn the culture by direct contact. The clair businessman then somberly characterized the intellectual's rejection of his offer: "Se te kesyon kouleu a" [It was the color question], which had consumed us for nearly an hour of conversation. We left the subject at that. It was nonetheless not hard to see why a noiriste intellectual would subsume the clair businessman's social and political engagement in his mulatto identity.

For all his substantial work in concrete projects that speak to the condition of the poor, his wife and children being also distinctly clair, the erudite clair businessman is again the mulatto subject who, irrespective of intent, effects the biological reproduction of color (Trouillot 1990a). His family is situated in a network of mulatto genealogies, notwithstanding a brother's marriage to a black woman. It remains that—from the little of it that I have read and from others' comments about it—the noiriste intellectual's body of work calls for critical attention to the condition of Haiti's dispossessed population. He is a leading figure of Haiti's intellectual elite. The erudite clair businessman is a leading figure of the country's economic elite. They say similar things on the condition of the nation. Yet they could not speak together on the condition of the nation. In the noiriste intellectual's rejection of the erudite clair businessman's proposal of the cultural workshops—presuming it was indeed grounded in the "color question"—the politics of color ruptured the circulation of a Haitian political liberalism.

The day after I was in the office of the clair businessman, I visited the mulatto entrepreneur in the early evening during Sandy's trailing rains. Like well-to-do residences in Boutilliers, the house sits on a relatively large parcel of land amidst lush vegetation. When I arrived in his open-air sitting room, as rain pelted the roof, water dripped steadily from a leak in the ceiling, and he was arranging rags with his feet on the tiled floor to soak it up. The leak was not new, and arranging the rags on the floor seemed a practiced routine. Life in the economically squeezed middle classes of the neoliberal age was actually not new to him. After he got married, he and his wife lived in her native France in the 1990s. He dabbled in real estate and other occasional employment. He said of those years, "on vivotait" [we scraped a living]. They eventually returned to Haiti with their young children and later divorced. He had since lived alone in his childhood home, and arguably he still "vivotait" with a small business in a chronic crisis of liquidity.

As we sip Cuban rum on the patio and Sandy's unrelenting rains seep through the leak in the ceiling, the mulatto entrepreneur inveighs against the decimation of local agriculture by the import of foodstuff. His anger reaches a peak as he argues that Haiti is "une société qui n'a plus une élite rurale" [a society that no longer has a rural elite] due to the collapse of agricultural production. Evoking Price-Mars's (1919) theme of *La vocation de l'élite* [The Mission of the Elite], he finds "enpòte du riz, se pa wòl yon elit" [importing rice, that's not the role of an elite], which—to him—should lead national development in all its dimensions. He remains angry when he speaks of oligarchic families' clientelist relations with the state. During our conversation, he objects more than once when I substitute "mulatto elite" for "economic elite." Over the course of the evening, I twice effectively speak of "mulattoes" as an undifferentiated formation, lapsing into a black-nationalist habitus, I suppose. The second time, with a hint of frustration, the mulatto entrepreneur repeats almost verbatim in French what he said the first time:

"Il n'y a pas une tête de pont qui mène les mulâtres" [There's not a head of the pack leading the mulattoes].

Like the erudite clair businessman, the mulatto entrepreneur did not vote for Charles Henri Baker in the elections of 2010. Although he voted for Martelly, he identifies with PAIN, the Parti agricole industriel national [National Agro-Industrial Party], which was founded by Louis Déjoie, François Duvalier's mulatto opponent in 1957, and is now led by a black agronomist.[13] According to international monitors of the 1990 elections led by former US President Jimmy Carter, "PAIN's progressive platform was similar in some respects to that of Aristide's FNCD" (International Delegation to the Haitian General Elections 1991, 45). With Sandy's rains pounding the roof of his patio, I ask the mulatto entrepreneur whether he has been in any private or civil society conversation on national politics with any black Haitians. He has not. I then ask him whether he has discussed his views on the oligarchic families' relations with the state with other mulattoes. He shakes his head with an ironic chuckle as he answered, "Teren an glise" [The ground is slippery]. Hearing this the day after the erudite clair businessman told me of his failure to engage the noiriste intellectual, the politics of color seems exceedingly effective at fragmenting a progressive politics on the national condition in Haiti's civil society.

CHAPTER SIX

UNITY IN COLORISM
AND CLASS IDEOLOGIES

Maids at the home of the wealthy fair-complexioned executive, like maids in elite households in general, serve in uniform during their workday. In upper-middle-class homes, although domestic servants tend not to wear a uniform, they are also expected to enact their service with noticeable self-effacement. One evening as I surfed the Internet on my laptop at the dining table of the math teacher, the groundkeeper fleetingly walked down a corridor perpendicular to my line of vision about fifteen feet away. In two or three steps, he disappeared past the corner of the corridor. The math teacher stepped up to the table to tell me in a mix of French and Creole: "Excuse-moi, Philippe. Gason an te oblije al debouche twalèt la" [Sorry, Philippe. The groundkeeper had to go unclog the toilet]. She earnestly apologized to me for that fleeting presence of the groundkeeper within the living area of her home, a section of the privileged household in which the servant staff shall not unduly be seen.

Class is the terrain on which both the math teacher and the fair-complexioned executive perform their distinction from Haiti's poor and culturally marginalized subjects. They share a corpus of class ideologies, which include color ideologies and in aggregate regulate sociopolitical-economic stratification in Haiti. In the first part of this chapter, I theorize diachronic linkages between the colonial regime of racial classification and today's sociocultural practices around color in the privileged classes. I then map, in literary and musical productions and in the ethnographic moment, discursive ways in which bilingual privileged blacks and mulattoes—as Western bourgeois subjects—alternately blacken the poor Haitian and distance themselves from social blackness. I end the chapter with a critical reading of the moment in 1960 when noiristes and mulattoes of the privileged classes celebrated the "crowning" of Claudinette Fouchard, a daughter of the mulatto elite, as a "beauty queen" on the global stage. The analysis ultimately reveals the transcendent unity of the privileged classes and the externality of the peasantry in that celebration of the nation's bourgeois pedigree.

Saint-Domingue's black and mulatto creoles, who generally marginalized native Africans, were variously "Latinized," and the creole Revolutionary elites' descendant social formations have culturally and sociopolitically marginalized the bossales' descendants (Casimir 2000, 2009b). Simplistic use of the terms "black" and "mulatto" in contemporary contexts erases this history and mystifies problematic everyday realities in Haiti (Casimir 2000). The system of color classification in the colony recorded a residual blackness with arithmetic precision as a social subject approached phenotypic "whiteness" through the generations. The colonial *mulâtre* is a biracial child of racially "pure" black and white parents; a mulatto's child with a white is a *quarteron* of one-quarter black "blood" inherited from the black grandparent. Keeping track of any minimal trace of blackness in an apparent whiteness, the taxonomy went on for a staggering 128 degrees of racial admixture over seven generations (Schuller 2010).

In contemporary Haiti, too, the typology of color is obsessively concerned with measuring embodied race. In the colonial era, the object of the state's measurement was European supremacy in the civilizational hierarchy of the Atlantic world. European power decreed that only in total whiteness was humanity fully achieved, and it insisted on bringing forth any underlying blackness one might bear wherever one was on the scale of whiteness. In today's Haiti, the object of the measurement of embodied race remains *Europeanness*, but the colonial logic is reversed. Now colorism aims alternately to foreground traces of whiteness or to efface traces of blackness in the person.

Mulatto Haitians can be resolutely nationalist, even black-nationalist, while they seek to leave behind any apparent vestigial blackness of the *body*. That is why mulatto color praxis remains highly attentive to distance gained in the approach to "true" mulattoness, in which somatic features are little if at all distinguishable from those of whiteness. In a related logic, privileged dark-skinned Haitians discursively seek to move away from blackness to achieve a deblackening of the *person* rather than the body. This silencing of *personal* blackness concomitantly imbues the social subject with a measure of imaginary lightness. This dual phenomenon is generated through the exceedingly elastic vocabulary of social color. Such terms as "brun," "griffe," "marabou"—for the most part with no precise somatic referents—are so many alternatives that altogether sidestep "black" in the description of the dark-skinned privileged Haitian. Although "black" and "mulatto" remain the semantic poles of the nation's nomenclature of color, in everyday social practice, through the alternate terminology, the social color of relatively dark-skinned privileged Haitians effectively becomes *not-black*.

On the one hand, the alternate terms that denote a nonmulatto are applied in the presence of various requisite capitals (wealth, education, genealogical prestige, and so forth). On the other, the privileged black bearing such other forms of capital in sufficient quantity can—albeit seldom—breach the mulatto endogamy and marry into the mulatto formation despite the deficit in lightness of complexion. The "masses" of Haiti are who remain invariably "black" in everyday practice. The situation is consistent with the fact that the Revolutionary and post-Independence elites, which yielded the contemporary formations of privilege, mapped the colonial logic of sociopolitical organization onto a postcolonial iteration of colonial economics. Whiteness was expelled from all strata of the new nation's elite, but the laboring classes at the bottom of socioeconomic organization remained marked in their *bossale* African ascendance. Notwithstanding Dessalines's short-lived experiment uniting his elite in a nominal blackness, the nation's privileged blacks and mulattoes, congruently with their colonial formations, have systematically suppressed African cultures in dominant national expressions (Casimir 2000).

The full scope of colorism in Haiti could not be apprehended solely in mulatto color prejudice but in the conjunction of material conditions and cultural practices of privileged people irrespective of color. The ballad "Haïti chérie" (Darling Haiti) has been said to be Haiti's "second national anthem" (Meehan 1999, 112). The song, adapted from a 1920 poem written by a physician, is deeply affective and universally admired. However, its lyrics articulate the color nomenclature with social privilege:

When you're in the whites' country, you see all faces in one color.
There are no mulattas, beautiful marabous, creole griffes,
Who like nice dresses, good powder and good scent
Nor beautiful young negresses who can say sweet nothings.[1]

The song invokes four different figures of Haitian womanhood, and it groups the first three together. Let us recall that "mulatto" indexes social lightness that is accessible to a dark-skinned subject with enough alternate capitals to compensate for the relatively dark complexion, and the skin shade of the clair executive—situated around the peak of the mulatto elite—is more or less similar to that of black US President Barack Obama. A *griffe*—in the mulatto typology—would have more or less the complexion of the American golfer Tiger Woods and unmistakably "black" nappy hair; and a marabou—in the black typology—would have relatively deep-dark skin and naturally straight and supple hair.

Thus, of the four types of Haitian women invoked in the song, the "negress" is alone in being irreducibly black. That is, although her blackness is nominally stated (in the *negro* racial type), it does not differentiate her somatically from the other three types that are grouped together. Her negroness in no way tells us whether her complexion, or hair type or shape of the nose is any different from that of any of the other three. Her differentiation in social color, the *emphatic* statement of her blackness, is realized in social characteristics. More specifically, she becomes black—she *is* a negress—in her distance from determinate cultural practices that define the other three women.

"Haïti chérie" operates across the boundaries of Haiti's two colorized social formations of privilege to define those other three types of women *together* as Haitian. They dress fashionably, make themselves up tastefully, and wear the right perfume. In so imagining them, the song puts them in a singular formation of Haitians defined—by clothing, make-up and scent—in the aesthetics of Western bourgeois sociality, and it makes the negress their *other*. Within this formation of Western bourgeois people, the social color of subjects who would constitute the black socio *political* formation of privilege is effectively not-black, in contradistinction to the color of the negress—as it were, an "unqualified" black. This scheme of blackness remains discursively and practically coherent within the privileged classes, because the black *formation* of [bilingual] privileged

Haitians is indexed by the *historic* Blackness that the nation inherited from its forebears, *not* by the blackness of Haitians actually existing outside the country's bilingual formation of bourgeois people. Folks like the negress of "Haïti chérie" are *being* black in national everyday realities of poverty and pernicious social degradation.

Blackness as a trope of life conditions at the bottom of the social hierarchy transpired in the language of a development executive, when he expressed outrage at what he asserted was rampant color prejudice in President Michel Martelly's close entourage. He and I were having lunch with two Haitian mutual friends. The four of us went to secondary school together and reunited at an Indian restaurant on the Upper West Side of Manhattan in New York City. A black man in his fifties, the development executive had been one of my collaborators on the project since my first trip to Port-au-Prince in March 2011, two and a half years earlier. Then, he worked for a US government development agency in Port-au-Prince, while also engaged in entrepreneurial pursuits. Prior to that, he had worked in the upper ranks of Haitian finance and as an entrepreneur in the US telecommunication industry. He has since completed coursework in an online PhD program of an American university. Currently, he still works in development in Haiti for an international NGO, and he is still a telecom entrepreneur with a niche service marketed in immigrant communities along the US east coast. He considers Martelly a friend, and at the time I first arrived in the field in Haiti he enthusiastically looked forward to Martelly's presidency.

I am at the restaurant with the development executive while he is temporarily in the New York metropolitan region to work on a business venture. He is thoroughly disillusioned about Martelly's performance as president of Haiti. In a wide-ranging conversation in Haitian Creole among the four of us at the table, he returns to the theme of color, which he and I have intermittently discussed over the past few years:

There again, it's not Michel himself. He's a good man. It's those he surrounds himself with. Those guys brag even their mistresses are white women or mulattoes. How do you tell me you don't fuck black women? I've got an issue with that. 98 percent of the country's women are black. That's not Michel; he'd never say such things. Michel fucks anybody. He'll fuck servants, he'll fuck street vendors. He'll never have a problem fucking black women.

Haitians can and do innocuously identify one another in everyday practice by the empirical shading of their skin—"nèg klè lòt bò a" [the light guy over there], "eleman nwa devan n an" [the black fellow ahead of us]. However, to make Martelly's sexuality ecumenical in the field of color, the development executive does not evoke *dark-skinned* women as such. The women that he evokes to illustrate Martelly's noncolorist taste in "fucking" *become* black in such life conditions as domestic servants and street vendors. Here again, the Haitian woman is being made to mediate the nation's codes of class and color (Ulysse 2007). This phenomenon is found in Haitian pop music well beyond "Haïti chérie."

"Choucoune," another universally admired ballad, like "Haïti chérie," originates in the privileged classes. It is based on a work by the nineteenth century clair poet and politician Oswald Durand, grandson of the mulatto historian—and Henri Christophe's secretary—Pompée Valentin de Vastey (Lynelle 2015). Also like "Haïti chérie," as a work axiomatically addressed to the literate classes, the source poem is notably innovative for its use of Haitian Creole as literary medium. Not surprisingly, Durand, "Haiti's national poet," seeks to reconcile the tradition of French Romanticism "with a [complex] Haitian identity" (Reinsel 2008, 26). Choucoune is the titular object of Durand's—and the singer's—romantic longings, and, we are told, "Choucoune, se te yon marabou" [Choucoune, she was a marabou]. As it happens, "marabou" is one Haitian term of social color that is rather precise, referring to a deep-dark complexion together with hair that is straight and not "kinky." Choucoune is nonetheless not black, because "marabou" and "black" are not interchangeable colors. Proposed in a literary text as the vicarious object of bourgeois Haitians' legitimate sexual feelings, Choucoune *could not* be black. In fact, in the repertoire of romantic ballads directed primarily at an audience in the middle classes, where the color of the loved one is invoked, I could not find any in which the character's social color is nominally black unless she is specifically situated among the working poor, the destitute, or the peasantry.

The band Super Jazz des Jeunes, popularly kown as "des Jeunes," and its lead singer Gerard Dupervil offer a sliver of musical history in which the terminology of not-blackness expressly articulates with an aspirational social situation. Founded in the early 1940s in a then middle-class neighborhood of Port-au-Prince and playing "dance-band arrangements of 'folkloric' music" as well as "French-style café songs," the band embodied "*noiriste* ideology"

(Averill 1997, 58). In addition to a rendition of "Choucoune," the des Jeunes-Dupervil discography includes three other songs in which the object of romantic or sexual longings is identified by her social color. In two of them, "café" songs, the color is the title of the song: *Marabou* and *Ma Brune* [My Brown]. The first is from a text by Emile Roumer, a mulatto *indigéniste* poet, perhaps the fiercest voice in the intellectual resistance to the 1915–1934 US Occupation (cf. Berrou and Pompilus 1975, 92). Dupervil croons (in French): "Marabou de mon cœur aux seins de madarines, tu es plus savoureux que crabe à l'aubergine" [Marabou of my heart with breasts of mandarins, you're tastier than crabs with eggplant]. Or: "Écoute mon cœur qui te parle et ma voix qui t'implore. [Ma] brune, entends ma chanson" [Listen to my heart, which speaks to you, and my voice, which implores you. [My] brown, hear my song]. In these songs, Dupervil longs for a personalized color rather than a colorized person. That is not the case in the third, "Machann Kasav" [Kasav Peddler].

In "Marabou" and "Ma Brune," the titles announce a social color, which itself will remain the object of longing, dissociated from a person. In effect, Dupervil loves a color standing on its own merit apart from the person. In "Machann Kasav"—from a des Jeunes album released in 1961 and reissued in 1969—the title announces an occupational status, a street peddler, and it is *not* what Dupervil longs for. The object of Dupervil's longing is distinctly a woman. She is a black woman, but he is very clearly not longing for her color either. Her blackness *cannot* in fact stand on its own. Her black color and her social status are inseparably linked as Dupervil sings (in Haitian Creole), "M te gen w ti nègès bò Tigwav. Se te yon ti machann kasav" [I had a little negress near Tigwav. She was a little kasav peddler]. Moreover, not only is the woman's unmitigated blackness inextricably linked to her occupation as a street vendor of kasav, a cassava bread that is a staple of the poor, she is also spatially situated *outside* Tigwav, which is itself already a provincial town.

"Marabou" and "Ma Brune" appropriate the musical syntax and sentimental vocabulary of the post-World War II French chanson to inscribe the worldly modern in a black Atlantic middle-class subjectivity. In "Machann Kasav," part of the des Jeunes repertoire Averill would classify as "dance-band arrangements of 'folkloric' music," this black middle-class subjectivity simultaneously delineates its paternalist affection for and its distance from the black poor and the peasantry. Significantly, Dupervil sings of a "*ti* machann kasav." In Haitian, the meaning of the modifier "ti" can be similar to that of the suffix "ito" in Spanish or the contraction "li'l" in English, evoking camaraderie or affection. In a different register, as is the case here, it can also be more literally akin to the English "little," used to diminish a social subject in relation to one's own situation in a hierarchy: "ti bòn" [little servant], "ti abitan" [little peasant], "ti machann." Dupervil nonetheless reassures us this girl is "moun bò Tigwav, se moun nan mòn, se moun de bien, se li m renmen" [someone from near Tigwav, she's mountain people, she's good people, it's her I love]. It is also significant that, in his Haitian Creole delivery, Dupervil does not say "debyen," as a machann typically would but rather uses the French pronunciation "de bien." The French inflection marks his place in the middle class, of which he makes the machann and the moun nan mòn—the peasantry—an *other*.

Dupervil insistently asserts the symbolic power to objectify this other Haitian: "M te bal yon bèl ti non kreyòl. Ow, se nègès ki pwotokòl. Li gen w ti mach kloutoup-kloutap. Se kou yon ti machin Fòd kat" [I gave her a nice creole nickname. Ah, it's a negress who presents herself well. She's got a li'l gait kloutoup-kloutap. It's like a li'l Ford "kat"]. Thus, where Dupervil appropriates a trope of bourgeois romanticism to identify with his "brune," lamenting being "un esclave amoureux à tes pieds prosterné" [prostrate at your feet, a slave in love], he foregrounds his social distance from the "black" machann kasav in telling of his love for her. The measure of his feelings for the machann is in the breadth of the chasm between their social locations, which he both cultivates and breaches.

I asked an octogenarian to help me grasp the allusion to the Ford vehicle in the song. He was born out of wedlock in Tigwav of a poor peasant woman and a scion of the local bilingual landed elite. The father became a physician, married, and established residence in the capital, where he held rental real estate in a few middle-class neighborhoods. He also provided for his son and brought him to Port-au-Prince for secondary school. The boy eventually became a schoolteacher and heir to his father's holdings together with his half-siblings from the father's marriage. Through his father's and his father's wife's families, he entered the respectable middle classes and became part of the des Jeunes audience during the band's most productive and popular decades through the 1960s. After he told me he knew the song, I spoke the verse about the car and asked him to help me understand it. Before answering me, he first hummed the verse, then repeated the line about the machann walking "kloutoup-kloutap" like a Ford kat.

The "kat" (four) qualifier referred to the number of wheels on a Ford vehicle that was used in public transportation between Port-au-Prince and the provinces in the early decades of the twentieth century, before the introduction of sturdier, six-wheeled buses. The "kloutoup-kloutap" of the machann's gait is a metaphor for the bouncing of the less steady Ford kat on the road. After explaining this to me, the octogenarian contextualized the singer's interest: "Se w ti fanm musyeu te gen yen nan zòn Tigwav lan" [It's a little woman the fellow had in the Tigwav area]. Where Dupervil sings of a little "negress," the octogenarian hears—interchangeably—little "woman," which distinctly denotes a mistress. "Black" or "little," the woman-machann is a less-than-legitimate object of Dupervil's sexual interest. Such a woman could not be "his" black because, in her social context, black is not a color that can respectably stand on its own for Dupervil to identify with and love for itself. Conversely, the disembodied brune, whom Dupervil loves *as* color, could not stand for a woman-machann in the imaginary of the privileged Haitian.

The discursive creativity that keeps blackness at bay from the privileged person is not limited to such specific terms as "brun," "griffe," or "marabou." This transpired as I drove to a funeral in Montreal in the summer of 2012, between trips to the field in Port-au-Prince. With me in the car were two black Haitians, an octogenarian widow, who was a lifelong friend of the deceased, and another woman in her late thirties of a relatively darker skin shade. One of the widow's sons, the youngest of her children, was a high-ranking executive in Haiti's banking sector and one of my collaborators. Of her four other children, the eldest, a daughter, was a physician in Haiti and three had successful careers in the USA. After the death of her husband five years earlier, she leased the family home in Pétion-Ville to a foreign NGO and relocated to the New York metropolitan area.

The octogenarian widow was motivated to relocate in part to look after grandchildren—children of her physician daughter—who had left Haiti to continue their studies in the USA. She now lived with them in a house that she and her husband bought in the late 1980s, while they lived in Haiti. They bought the house as four of their children began to leave Haiti successively. The oldest left upon completing medical school with plans to prepare and sit for the "matching" exams that control entry to US medical residencies, and the other three upon completing the *baccalauréat* to attend college in the New York area.[2] After graduating with a business degree, the youngest return to Haiti, and the house served as a stepping-stone for the others as they established their careers in the USA and eventually bought their own homes.

The younger woman in the car on the drive to Montreal was of a more modest social background than either the widow, who had known her since infancy, or I. The woman's parents were from the Port-au-Prince working class; of limited formal schooling, they were not French-speaking Haitians. When they left Haiti in search of job opportunities in the USA, they left the woman as a baby in the care of a relative. The relative was a niece of the deceased, whose funeral we were on our way to. The relative and the octogenarian widow riding to Montreal with me were next-door neighbors in Pétion-Ville for decades.

The younger woman in the car with us eventually joined her parents in the USA in early adolescence. After high school, she briefly attended a local community college before enrolling in a vocational school. A few years after she began working in her present job as a nursing assistant, she and her husband purchased a house in the neighborhood of the octogenarian widow. They live there now with their daughter. Her residential proximity to the widow has renewed bonds of community formed in Haiti during her childhood in the care of the widow's neighbor in Pétion-Ville. As I drive them to the funeral in Montreal, a social distance still obtains between them in the Haitian class context, and the younger woman manages it in the aspirational margins of the moment.

The octogenarian widow is fluent in French and of very limited competence in English. The younger woman speaks French haltingly, and not more than a few sentences or sentence fragments at a time. All three of us in the car are fluent in Haitian Creole, which the widow does not seem to mind speaking. Yet, throughout the drive to Montreal, the younger woman returns to French every once in a while, and, although the widow clearly struggles to comprehend the English passages of the conversation, she speaks in English as least as often as she speaks in Haitian Creole, Haiti's vernacular tongue. Altogether, considering that Creole is the common language that the three of us speak fluently in the car, the younger woman uses it relatively sparingly. Eventually, the younger woman and the octogenarian widow come to speak of the premature death of a daughter of the deceased whose funeral we are going to in Montreal. The daughter died of AIDS fifteen years ago.

The younger woman in the car with me is particularly effusive about the dead woman's beauty, telling me in a mixture of English and Haitian Creole:

"She was gorgeous. Ou konn tande y ap pale w yon dam ki byen kanpe? Leu dam sa a ap mache nan Petyonvil, meusyeu yo kanpe sou deu ran pou yo gade. Li te gen w ti kouleu" [You've heard of a well-shaped lady? When that girl's walking in Pétion-Ville, guys line up in rows of two to watch. She had a li'l color]. Over the years, I have heard Haitians use the phrase "yon ti kouleu" [a li'l color] to describe somebody's color, but I never paid critical attention to the usage. This time, I do. I find it significant that "yon ti kouleu" is not somehow or other followed by an actual term from the Haitian vocabulary of color. No precision is forthcoming.

After the younger woman in the car said that last sentence about the dead woman's li'l color, without ado, the octogenarian widow interjected some remarks of her own around the premature death of her deceased friend's daughter. After the widow finishes speaking, I seek some clarity from the younger woman: "Ki kouleu l te ye?" [What color was she?], I ask. "Yon ti kouleu kòm si m ta di w" [A li'l color as if, say], she answers, and her voice trails off for a fraction of a second. She then speaks a new thought: "Li te reyèlman ou bote" [She was really a beauty]. I will know nothing more about the color of that beautiful woman, who died prematurely of AIDS. In the imaginary of the younger woman telling me the story, she simply sees no need to add clarity to the dead woman's color. "Yon ti kouleu," I am realizing, for all its literal vagueness, is in fact practically precise in describing the social color of a Haitian person of or aspiring to the respectable middle class. The phrase is not found in the vocabulary of color in the literature on colorism in Haiti, but Haitians do use it in everyday practice for a meaningful indication of a person's color. Now, on the drive to Montreal, using "yon ti kouleu" intentionally and meaningfully, the younger woman in the car has just told me that the beautiful woman who prematurely died of AIDS was not-black. In her not-blackness, I was left to know very precisely that she was not from the "masses."

At the time I began my conversations around the color issue in Haiti in early 2011, relatively dark-skinned Haitians had begun using imported creams and bleach-based homemade concoctions to lighten their skin systemically. The black physician, with whom I went to Kay Atizan, brought up the practice as we spoke about the politics of color in his office. He believed it to be a relatively recent cultural development; he had begun to notice it after the 1990s. A tell-tale sign of skin-lightening, he told me, is the contrast between the color of the cavity between the knuckles and the color of the rest of the back of the hand. In such cases, the lightening agent did not adequately penetrate the folds of the skin between the knuckles during application. He spoke of lower-class female patients who lightened their skin using homemade mixtures.[3] He saw their choice pragmatically. These patients, he told me, were generally economically insecure young women who relied considerably on amorous relationships for their subsistence. They lightened their skin, the physician said, because they believed that would give them an advantage with potential lovers over women who appeared darker-complexioned.

None of the privileged Haitians with whom I broached the subject in Haiti admitted to or showed signs of engaging in the practice of skin lightening. The owner of the beauty salon in the Delmas courtyard was the only practitioner with whom I discussed it at some length. Her husband drives a minibus between Port-au-Prince and his hometown of Saint-Marc. She acts as de facto property manager of the two-family house where she operates her shop, keeping the books on the property for the absentee owner living in the USA. She has rent-free use of two rooms, the one in which she lives and the one for the salon at the back of the main house. She lives with her husband and their two young daughters in the smaller of two rooms of an outbuilding, which would have been servant quarters when Delmas was a solidly middle-class destination in the 1970s and 1980s. An older woman, who is unrelated to her, rents the larger of the rooms. The residents of the outbuilding do not have access to the four modern bathrooms in the two apartments of the main house. They share an outhouse and an outdoor bathing alcove tucked in a corner of the backyard.

Although the beautician's natural complexion is similar to or perhaps slightly lighter than that of US President Barack Obama, given the social context of her everyday life, her skin color would not count for much in the socioeconomic hierarchy of privileged Haitians. Her clientele is strictly from the ranks of the working class. She would not be meaningfully clair in social transactions with elite subjects, because her person is socially defined in the world of Haiti's working poor. However, she is not unaware of her skin color in managing her status within her social plane. Despite her relative lightness of natural complexion (in the Haitian context), she applies a lightening cream to her face. According to her, skin lightening is widespread among her clients and more or less overt. However, she makes a clear distinction: "Mwen, m sèvi avè l pou fè figi m fre men lòt moun yo, yo black, yo fè l pou yo ka vin klè" [Me, I use it to freshen my face, but the other people, they're black, they do it so they can become light]. She makes a point of telling me that she only uses one cream whereas "lòt yo ta gen dwa sèvi ak menm ven krèm yo melanje ansanm" [the others could use up to twenty creams they mix together]. She adds that for her the practice is a *foli*. Like its French origin "folie," the Creole word means "madness," with a connotation of extravagant fancy in a context like this.

I ask the beautician whether she knows anyone who uses a homemade product, and I read her own socioeconomic aspiration in her answer: "Mach-ann nan lari a. Yo pa kab achte krèm yo. Yo ka itilize zafè pa yo. Yo mete l sou figi yo pou solèy la. Yo chita nan solèy la tout jounen" [Vendors on the street. They can't buy the creams. They might use their own stuff. They apply it to their face for the sun. They sit in the sun all day]. Incidentally, not much later, her husband was to confide in me: "Now that things are working out for her, she doesn't need me anymore. I'm there, it's as if I wasn't. I'm not enough for her now." With her salon relatively thriving, the beautician defined her distance from street vendors "below" her in the meanings of social color, while she left her husband to feel that she now wanted someone "better" than him.

Significantly, even though the beautician does not speak English and has never traveled out of Haiti, while our conversation was in Haitian Creole, she used the English word "black" ("lòt moun yo, yo black") to refer to the darker-skinned Haitians she knew to be using skin-lighteners. In doing so, she appropriated not an Americanism or a Briticism, but a French usage. Since at least the late 1980s, black and white French urbanites have routinely referred to a black person as "un black" rather than "un noir." The usage is nonetheless rare in Haiti. The mulatto entrepreneur, who could not coun-tenance the thought of a white Haitian, is the only other individual who would use the term with me—a few times in casual conversation—during my fieldwork. However the word entered the beautician's lexicon, her use of it as the French do suggests how much colorist operations in Haiti are informed by an aspirational encounter with the dominant modernity of the global West. Moreover, the beautician's engagement with color suggests that colorism in Haiti is a totalizing system of thought and action, inhering in the everyday life of subjects far down the social scale who aspire to emulate dominant sociopolitical-economic lifeways of the West.

❀   ❀   ❀

About two weeks after the development executive and I had lunch at the Indian restaurant in Manhattan, *Le Nouvelliste* reported in its issue of October 30, 2013, that "Miss Haiti Univers 2013" would be representing the country at the Miss Universe pageant in Moscow on November 9. The article refers to Mondiana J'hanne Pierre, the twenty-one-year-old woman in question, as a "brune." She is a relatively dark-skinned daughter of *black* middle-class parents. In the photograph that illustrated the article and in public photographs of US statesperson Condoleeza Rice, the two are more or less of similar complexion. That Pierre would be a brune to the *Nouvelliste* readership was hardly remarkable. That the newspaper had also celebrated Claudinette Fouchard, Miss Haiti 1959, as a "brune" was very remarkable.

Haitians do not generally deploy the vocabulary of color in a social vacuum. In public photographs, Fouchard, who was also twenty-one years old at the time she became Miss Haiti, appears noticeably lighter than the late US entertainer Lena Horne. In Haiti, the difference in phenotype between Pierre and Fouchard would be significant in social economies of the middle and upper classes. Moreover, Fouchard was the daughter of a prominent scion of a well-to-do mulatto family. By the descriptive scales in effect in the colorized social landscape of the 1960s (Price-Mars, 1967, 36–37) and early 1970s (Labelle 1987, 119, 121) as well as after the turn of the twenty-first century, and by the contextual class indices, Claudinette Fouchard could alternatively be described as a *claire* or a *mulâtresse*.[4] Thus, it is not because of a change in the valance of "brune" over the intervening decades that *Le Nouvelliste* assigned the same social color to the relatively dark-skinned Pierre from the black middle class and the relatively light-skinned Fouchard from the mulatto elite. Rather, *Le Nouvelliste* exceptionally made Fouchard "brune" in 1960 because of contextual requirements. The elasticity of brune silenced both her relatively light complexion and her mulatto belonging.

What I call here the Claudinette Fouchard moment was a definite nationalist euphoria in January 1960, when the privileged classes celebrated the young woman's triumph on the global stage as exemplar of [Western modernist] grace and beauty. That month, she won a beauty pageant in Cali, Colombia. François Duvalier had become president just over two years before in elections explicitly contested on grounds of color and concluded—on September 22, 1957—by firefight in the streets of Port-au-Prince. At the time Fouchard won the beauty contest in Colombia, Duvalier had already shown ominous signs of gathering dictatorial powers. Nearly a dozen figures associated with the 1957 government of Provisional President Daniel Fignolé (May–June 1957) had been living as asylees in various foreign embassies in the capital. Duvalier exiled them in the fortnight that Fouchard returned to Port-au-Prince. Four months later, in May, the regime would round up and summarily jail several middle-class mulattoes for allegedly plotting the return of the exiled politician Louis Déjoie, Duvalier's mulatto opponent in the 1957 elections. This is all to say, in the historical moment around the national celebration of Fouchard, Duvalier was hardly timid in his powers and in his political instrumentalization of color.

Fouchard had left the country as Miss Haiti at the end of December 1959 to participate in the pageant in Cali. In an interview at the airport before boarding her flight, she declared to a *Nouvelliste* reporter (her words featured as a subhead across two columns at the top of the front page): "I will do my best for my country and for my race." Fouchard thus erased the color of both country and race in the joint tradition of privileged blacks and mulattoes, when they wish to transcend their political fragmentation in color to assert their common pride in the nation.[5] When she returned to Port-au-Prince in early January crowned *La Reine mondiale du sucre* (The World Queen of Sugar), the news media copiously covered her celebration as national avatar, possibly none more than *Le Nouvelliste*, the establishment daily.[6] All segments of the elites and the middle classes celebrated "La Reine" as the epitome of national beauty. Fouchard paraded through Port-au-Prince in a Mercury convertible, the mayor gave her the key to the city, and she addressed the populace at the soccer stadium. The producers of the bourgeois pageantry around her triumphant return included prominent noiriste state actors alongside exclusivist mulatto "society Circles of Port-au-Prince."[7]

Although Jean Fouchard, Claudinette's father, was arguably a black-nationalist historian, his marriage, the marriage of his older daughter to a white European, and Claudinette's pending marriage to a German industrialist very much reproduced the mulatto endogamy of color, and La Reine was lavishly feted in private clubs generally taken to be exclusionary mulatto bastions. President François Duvalier, a most aggressive "noiriste" ideologue, nonetheless received her with great pomp at the National Palace (fig. 6.1). He gave her "a beautiful car, a magnificent and so generous gift."[8] A number of florid poems celebrated her charms in the pages of *Le Nouvelliste*. In all of them, her mulattoness remains as unspoken as the national race remains free of color when it is invoked. To an anonymous "Admirateur Patriote"

Lynn Grossberg

)l **The Queen And The President:** After decorating Haitian beauty, Claudinette Fouchard with the Order of Honor and Merit, the rank of an officer, President Francois Duvalier congratulates her for winning the "World Sugar Queen" title (see Foreign) at an official palace reception.

Figure 6.1. François Duvalier shared the global stage with *La Reine du sucre* Claudinette Fouchard in the February 4, 1960, issue of *Jet* magazine.

[Patriotic Admirer], she is a "Fine Flower of the Race." Another admirer adoringly asserts "ta brune couleur, la plus belle du monde" [your brown color, the most beautiful in the world].[9] In four of his other nineteen verses, the author—a black man—addresses her four times by name: twice as Claudinette, twice as "Brunette," an affectionate diminutive of brune. A clair man effusively exclaims: "Louant sans y penser cette race qui la moula . . . Elle est brune : Grâce Créole! Elle ondule : Grâce Créole! Elle est Choucoune : Beauté Créole!" [Praising naturally this race that molded her . . . She is brown: creole Grace! She sways: creole Grace! She is Choucoune: creole Beauty!].[10]

Le Nouvelliste also published a partial inventory of "The Presents Received by the Queen" in fifteen column inches of front-page news. They were from cabinet ministers, industrialists and businesspeople, and assorted privileged blacks and mulattoes. The gifts included "a television set, the most beautiful model in town . . . the keys to the City in a tortoiseshell case set with gold labels . . . bouquets . . . flowers (orchids, roses, gladioli . . . etc) . . . a silver brush . . . a porcelain vase from Bavaria."[11] A sleight of discourse concludes the enumeration of the presents: "Fruits and vegetables—and that is the most touching of gestures—brought by peasant families from Boucassin."

That final sentence of a catalogue of La Reine's gifts operates discursively at two levels as it notes with paternalist pathos the "touching" gesture of peasants bearing gifts of foodstuff devoid of bourgeois cultural polish. On the one hand, the language innocuously, but emphatically, asserts the externality of the rural folks in the celebrations. On the other, in doing so, it affirms the transcendent unity of the privileged urbanites who basked in Claudinette Fouchard's triumphant assertion of the nation's bourgeois pedigree to the world (fig. 6.2). In effect, in the Claudinette Fouchard moment, blacks and mulattoes, the elites of Port-au-Prince, jointly articulated the power to author the nation's cultural ideals.

In the euphoric cross-color nationalism of the celebration of Claudinette Fouchard, a relatively light-skinned daughter of the mulatto elite, the race that produced her remains without color; she is imagined brune, the immensely elastic color of privileged Haitians; and she is identified with Choucoune, an iconic fictional beauty who is otherwise a marabou, a not-black of deep-dark skin. Altogether, in their public celebration of triumphant national feminine beauty in Claudinette Fouchard, privileged Haitians across color boundaries made her the ideal creole, a cultural subject who since the

Wide World

⚋ **Haiti Queen:** Placing a crown on Claudinette Fouchard, 21, Jean Jacques Honorat, head of the Tourist Bureau, officially proclaims her "Miss Haiti of 1960." The shapely (36-24-36), beauty speaks five languages, has attended Georgetown U., and the Sorbonne, majoring in art, music.

Figure 6.2. Claudinette Fouchard and tourism chief Jean-Jacques Honorat—a daughter of the mulatto elite and a privileged noiriste—jointly affirmed Haiti's bourgeois pedigree to the world in the pages of *Jet* magazine, February 4, 1960.

colonial era has been distinguished not in a distinct color or race but in a definite non-African-ness.

Overall, the Claudinette Fouchard moment, comprising mulattoes and blacks, suggests that colorism and elitism are mutually productive and are each a modular modality of social stratification, lending themselves to contextual deployment singularly or in tandem. Mulattoes continue to reproduce their endogamy through prejudice of color in personal relations that are actually or potentially prefigurative of biological reproduction. Privileged black nationalists continue to deploy the nation's presumptive Blackness politically, while they distance themselves from the blackness of the dark-skinned poor through the color nomenclature. Privileged blacks and privileged mulattoes can also jointly deploy duly calibrated expressions of colorism in conjunction with other ideologies of class to set boundaries between themselves as a singular aggregate and the lower strata of the social order.

CHAPTER SEVEN

MATERIAL UNITY IN PRIVILEGE

I first met the fair-complexioned executive at a coastal real estate development that she owns with her husband a few hours from *Portail Léogane*, a
roundabout that was once the capital's southern gate. The engineering contractor had taken me there with him to inspect work on a renovation project.
When we arrived, he met up with a crew of technicians from his company
reconfiguring a room in a building. After briefly reviewing their progress, he
made his way to a suite that two masons were rebuilding in a different wing
of the building. A light-skinned Haitian man bantered amiably in Haitian
Creole with the masons, while he inspected their work. He was the architect
of the renovations, not the owner of the property as I initially thought, and
he had overall responsibility for the project. The contractor introduced us to
each other in French; the three of us were soon alternately speaking Haitian
Creole. The architect had a droll sense of humor. The contractor occasionally
appeared in local venues as a humorist. Inveterate jokesters, they maintained
a stream of humor in idiomatic Haitian Creole as they discussed their coordinated work on the renovations. The day felt propitious for my own work
as I looked forward to observing and participating in the collaboration of a
black Haitian and a *mulatto* Haitian in an easygoing business relationship. It
was my fifth full day in the field. The ethnographer would later grasp what
I, the *Haitian*, perhaps the *black* Haitian, or yet the *black-nationalist* Haitian
had experienced.

After I returned to the USA and began analyzing my field notes, I incidentally reread the architect's features in pictures on his Facebook page. I realized then, in New York City his complexion together with his dark eyes and close-cropped supple black hair would have made him white to me, perhaps one with origins in Mediterranean Europe. I also grasped then two significant phenomena that occurred in parallel at the real estate complex. On the one hand, as a Haitian, I mulattoized the architect at my first sight of him, because he was fluently speaking Haitian Creole with the two masons without the slightest trace of a foreign accent. As I took it for granted that he was Haitian, the mulattoization ensued. In that moment, the Haitian praxis of color fragmented the field of research in lines of color. On the other hand, as an anthropologist, I also began to apprehend existential commonalities between the architect and the engineering contractor, which underlay my perception of a societal cohesion that they embodied throughout the day. My anthropological imagination would eventually grasp their *unity* that day in social relations that were reproductive of their respective situations in Haiti's privileged classes.

This chapter explores spatial and temporal dimensions of the unity of privileged Haitians across the boundary of color in the articulation of class reproduction. I draw below intersecting diachronic genealogical trajectories that link a Haitian rural elite and urban privilege in Port-au-Prince and the Western metropolis beyond. They represent a history of lived experience that encompasses the class position of the math teacher and the engineering contractor. I then make salient that the social situation of the two inheres in a cohesive sociality that also encompasses the position of the fair-complexioned executive. I map this sociality yet further to situate within it the poet-engineer and his childhood neighborhood, which, as it happens, is also the childhood neighborhood of the fair-complexioned executive and the architect of the renovations at the real estate complex. To illustrate cogently the material unity of the two colorized formations of privilege as a modality of class formation, I conclude the chapter with an ethnographic moment, in which the prejudiced mulatto entrepreneur enacts the reproduction of his class situation in concert with that of a black peer at the expense of poor monolingual creolophone Haitians.

A technologist in an allied health profession introduced me to the math teacher, the wife of the engineering contractor, in the summer of 2009. The three of us were at a fund-raising party for a prospective candidate in Haiti's 2010 presidential elections. The latter ultimately did not run, but my friendship with the math teacher did take hold. The fund-raiser was hosted by a physician couple at their suburban home near the New England coast of the United States. Both hosts were products of rural privilege and first-generation urbanites, and both practiced in one of the more lucrative medical specialties in the country. As it happened, at the Faculty of Medicine and Pharmacy of the State University of Haiti, both hosts of the fund-raiser were students of the father of the architect of the renovations at the real estate complex of the fair-complexioned executive. The party was in fact the site of a convergence of social trajectories with origins spatially and temporally deep in Haiti's landowning peasantry.

The husband who hosted the fundraiser is the brother of the allied health technologist, and the two are first cousins of the math teacher. The wife, a daughter of the provincial petite bourgeoisie, went to primary school in her hometown and to secondary school in the capital, where she attended Institution Sainte Rose de Lima, a parochial girls' school founded in the nineteenth century whose elitism is the stuff of legend. For his primary and secondary education, the husband attended Institution Saint-Louis de Gonzague, which was through most of the twentieth century the most prestigious parochial boys' school in the country. Both moved to the USA after medical school and successfully sat for examinations that control access to residency training at US hospitals.

The math teacher's father was the older brother of the father of her cousins, the allied health technologist and the husband who hosted the fund-raiser. Their common grandfather, their respective fathers' father, was born after the turn of the twentieth century in a remote mountain village, where he spent his entire life, inland from the southern coast of the country about three hours from Port-au-Prince. Today, the village remains inaccessible by car. When I visited it with the math teacher and the engineering contractor, the latter drove about ten minutes on a dirt road after branching off the nearest paved street, and then parked his SUV in a clearing where the road became impassable (fig. 7.1). We then walked for more than half an hour at a brisk pace over a terrain of steep hills to arrive at a plateau far up the mountain. The grandfather was the largest landowner in the area, some of his holdings inherited from his own father, some acquired, and he could speak and write French, the cultural competence that is a foundational index of the nation's privileged classes. He and his wife also had two daughters—the two older children—in addition to the respective fathers of the math teacher and her two cousins.

Figure 7.1. As the engineering contractor parked his SUV in a clearing, the math teacher (in hat), her daughter (partly obscured) and her cousin, the allied health technologist, headed toward their ancestral home. We eventually walked thirty minutes up and down steep hills to get there, June 2016. Photo by the author.

The respective fathers of the math teacher and of the host of the fundraiser were born in the mid-1930s and died in the 1990s. They walked more than an hour each way to attend school in the town nearest their village. The curriculum only went through the first half of the secondary cycle. After that, the brothers went to live at a pension in the urban center of the region, where they continued their schooling through the *baccalauréat*. The pension then in Haiti was a middle-class family home providing room and board and—of no small social significance—the habitus of the petite bourgeoisie. During that time, the two brothers met the young women—lifelong friends—who would become their respective wives. The fathers of the young women were not landowners. However, they were dominant tradesmen in their respective fields and well established in the city's respectable middle class. Both young women were of proper petit-bourgeois upbringing, with the all-important fluency in the French language and French-derived social etiquette.

The two brothers and both young women independently migrated to Port-au-Prince. The brothers eventually completed their university studies, married, and established themselves professionally in the capital. The father of the host of the fund-raising party and the health technologist was himself a doctor, and a colonel in the FAd'H during the Duvalier dictatorship. His brother, the math teacher's father, was a lawyer. The two brothers left their children significant residential real estate that they acquired in Port-au-Prince and its suburbs. Their children are the first generation of the family to be born in the city. After the math teacher launched the engineering contracting firm with her husband in the mid-1980s, she drew on her family's connections in the Duvalierist state bourgeoisie to build their initial client base. She has also managed the family land in the ancestral village, and she does so with nationalist pride (fig. 7.2).

The mother of the allied health technologist and the host of the political fund-raiser eventually migrated with her siblings from their native provincial city to Port-au-Prince, where they also entered the orbit of the Duvalierist state bourgeoisie. One of her sisters left Haiti in the mid-1960s to study nursing in central Europe on a scholarship from the Haitian government. After completing her degree, the sister successfully applied for a professional immigrant visa that allowed her to settle in the USA. She then sponsored her siblings for a US Permanent Residency permit. Upon thus receiving a "green card," the mother of the allied health technologist and the host of the fund-raiser in turn sponsored them, along with their two siblings, for the Permanent Residency, passing along to her children the mobility capital that would ultimately give them access to US professional careers. In the summer of 2009, when the math teacher and I met each other for the first time at the fund-raising party as guests of her cousin and his wife, the two had been in their medical careers for over a decade. Our meeting was a contingent culmination of a web of diachronic relations, which, in their articulations over more than a century, linked Haiti's rural elite in the country's remote interior to the state bourgeoisie in the capital, and thence to spheres of privilege of the global bourgeois West.

❧   ❧   ❧

The math teacher introduced me to her husband, the engineering contractor, shortly after I arrived in Port-au-Prince on my first trip to the field. A few days after that, he took me with him to inspect the work of his company on the renovation project at the real estate development of the fair-complexioned

Figure 7.2. The math teacher and her cousin, the allied health technologist, in front of their fathers' and grandparents' grave at the edge of the family's land in their ancestral village. Photo by the author.

executive. After he and the architect of the renovations discussed the state of the project, we separated. I followed the architect; the engineering contractor went elsewhere on the grounds.

As I walk with the architect along a pathway bordered by a flowerbed, a helicopter with a prominent logo of the United Nations flies overhead. Earlier in the day, a business errand took the engineering contractor and me past a UN military pickup truck a quarter of a mile or so outside Cité Soleil, a sprawling slum on the outskirts of Port-au-Prince that has been notorious for extreme poverty and extreme gang violence since the 1990s. We were on Route 9, a thoroughfare itself infamous for gang and kidnapping activity. The truck was parked on the shoulder of the roadway, facing the street strategically at a ninety-degree angle. Foreign soldiers standing in its bed with machine guns watched intently over the roadway. As the sight drew my attention, the engineering contractor stated matter-of-factly: "They're supposedly here to keep order. Terrorizing is what they're doing to people in places like around here" (fig. 7.3). The poet-engineer, the cultural impresario,

Figure 7.3. Wary eyes on a UN Peacekeeper. Photo courtesy of IOM Haiti.

and several other middle-class Haitians had similarly expressed disdain or bitterness to me about the UN military presence in the country. Now, as the UN helicopter flies over the real estate complex, the mulatto architect becomes another one, with a classic US obscenity. He stops walking and, looking up with a smirk and both arms raised above his head, he gives both middle fingers to the aircraft.

Eventually, the architect and I rejoined the engineering contractor, and the three of us walked over to a restaurant located on a veranda of the complex. There, we met up with the civil engineer on the project, a man of a noticeably darker complexion than the engineering contractor. I noted the difference, because gradations of skin tone can unpredictably become significant at the intersection of identity, color, and privilege in Haiti.[1] The four of us waited at a table for the fair-complexioned executive, who was delayed at a staff meeting elsewhere on the property. Meanwhile, we made small talk.

At the table, the architect and the contractor begin trading humorous stories of grueling experience around the theme of travel. The contractor, who unabashedly admits to his predilection for modern comfort, good food, and fine drink, tells with mock horror of his wife making him walk a trail through the mountains east of Port-au-Prince to the city of Jacmel in the

South-East Department. The architect, whose mother is a white European, speaks of juggling his luggage and that of a gaggle of younger cousins in a rainstorm outside a train station in his mother's native country. The settings of their experiences are vastly different, but they are otherwise two modern professionals humorously telling tales of woe on a distinctively bourgeois pursuit of leisure. The civil engineer, apparently the youngest at the table, is of a more reserved demeanor and laughs at the jokes with considerably more restraint than any of us. I have noticed a pronounced provincial accent when he speaks either French or Haitian Creole; perhaps he is from the proverbially conservative rural elite.

When the fair-complexioned executive arrives on the veranda, she approaches the table from the direction I am facing. In that moment, she is a white woman to me, because I take her to be a foreigner. She is wearing Capri pants, a pastel polo shirt and tasteful mules, her blond hair reaching to her shoulders. Her skin tone is reminiscent of that of the French actress Catherine Deneuve, an international icon of whiteness that will randomly come to mind when I write my field notes later. The fair-complexioned executive sits down next to me at the table, and the contractor introduces us. As the two of us make small talk in French, the architect announces to her with mock seriousness in English: "Anthropologist is here to study our customs." I will not have an opportunity to discuss with him what might be behind his irony, but, given the hint of ridicule in his tone, he seems to be alluding to the "Haiti [of] the 'anthropological imaginary'" (Magloire and Yelvington 2005, 2), a Haiti axiomatically defined in tropes of race and color. Not for the last time, I become cognizant of doing the anthropology of a Haiti that can talk back to the discipline with the symbolic wherewithal to challenge its assigned meanings. I repeat a mental note that I made while having dinner with the engineering contractor and his family two days earlier: situate this Haiti in the West's modernity without such qualifiers as "periphery" or "alternative."

The fair-complexioned executive soon asks a waiter in Haitian Creole, "Ki sa w gen pou w ofri envite n yo?" [What do you have to offer our guests?]. Her amiable paternalism—accentuating rather than negating the class positions in the exchange—is often deployed by privileged Haitians across the colorized map toward their domestic servants and "le petit personnel" [the little personnel] of their businesses. Now, I know she is Haitian. In retrospect, this is probably when I begin to cease seeing her whiteness. It is about five minutes after she joined the other four of us at the table. When I leave the complex in a few hours, she will have become a *mulatto* collaborator to my research.

The waiter brought us a large plate of ceviche that he put in the center of the table. As we eat chunks of fresh fish marinated in vinegar, the conversation remains centered on the progress of the renovation project, or lack thereof from the perspective of the fair-complexioned executive. At some point, she remarks with pride that the kitchen is supplied by local fishermen. All the while, amidst talks of ballooning cost overruns and missed deadlines, the mood at the table remains relaxed and friendly among four Haitian professionals of diverse social and ethnic backgrounds negotiating the realities of a business process.

The engineering contractor is a product of the public-sector petite bourgeoisie. His father led a government development agency in the 1970s and 1980s in the southern city of Les Cayes. His brother is a mathematics PhD and the chairperson of his department at a US university, and two sisters are civil servants married to well-known physicians. The architect's father was a light-skinned physician, whose ancestors migrated to Haiti from elsewhere in the Americas in the early nineteenth century. He was a respected teacher and mentor at the Faculty of Medicine of the State University of Haiti and was known for his volunteer work with the disabled. Unlike the architect and the engineering contractor, the civil engineer does not live in the Port-au-Prince metropolitan area, and he shows little of their worldly jollity. He lives in his hometown, which, with a population of around sixteen thousand, is the urban center of a provincial administrative district that is over eighty percent rural. The social unity of the five of us at the table is nonetheless not forced, and the arrival of the daughter of the fair-complexioned executive makes it quite salient.

As we finish off the succulent ceviche, the fair-complexioned executive's daughter arrives at the table on the side where the architect sits. Her complexion is as fair as her mother's, and her straight blond hair drops on her back well past her shoulders. Stopping by the architect, she leans down and forward, and plants a kiss on his cheek. This greeting is a defining ritual of the well-bred Haitian child, and the young woman, who is about twenty-six years old, repeats it with each of her mother's three other guests around the table. Although the practice principally marks a generational rather than gendered hierarchy, it is inflected by gender in this instance. Generally, by late adolescence, boys stop greeting their male elders with a kiss and greet them instead with a handshake. Be that as it may, as sociologist Alex Dupuy will point out on the significance of class in that moment (private communication), the fair-complexioned executive's daughter would not similarly kiss her parents' domestic staff.

A kiss on the cheek is hardly uncommon in fashionable precincts of urban life in the Americas or Europe. The practice may be termed "air-kissing," when the parties' respective cheeks make tangential contact as the lips go through the motion of a kiss more or less in the air. This is a reciprocal gesture, and it indicates more or less effervescent friendliness. This is how the math teacher, the engineering contractor's wife, and I greeted each other, when I arrived for dinner at her home the previous Sunday. In a quintessentially Haitian variant of the practice, the kisser's lips squarely press against the recipient's cheek more or less at a right angle. There is no expectation of reciprocity in this version. The receiver of the kiss makes a cheek available to receive an expected expression of respect for one's elder. This is how the contractor's daughter greeted me, when I arrived for dinner on Sunday. She was doing schoolwork with a classmate, who had never seen me before. As the classmate left shortly thereafter, she successively kissed goodbye to the contractor, his wife, and me in the same manner.

The daughter of the fair-complexioned executive is being a quintessential Haitian as she follows the practice with ritual precision at the table on the veranda of the real estate complex. She first kisses the architect, then me. After walking around the end of the table where her mother is sitting, she kisses the engineering contractor. The civil engineer is sitting next to the contractor and directly across from me. The young woman leans down toward him in the same gesture of understated deference she has just done thrice. I watch her fair lips press softly against the jet-black skin of the civil engineer without hesitation, and this utterly innocuous gesture of Haitian social life has just made Haiti a much more complicated place than the one in the Black Republic schema that I brought with me the previous week from the North American academy. A fair-skinned daughter of the mulatto colorist elite, educated in the techniques of the endogamy of color by her mother, has just earnestly greeted with deferent humility three men whom—or whose sons—she would not date, much less marry, because they are black.

Incidentally, the real estate complex where we are now—her mother's property—comprises several buildings, a pool, and a private beach, with ornamental shrubs and flowering plants dotting the grounds. It is neither an ephemeral nor a movable investment. It is the object of a grounded elite. Moreover, through a maternal great-great-great-grandfather, the fair-complexioned executive's roots in the nation extend to the late colonial era. Although neither she nor her daughter foregrounds the African heritage in her Haitian identity, they are both bona fide Haitians. It is little wonder that the daughter embodied the unity of the six Haitians around the table through a typically Haitian practice. It is also little wonder that the daughter's kiss on the cheeks of her mother's three black and one mulatto guests around the table proceeded from the four men's class, wherever they might be individually situated on the scale of wealth. Haiti is after all a postcolonial Western bourgeois society. When her mother asked the black man of her petit personnel what he would offer "our" guests, she ritually reaffirmed his class position below all of *us* at the table, not merely below her. Whose blackness and whose nation does the "Black" Republic then stand for? What of my subjectivity that ceased seeing whiteness in her, when she became Haitian therein? The politics of color and race truly is a mystifyingly intricate code that regulates a national economy of privilege.

As we rose from the table after the business meeting ended on the veranda, I gave my business card to the architect. He gave me two distinct cards, one representing his professional practice in the construction industry and one representing his volunteer engagement in Haiti's environmental movement. I gave a card to the fair-complexioned executive, and she handed me two, one for her and one for her daughter. The latter humorously repeated their respective names to ensure that I remembered who was who of the two. The civil engineer did not have a business card, and I had none left. We each wrote down our respective contact information for the other on a piece of paper. After we all said goodbye to one another, the civil engineer, the contractor, and the architect strolled away. I stayed behind by the table long enough to ask the fair-complexioned executive (in French) whether she might want to participate in my research on *le sentiment d'appartenance, l'identité et l'engagement socio-politique dans les classes privilégiées du pays* [the sense of belonging, identity, and sociopolitical engagement in the privileged classes of the country]. She agreed instantly. I thanked her for her hospitality and bid her goodbye again before walking away to join the engineering contractor in his car.

As the contractor began the drive back to Port-au-Prince, I read the family name on the business cards of the fair-complexioned executive and her daughter. I was not at all familiar with it. To be certain, I asked the contractor whether they were Haitians. He said they were, and he identified the fair-complexioned executive by her maiden name. I recognized that surname. Although I had no recollection of ever having seen her before today, she and the poet-engineer grew up about half a mile apart in a neighborhood not far from the Boutilliers hills. In my youth, two first cousins and a number of friends of mine lived in the area, and I easily recalled the family of the fair-complexioned executive in its social landscape. As the engineering contractor drove on toward the capital, I made a mental note to speak with the poet-engineer for what contextual insight I might gain on the fair-complexioned executive's current position in Haiti's business elite.

About twenty minutes down the highway, we encounter a civil disturbance. We are now perhaps half a mile from a state office building, where we saw a commotion on the way from Port-au-Prince in the morning. Broad, unpaved footpaths on either side of the highway separate it from bordering communities. We have been seeing increasingly more people milling around, looking in the direction of the state office building, with increasing pedestrian traffic crossing the roadway. We eventually realize that a mass of people occupies the breadth of the road about a quarter of a mile ahead of us. We happen to be traveling directly behind a UN military SUV on the highway. I suggest that behind a UN military vehicle is not a bad place to be, whatever may be going on up ahead. The contractor does not answer immediately as he keeps his eyes intently far down the road ahead of him. Slowing down, he eventually answers, "That depends." He pulls up to the side of the road and lowers the glass by me to call out to a passer-by: "What's happening up ahead?" The amiable answer from a man on the dirt path is as succinct as it is cavalier: "Action." When I eventually write my field notes, the nonchalant answer will seem quite ironic, but it is not in the moment it is spoken, given the gathering anxiety in the contractor's air-conditioned SUV. Meanwhile, another SUV drives past. It is a sleek late-model vehicle with a metallic black shine.

The contractor begins driving again, moving cautiously. When we are within several hundred feet of the state office building, it is clear that a protest is taking place. The contractor pulls to the side of the road again. He lowers the glass on my side again to speak with a woman sitting in front of a cement-block wall on a *ti chèz*, a scaled-down chair that stands about half a foot from the ground. He asks the woman whether there is a way to that side of the state office building. The woman recognizes him from some television appearance that he made as a humorist and advises him warmly. Following the woman's directions, the contractor eases his vehicle off the roadway and goes through an opening in the wall beyond the spot where the woman is sitting. We drive through an empty lot, then cross a footpath to arrive in a narrow passage behind a house, possibly part of the backyard. An older man and a child good-naturedly get up and step back to make room for the vehicle to get through. The contractor asks the older man whether he is on track to get to the road that runs alongside the state office building. The man nods and tells him to keep going straight, pointing ahead of us. We eventually come out of the narrow passage and cross some vague expanse that seems to be another empty lot or a commons. After that, we are on the sidewalk of the paved road that will take us to that side of the state office building at the intersection with the highway, up ahead to our left.

When we get to the intersection, to our right the highway continues toward Port-au-Prince. From what I can see to our left, there is a diffused tension among a sizable group of people milling outside the building. The contractor turns right. Not a hundred feet later, we are in crawling traffic. Further, there is a roadblock, which we cannot see. Traffic soon comes to a standstill. Moments later, the shiny black late-model SUV drives past in the opposite direction. I presume it reached the roadblock and has reversed course in search of a way out of the blockage. I have a clear view of the driver. He is a light-skinned man, who gazes intently ahead of him with noticeable anxiety. When I notice his expression, I conjure the image of someone frantically looking for an exit from a boxed-in yard that has none. The contractor lowers the glass by me to ask a passer-by what is going on. The full answer is thoroughly vague: "Mè a ak ekip ki pa dakò ak li" [The mayor and groups that don't agree with him]. The man continues on his way. The only moving vehicular traffic is of motorcycle taxis easing their way past the engineering contractor's car among the pedestrians on the dirt path alongside the road. That, too, soon stops.

Suddenly, stones begin raining down on the road, and the pedestrians dart this way and that. The stones hit cars or land on the pavement every few seconds, sometimes a few at a time. They are coming down with such frequency and such intensity that it cannot possibly be a lone individual throwing them. I cannot tell the radius of the target field; it is at least two car lengths in front of the contractor's SUV and probably the same behind it. From my perspective in the car, the stones are coming at a slight diagonal angle from an elevated position to the left ahead of me. Across the road, there are houses lining the dirt path, then a clearing where a slope rises from the dirt path. The stones seem to be coming from quite beyond a tree that stands on the slope about ten to twenty feet from the edge of the highway. They are relatively big; none seems smaller than an adult fist.

Neither the engineering contractor nor I saw it coming, the first stone that hits his car. A dull but violent thud simply popped inches away from his head. The stone hit the metal band between the front and rear doors. We are startled, but we both remain calm. Through the windshield, I have a clear view of the next stone hurtling toward the car; it seems to be the size of a grapefruit. I am relieved, when it lands on the hood of the vehicle and not on the windshield. The vehicle behind us is slightly more toward the middle of the roadway than we are. It is a large commercial bus. In a flash of inspiration, the contractor eases the car forward; then, with the two right wheels now onto the dirt path bordering the roadway, he switches gear into reverse. He eases his way backward until his SUV is completely in the shadow of the bus. Now sheltered, the contractor's car cannot be hit. We do hear stones occasionally hitting the other side of the bus. We are so close to the bus, and it is so tall next to us, that I cannot see its roof. I lean forward but can only see the bottom edge of the roofline. Generally, whatever else might be on the cargo rack, there quite likely would be foodstuff and perhaps some small animals of country people heading to market in the capital.

Thus, in this palpably concrete experience of Haiti's political volatility, our cover is a bus full of poor, possibly mostly rural Haitians. As I live the moment, its allegorical power is not lost on me. Two local women were scrunched up behind the driver of the last moto-taxi that rode past the contractor's SUV on the dirt path after car traffic came to a halt on the highway. I imaginatively substitute the motorcycle for the contractor's air-conditioned SUV alongside the bus. In my imagination, the driver of the motorcycle and the two women scrunched up behind him, three Haitians more or less as dark of skin as the contractor, are now the ones taking cover from the stones in the shadow of a bus full of poor folks. The allegorical significance no longer holds. Poor people finding protection from the contingent chaos of daily life at the expense of other poor people could not be much of an allegory on asymmetrical class relations. I imaginatively replace the contractor's vehicle with the light-skinned driver's shiny black late-model SUV and, this time, the allegory holds again. The stones stop when security forces in army fatigues show up on the scene. I ask the engineering contractor whether they are from MINUSTAH, the diplomatic framework of the current UN military control of the country. They are not; they are from CIMO, Haiti's riot police. Traffic eventually starts moving again.

I never found out the precise cause of the disturbance on the highway to Port-au-Prince. The next morning, the fair-complexioned executive invited me via email to visit her the day after that at the headquarters of the family firm in downtown Port-au-Prince. In the evening, to prepare for the visit, I telephoned the poet-engineer to chat about how their childhood neighborhood had changed and how it had not since I left Haiti. Incidentally, he had returned to live in his childhood home after losing his house in the earthquake of January 2010. On the phone with him that evening, I brought up the fair-complexioned executive by her maiden name, and I asked him whether anyone in her family still lived in the house in which she grew up, about eight blocks away from his. He had been an acquaintance of one of her brothers in their youth. He told me that he did not know who now lived in the family home. I would later learn that the fair-complexioned executive and her husband did.

As we spoke, to illustrate social continuity in the neighborhood, the poet-engineer invoked by name the architect in charge of the renovations at the fair-complexioned executive's real estate complex. He told me that the architect still lived nearby. I was flabbergasted. I told him that, incredibly, I was introduced to that man just the day before. The poet-engineer now was the one surprised: "Don't you remember him?" he asked me. "I knew him?" I asked in turn. "Maybe you don't remember him, but you have to have known him. When I was at the faculty, he was often at my house. We studied together. Very funny guy, always telling one joke or another." The poet-engineer further pointed out that the architect grew up in the neighborhood as well and that he, too, still lived in his childhood home. The two no longer socialized together, but "we nonetheless see, we greet each other every morning when he drives past my house," the poet-engineer added. He enumerated others besides the architect who made up a study group that gathered at his house in their days at the Faculty of Sciences of the State University of Haiti. I remembered several of them. I was in secondary school at the time and was frequently at the house, linked to the poet-engineer and particularly to his younger brother, who was closer to me in age, by our common interest in soccer and other youthful pursuits.

In our telephone conversation that evening, the poet-engineer effectively traced a social history of the neighborhood, which "was spared by the earthquake," in the words of a lifelong resident in her fifties who lives on his street. It has remained remarkably stable, its name still resonating with the well-to-do as an elite locale. Focusing on the seven blocks of the street on which the poet-engineer grew up, I mapped a microcosm of the material unity of the privileged classes and the tension around color that it contains.

The poet-engineer's house is impressively set amidst lush vegetation behind seven-foot whitewashed walls and a wrought-iron gate, although some sections of the house are in considerable disrepair. The poet-engineer's younger brother has lived there all his life and has not been able to afford decorative maintenance and necessary repairs. It nonetheless remains an imposing two-story, twin-turreted structure with thirteen wide steps rising to a wrap-around porch from a cobblestone driveway. In photographs from our youth, the house appears resplendent in a red-and-white color scheme. In those days, foreigners occasionally stopped to take pictures of it from across the street as a representative of gingerbread architecture. At the time—in the Duvalier years—at one end of the street lived a pillar of the business elite, a (mulatto) family whose eponymous trading house was among the largest of the day. At the other end, another (mulatto) family lived in what was remembered in the neighborhood as a "Déjoieist" house, because in 1957 its residents supported Louis Déjoie, François Duvalier's mulatto opponent in the presidential elections. On the intervening seven blocks of the street lived a remarkable array of families of various degrees of privilege, some less anonymous than others.

Between the Déjoieist house and that of the poet-engineer, an upscale rental property with a gate at either end of a crescent driveway was home for years to US diplomats. Today, it remains home to expatriates of significant status. About three hundred feet down a perpendicular street outside one of its gates, a post-Duvalier former prime minister keeps his private offices in a genteel hillside house . Then, on the other side of the poet-engineer's house lived a (clair) civil servant of august stature, the nominal head of a branch of government. The Duvalier in-laws lived inconspicuously in a residential complex six houses further up the street. A (black) cousin of the Duvalier in-laws on a different kinship line occupied the second house of the complex. Diagonally across the street, lived the middle-class mulatto family whose younger daughter was friends with the Duvalier in-laws' daughter.

Next door to the Duvalier in-laws lived a (black) household that produced a presidential candidate who became prime minister in the years after the second coup against Aristide. A (clair) civil servant, who was one of the nation's most important finance officials under Jean-Claude Duvalier, was the other next-door neighbor of the household that produced the presidential candidate and prime minister.

One of the sons of Jean-Claude Duvalier's finance official has been a key member of the cabinet of René Préval, the current president. However, he is not the most remarkable link of the street's past to present political power. It is rather the Duvalier in-laws' cousin, who lived in the second house of their residential complex. The cousin, at whose house I met Jean-Claude Duvalier once when he was president, was also a second cousin of President Préval on yet another kinship line.[2] Thus, in 1991, when President Jean-Bertrand Aristide embodied the Lavalas movement's euphoric promise of transformative change in the aftermath of the Duvalier dictatorship, the Duvalier in-laws' cousin, who hosted President for Life Jean-Claude Duvalier at his house during the dictatorship, was also a cousin of the first Lavalas prime minister, René Préval.

If the social history and geography of the poet-engineer's neighborhood since his childhood suggests the societal unity of Haiti's privileged classes, it also suggests that defining political agency in the color (or race) of political actors can produce a poor map of political possibilities. Incidentally, a few days before the telephone conversation in which the poet-engineer retraced that history with me, I detected the limits of his political engagement in a praxis that marked his class position and could not have marked his color.

It is the last Sunday morning of March 2011, two days before I will be at the real estate complex of the fair-complexioned executive for the first time. The poet-engineer and I are discussing *bidonvillisation* on the porch of his house. I say to him that I have noticed an encroachment of informal, small-scale sidewalk retail commerce in several hitherto elite neighborhoods of Port-au-Prince, but that does not seem to have happened in this area. He tells me that is indeed the case but that it may be a matter of time. He tells me of his concern about that possibility and of his vigilance about preempting it. He mentions a formerly residential house on his block that is now the headquarters of a political organization. He deplores the garish letters—style, size, and color—of slogans painted on the wall facing the street. "Yo defigure blok la, y afekte imaj katye a" [They disfigure the block, they affect the image of the neighborhood], he complains to me. To illustrate the situation further, he invokes a homeless woman, apparently mentally ill, who for years bathed and did her laundry in water running down the gutter on his block. His concern about the "quality" of life in the neighborhood eventually led him to ask a personal acquaintance in the municipal authority to address the situation. Sometime after that, the homeless woman was no longer seen bathing or doing laundry in the gutter on the block. The poet-engineer does not know exactly what his acquaintance in the city government did, but he is certain that the latter intervened somehow.

Rather surprisingly, I was not at all upset after the poet-engineer told me the story. However, as I was apprehending social realities of Haiti's black-nationalist postcolonial present, I was critically interested in his intervention against the poor woman's use of the public space of his neighborhood. My interest was less in the fact of the limit of his progressive politics, which the story reveals, than in the fact that he arrived at the limit in the management of the neighborhood's elite value. His concern with the social *standing* of the neighborhood made salient to me that he was a modern bourgeois subject— that is, a class subject—before being a *black* Haitian nationalist. The neighborhood was in fact an object of class solidarity in motivating the poet-engineer to act against the poor woman's agency for the sake of its value as an elite place. In October 2012, I was to observe the prejudiced mulatto entrepreneur similarly enacting a solidarity of class with a black associate over against the socioeconomic interests of his monolingual creolophone workers.

The morning the mulatto entrepreneur told me of his color prejudice, he was acutely broke. By the end of the day, he would momentarily resolve his pecuniary jam expressly at the expense of poor Haitians, and he articulated the momentary solution with the interest of a fellow middle-class profes-sional, who was incidentally black. After he picked me up that morning on his way to work, his cellular telephone rang as he drove through a maze of side streets in the Delmas area. When he answered, without any greeting, he humorously chastised the caller, evidently a friend, for not having returned his phone calls earlier. He laughed at whatever the man responded, and they chatted for a few minutes. After he hung up, I asked him whether the man was a black or a mulatto. He told me it was a black friend, who called him to announce that the US consulate had granted him a visa to visit the United States. He chuckled again as he related what had made him laugh on the phone. After telling him about the newly granted visa, the friend added with mock condescension, "M se w kapitalis kounye a. M pa gen pasyans pou nou" [I'm a capitalist now. I have no patience for you folks]. For context, he told me that the friend, who worked for a development NGO, was a former member of the Haitian Communist Party and had lived for seven years in the former East Germany, where he studied political propaganda.

As the mulatto entrepreneur drove on, he joked about his friend being a lapsed communist, and that got us back to the theme of political engagement in the elites of Haiti. We had spoken about that at length on his patio during the final rains of Hurricane Sandy about a week earlier. He told me that there was a strong discourse about social engagement but little actual action. He said people who seemed to be "elite" are often in the middle class and financially stressed. He said that he belonged to a group nominally involved with environmental renewal, but the group did not meet, and he had not done anything concretely that he could call engagement. He told me his business was struggling, then turned to look at me to add, "M pa gen kòb pou m fè makèt" [I have no money for grocery shopping]. He stopped at a gas station and got out to have the attendant fill a five-gallon plastic container in the trunk of his SUV. As I waited in the car, I recalled a conversation several months earlier in which the moneyed black intellectual—the husband of the wealthy clair executive—described realities within the mulatto formation: "Gen mulat pòv, gen mulat rich. Sa vle di, lè m di w mulat pòv la, nèg la pa gen kòb menm jan ak nèg nan peup la wi. Nèg la plen pwoblèm wi" [There are poor mulattoes, there are rich mulattoes. When I tell you poor mulattoes, the guy's got no money like the guy from the people. The guy's full of problems].

After the mulatto entrepreneur got back in the car and drove out of the station, he said with resigned discontent that ethanol, the gasoline additive, was now imported and marketed to Haiti's poor as a substitute for kleren, the local rum that had been the poor's default liquor since time immemorial. I asked who imported it. Driving on to his factory near Boulevard Jean-Jacques Dessalines, he turned to look at me with a hint of contempt as he spoke the surname of an oligarch family.

At the factory, a mostly open-air plant that manufactures structural components for construction projects, fewer than a dozen monolingual creolophone black men were at work. After one of the workers removed the gasoline from the trunk of the SUV—fuel for the plant's machinery—the mulatto entrepreneur conferred with a supervisor. Throughout the ten or fifteen minutes we were there, his rapport with the workers was friendly and easygoing. We then left to visit a construction site on which his company had a contract. On the way, we stopped at the headquarters of Fokal, the prominent local NGO, to pick up a US$5,000 check. Fokal owned the project, a cultural-heritage initiative, and the money was a scheduled disbursement on his contract. After we left there for the construction site, he made a telephone call. While driving, he frantically negotiated the sale of a piece of equipment from the factory. The deal did not come through. After he hung up, I argued that selling a piece of equipment to raise cash seemed to be a prescription for a worse cash flow problem in the future. He shrugged and told me he would deal with the future problem, "leu futu a rive" [when the future arrives].

At the construction site, I left the mulatto entrepreneur conferring with a supervisor and walked around the area for five or ten minutes. When I came back, he was anxiously reviewing his home electricity bill with a (black) technician for the possibility of challenging it with Electicité d'Haïti, the power company. He also solicited suggestions on how he might more economically use his swimming pool's water pump. The technician was on the crew of a black engineer, to whom the mulatto entrepreneur had subcontracted some of his responsibilities on the project. On the way back, we met the engineer about a mile down the road. The latter was driving in the opposite direction to the construction site. He and the mulatto entrepreneur stopped their respective cars side by side in the middle of the street long enough to greet each other from behind the wheel. Before they moved again, the mulatto entrepreneur told the engineer to come over to his house in the evening.

We then drove on to a trading house on the other side of town to cash the Fokal check. The mulatto entrepreneur could not simply deposit the check in his bank account. He needed the funds that day and did not have a balance large enough in his account against which to draw the amount of the check. He asked me to wait for him in the car in the parking lot of the trading house and disappeared inside, maybe for a little more than five minutes, less than ten. After he returned to the car with the cash stuffed in an envelope, he told me that he was relieved to have the money; he would be able to pay the engineer later in the evening.

When the mulatto entrepreneur drives out of the parking lot, I am surprised that he heads away from the factory, which is not far from the trading house. I ask him why we are not stopping at the plant to see how things are going. He answers, "M pa kapab. M pa ka peye yo. Si m ale, l ap pi difisil, y ap atann m ap peye yo" [I can't. I can't pay them. If I go, it'd be more difficult, they'd expect I'm paying them]. As he says this, there is no trace of venality in his voice. His tone is not matter-of-fact either, not like the time he told me of his prejudice of color earlier that day. When he told me then that he would not have married a black woman, he effectively shrugged at the point he was making; it was a banality to him.

The mulatto entrepreneur's expression is different now. His tone is in the emotional register of someone arriving at an unpleasant resolution of an unpleasant dilemma. I am very conscious that, in a visceral experience of common class belonging, the mulatto entrepreneur gave joint priority to his and his black peer's social reproduction, *then* determined that he would have no money left to pay his employees. The moment is affectively reminiscent of the conversation in which the poet-engineer told me of his intervention against the poor woman who had been reduced to bathing and laundering in the gutter near his house. To my immense surprise in the current moment, as at the time of that conversation with the poet-engineer a year and a half earlier, I feel no outrage.

This afternoon the mulatto entrepreneur can stop at the supermarket on his way home, if he wants to, and in the evening, he will pay the black engineer. I am conscious that their solidarity is over against the interest of the poor people working at his factory. I am also conscious that throughout the day the mulatto entrepreneur remained a moral subject engaging with everyday banalities of national life, speaking concretely to social, political, and economic realities of the nation. It has been eighteen months since I began thinking through the intersection of color and class in the country. The complexity of the Haitian condition feels somewhat overwhelming. Eventually, I will read the political agency of the poet-engineer and that of the mulatto entrepreneur, and of my privileged collaborators in general, through a moral economy of bourgeois politics duly situated in its historical context.

In the global North, privileged radical thinkers and activists can and do organically reach a historical—and morally acceptable—modus vivendi with capital, and the negotiated compromise is routinely expressed in their privileged class situations within the opposition to bourgeois capitalist expropriation of surplus-labor. In Haiti no less than in the North, politically progressive people of privilege can and do engage in a moral economy that articulates with the organic reproduction of their privileged-class situation. Notwithstanding the persistent thesis of an exceptional Black Republic, neither the prejudiced mulatto entrepreneur's act of class solidarity with his black associate nor that of the black-nationalist poet-engineer with his [black and mulatto] neighbors is a historical aberration. On the one hand, they are politico-moral subjects of a bourgeois society, and the limit of the liberalism of bourgeois political actors does not generally encroach substantially on the reproduction of their class situation (Hacker 1992). On the other, and of more critical importance, both cases are historically congruent with the defeat of the African bossales by the Latinized creole Revolutionaries more than two centuries after the fact.

The class solidarity enacted by the black poet-engineer with his [black and mulatto] neighbors and by the mulatto entrepreneur with his black associate reveals an obverse disunity. The blackness of the woman who bathed and laundered in the gutter near the home of the poet-engineer did not preempt his defense of his neighborhood against her interest in the public space, even though he is a black man who sees himself—and whom I continue to see—as a progressive nationalist. Similarly, the eight or so employees at the plant of the mulatto entrepreneur were practically as dark-skinned as their boss's black associate, but their putatively common blackness did not preempt the mulatto entrepreneur's conflation of his and the associate's economic interests in the economic violence against those workers. In the moment of social violence—sociopolitical in one case, political-economic in the other—class is evidently the vector of the social solidarity of the privileged subjects standing together across the boundaries of color. As Haiti's French cultural heritage, the sine qua non of elite-class formation, mediates their solidarity, it ultimately also becomes the vector of the disunity of the bilingual black standing on this side of the boundary of privilege and Haiti's monolingual, Creole-speaking poor standing on that side.

CHAPTER EIGHT

THE POLITICAL ECONOMY
OF KNOWING WHITE

A little less than two years after I met the math teacher for the first time at the political fund-raiser in the USA, she invited me to her house in Port-au-Prince. When I arrived in late afternoon that day of March 2011, her husband, the engineering contractor, was not home. When he returned, the math teacher introduced us to each other, then left us on the porch and went inside to attend to dinner preparations.

As is customary among bilingual privileged Haitians meeting for the first time, the engineering contractor's first few sentences to me are in French. He correctly presumes that I speak the language. As a Haitian political subject in a similar situation in a different context, I might answer in Haitian Creole. That would be an ideological statement on prevailing linguistic norms. The ethnographer, conforming to customs of the community under study, answers in French. The engineering contractor continues to address me in French, and our conversation remains in French for about a half hour or so without either of us speaking a word of Creole. We speak about many subjects—Haitian politics, hip hop, the artist in society, stand-up comedy. He leaves me to think that he sees the two of us as sharing a common liberal political perspective on the Haitian condition. He then gradually switches to Creole, and eventually that is what we speak through the evening. In our innumerable conversations since then, we probably have not spoken more than two or three successive sentences in French to each other. That evening, he ceased to use French with me at the point he ceased to feel a need to state his social situation to me.

The computational linguist Michel DeGraff (private communication) has said that, growing up in middle-class Port-au-Prince, he believed he spoke "one and a half languages," given the strict marginalization of Creole in favor of French by teachers and parents. Haiti has continued its "long history of exclusion and miseducation rooted" in its elites' linguistic praxis (DeGraff and Stump 2018, e128). French-speaking Haitians do nonetheless routinely speak Creole in given settings. While the vast majority of Haiti's population consists of monolingual Haitian Creole speakers, there is a significant number of people from the lower strata of the petite-bourgeoisie—and to a lesser extent in the working-class—with functional competence in French that does not rise to true fluency. The relatively small minority that is fluently bilingual in French and Creole is also competent in the signals to engage one rather than the other language. It is a politically dominant "singular 'linguistic community,'" in whose bilingualism French is the language against which uses of Creole must "be practically measured" for appropriateness in any given exchange (Bourdieu 2001, 71).[1]

I theorize below the logic of a postcolonial black elite appropriating cultures produced by white colonial power to define itself locally and globally, while at the same time cultivating a secular worship of ancestors who implacably vanquished colonial white supremacy. This is effectively the theoretical framework in which I have critically interpreted the field experience at the intersection of color and culture in the reproduction of the Haitian privileged classes. It becomes relatively expansive as I wish to accommodate the challenging intricacies of containing race and class coherently in one analytic matrix.

I start by drawing a parallel between privileged Haitians' appropriation of French cultures and the French Revolution's violent imposition of the French language on the vast majority of the people of France, who did not speak it in the final decade of the eighteenth century. I follow that with a phenomenological reading of Pem Buck's (2001) history of an invention of the whiteness/blackness binary in a colonial political economic maneuver. As I read Buck, I discover culture becoming by necessity the marker of boundaries of privilege indexed by whiteness. These boundaries will inevitably become transracially permeable between the transmissibility of culture and the need of capitalist modernity to reinvent itself continually. I end this section of the chapter by noting the central importance accorded a Western "education" by other black Atlantic postcolonial elites, by way of arguing that, in the colony as much as in Europe, such education produces a certain subjectivity, not a certain physiognomy. Throughout the rest of the chapter, I engage critically with discourses and practices around French cultures that articulate with a privileged class situation in the ethnographic field.

❧   ❧   ❧

The French language is hardly a historical development that organically united a national population. Its emergence as the language of France itself just ahead of the founding of Haiti is an illuminating forerunner of its appropriation and its mapping onto the organization of social privilege by the Haitian elites. In 1794, parallel to Maximilien Robespierre's political Terror, the Revolutionary First French Republic began a brutal *terreur linguistique* that imposed the French language on more than twenty-two million people who spoke a collection of some thirty tongues (see Perrot 1997). Most of the fewer than three million people who spoke French at the time were concentrated in Ile-de-France, an administrative region with Paris, the seat of state power, at its center. The *Nouveau régime* undertook the forceful campaign of linguistic transformation in response to increasing rural resistance, which had exploded in the counter-revolutionary war of Vendée in western France in March 1793. In forcing linguistic homogeneity, it sought to repress regional identity in favor of national identity and to cultivate allegiance to the radical Republican experiment. Moreover, the *bourgeoisie* that will dominate the Republican project appropriates the French language from the defeated monarchy along with a host of institutions (*L'Académie française, l'Opéra de Paris, le Musée du Louvre*) and forms of expression (opera, ballet, music). The bourgeoisie will make them its own and redeploy them to mark its distinction throughout its rise to hegemonic social, political, and economic power over the following centuries.

Thus, the Revolutionary French state articulated the French language, a most cogent site of Western symbolic power, not qua culture but as political instrument. The political instrumentality is ultimately at the service of the interests of a class aborning as "bourgeois" in its confrontation with the aristocratic and clerical upper classes of the monarchic *Ancien régime*.

There would be nothing exceptional in the appropriation and redeployment of French cultures by the elites of Revolutionary Saint-Domingue and post-Independence Haiti as they asserted their sovereign presence in the globally emergent West, notwithstanding their dehistoricization into a token of "universal humanity" by Buck-Morss (2009, 147). The specific geographic origin of the French language and its broader cultural universe always remains inscribed in the collective memory of the global West, and its norms of standard practice are defined or sanctioned in a definite center of global Western power; that place is France. The French language is of France, it is of Europe. In the contextual history of Western modernity, it is seminally *white*. It is nonetheless neither a natural faculty nor a universal value, and in this dual fact begin the logic and the measure of its historico-political instrumentality in Haiti.

In twenty-first-century Haiti no less than in 1790s France, the French language is a social capital to which access is politically negotiated. The Revolutionary regime in France appropriated French as the language of power from the old order that it vanquished. The elites of Revolutionary Saint-Domingue and post-Independence Haiti did the same, not as a *black* people but as elites historically appropriating a symbolic instrument of power for the regulation of class formation and privilege contestation. They had to be mindful of their competence in the dominant cultures that articulated with global exchanges, including trade and investment, to which the national economy was inextricably linked (cf. Robotham 2000). Competence in dominant European cultures was thus to become politically instrumental in the formation of postcolonial nationalist elites in the orbit of the West in general because the authority to represent the nation on the global stage is premised on the capability to engage with globally dominant Western cultures. To claim such authority, the postcolonial elite subject must locally demonstrate competence in these cultures, which thus become politically operative objects of the formation of the postcolonial elite.

In proposing French as an object of whiteness appropriated by a people of color as vector of class formation, I do not wish to legitimize the fetishization of a European type of humanity and civilization, upon which planetary regimes of racialism have been built since the sixteenth century. Nor do I wish to overlook or diminish the uses of the phenomenon of whiteness in Western projects of colonial and imperial domination. Rather, in the proposition, and elsewhere in the analysis, "whiteness" is in effect a heuristic device.

I use the term to denote continuities from the colony to the postcolony in modes and modalities of power and privilege, which might be mystified by postcolonial somatic discontinuities in their embodiments. I seek to apprehend colonial legacies of power that can be controlled by postcolonial subjects who are not white to access privilege originally reserved for whites that might still be said to be white.

At the dawn of the global order around the Atlantic that eventually became the West, whiteness was an operational innovation developed by European colonists in the long history of race as technology of societal configuration. As an index of transcendent privilege in a global system of related local white supremacies, it has generated various kinds of colonial and postcolonial violence against racially dominated populations. The totalizing everyday violence of white racism has irrefutably sought to negate the past, the present, and the future of dominated nonwhite peoples. Only through a cathartic counterviolence could peoples of color dehumanized by European colonialism ultimately reclaim their humanity (Fanon 1991, 2011). The analytic aim here is to tease out of the history of whiteness how and why Haiti's postcolonial elites nonetheless adapted cultural ideologies and practices around race and social color that European colonial power produced to regulate sociopolitical economic organization.

In the colony, fairness of complexion became an early *signal* of whiteness. However, as phenomenon, whiteness was most cogently comprehensible in determinate privileges, which simultaneously produced and expressed its significance. The bearing of a light complexion did not ipso facto place or mark one in a dominant societal position. That left the mid-nineteenth-century southern US plantocracy, for example, to draw on "education [from] the days of European privilege and caste" to delineate its boundaries as an elite amidst the commonality of light complexion across the classes of whites (Du Bois 1935, 35). Nonetheless, given its foundational visibility in the phenomenal instantiation of whiteness, lightness of skin retained universal value over the history of bourgeois capitalist modernity. But it did not retain *indispensability* in the contestation of various forms of class privilege originally constructed as domains of whiteness by the European colonial enterprise and bequeathed to bourgeois capitalism. As Pem Buck (2001) traces an invention of the white/black binary in colonial North America, culture rather than physiognomy transpires in fact as the logical barrier to elite privilege.

Through an anthropological reading of the Bacon Rebellion in the British colony of Virginia in 1676, Buck lays bare the social architecture from which whiteness phenomenally emerges. The uprising presented the colonial aristocracy of royal representatives and rich plantation owners with a formidable alliance of yeoman frontiersmen, African slaves, and indentured European immigrants. The farmers wanted the power to expropriate Native Americans' land at the frontier. Enslaved Africans and indentured European laborers constituted a distinct faction. They had lived and loved and fought together in similar material conditions irrespective of somatic appearance and ancestral origins, and they were now together demanding better terms for their labor from the prevailing regime of labor extraction.

The strategic response of the colonial elite to worker solidarity was the introduction of modalities of radical social differentiation based on ancestral origins and somatic features. Africans' condition of bondage was made absolute and unforgiving. European laborers did not receive better wages as they had demanded. Instead, they were granted political rights denied people of African origins, which effectively included rights of violence with impunity against Africans and their descendants. These European laborers eventually came to an imaginary identification with the colonial elites based on apparent somatic commonalities. Altogether, the whole became one variously privileged grouping of *whites* (Buck 2001, 19–27).

In apprehending the functional interplay of race and culture that guards elite-class boundaries, it is useful to read a schematic phenomenology of race in the historic context captured by Buck. In colonial Virginia, skin complexion eventually indexes race, but this *racial* significance of skin color arises *after* the socio-juridical innovations by which colonial elites resolved their *political-economic* dilemma. Complexion becomes race in the wake of purposeful and capricious violence that now differentiates laborers. One category of workers in alliance with the elites can now inflict violence on another, whose bondage is extraordinarily intensified. The extreme degradation of Africans' existential conditions is what now makes them "blacks" in their somatic appearance—their distinctive physiognomy becomes the phenomenal signal of their existential degradation. Africans arrive at their racial condition, they experience racism, because of the degradation of their persons, not the other way around. Degradation of the person precedes racialization.

Laborers of European origins read the integrity of their person in that of the elites, a reading made possible by the nonexperience of the violence reserved for Africans. The arbitrary power to degrade what is not-white together with the integrity of the European person expresses the superior social condition of the "white." That is also to say, to obtain the significance of whiteness, the elites—ultimately united in cultural commonalities—must create the conditions of the African's social degradation. They must yet manage the exclusion of the nonprivileged white from spheres of societally transcendent power. In colonial Virginia, as in subsequent centers of Western bourgeois power, elite subjects of European origins structurally cordoned off domains of decisive political-economic authority from other subjects from Europe and its diaspora situated lower in the social hierarchy. They were all bound together in the "white" identity, but the elite retained the power to define the unstable social conditions of this identity. In the intertwined histories of whiteness and the West, not all fair-complexioned subjects of European origins will *become* white, and the valuation of *cultures* will manage attainment of whiteness and its privileges. Thus, whiteness begins at the phenotype but is fully realized in dominant Western bourgeois ways of being.

Through an "education" in the elites' cultural practices and ideologies—from aesthetics to language to management of the body alongside techniques of industry—elite power made itself legible as well as relatively accessible to intermediate social strata that articulated the colonial (and later capitalist) project on the ground with the laboring classes. Culture being fundamentally transmissible, Western social economies were to become quite elastic in the distribution of privilege within and across racial typologies in the elites and "middle" classes of a capitalism that requires constant social transformation. The nonwhite subject of bourgeois capitalism, without ceasing to be Europe's *other* and without ceasing to be the object of the pan-European racialist gaze, can deploy determinate cultural competencies to concrete sociopolitical economic power that is said to be a domain of whiteness.

Haiti presents two centuries of a Western postcolonial society managing the conjugation of race and culture toward the reproduction of elite privilege. Privileged mulattoes came out of the colonial experience equipped with the colonizers' education in normative modes of being social, which relatively articulate with social, political, and economic privilege throughout the world of Western capital. The country's black elites have assiduously pursued that education at least since Toussaint Louverture sent his sons to France to be so educated. Later postcolonial elites of the black Atlantic were to reaffirm the pivotal import of dominant cultures originating in Europe in the articulation of social privilege in the global West.

Introducing a seminal work of négritude and Pan-Africanist cultural identity, Léopold Sedar Senghor, the volume's editor, who will later become the president of Senegal, invoked with gratitude the decree that abolished slavery in April 1848 "and this other decree, dated the same day, which instituted free and compulsory schooling in the colonies" (Senghor 1948, 1).[2] Not incidentally, Senghor's celebrated volume was an anthology of a new kind of poetry, black—or Malagasy—*and* French. The schooling that "other decree" mandated in the colony was a historical education in the academic codification of Western ways of being social. By the very evidence of the persons of Senghor and the other creators of négritude, this education—elaborated in its full scope over "primary," "secondary," and "tertiary" (or "university") levels—did in the colonies what it did in Europe and its diaspora. To understand better the implications of what that education did do, let us first understand what it did not do: it did not produce people of fair complexion in the colonies any more than it did in Europe. What it did do, and still does everywhere it is historically dispensed today, is the formation of social subjects of various capacities to reproduce, and to adapt and innovate, the vast and unstable complex of symbolic, theoretical, and practical technologies articulating with global systems of economic production that emerged in the aftermath of Christopher Columbus's travels across the Atlantic.

In expressly nonwhite Haiti, as post-Independence privileged people generally made the pursuit of a bourgeois education a quasi-political project, *blackness* appeared soon enough as innovative an instrument of governmentality as whiteness. Like whiteness, blackness bore in its own political instrumentality any number of contradictions that it must manage. In a cohesive field of social practice across boundaries of color, relatively privileged subjects from the black formation expertly deploy determinate modes of bourgeois culture—including the alternate vocabulary of color explored in chapter 6—to arrest in *their* persons the existential degradation that arrives at social blackness. All the while, they deploy bourgeois culture again, at times together with privileged mulattoes, to conflate nonprivileged persons with their degraded life conditions in poverty, degrading them existentially, in order to render *them* socially black. Not surprisingly, the tactic is evocative of the rhetoric of "*white trash* . . . used by Americans of all colors" to make poor US "whites" not quite white because of their deficient embodiment of norms of bourgeois being (Wray 2006, 1).

Where in the USA social exclusion is sought through erasure of whiteness from a subject who might otherwise appear to belong in spheres of social practice in which whiteness is an operative instrument, in Haiti it is sought through accentuation of blackness in the subject who might similarly appear somatically indistinguishable from the respectable and the privileged. In both places, the object of the tactic is management of points of entry to social privilege. The parallel suggests, on the one hand, the versatility of race as instrument of sociopolitical stratification in the West and, on the other, the centrality of culture in the instrumentality.

※   ※   ※

In the days after my first conversation with the engineering contractor at his house, the cultural impresario and I went on a leisurely drive with the poet-engineer in one of the latter's two SUVs officially registered to the Haitian state. With us in the car were two younger friends of theirs, a man and a woman, lovers who seemed to be in their twenties. He is a surveyor for the Institute for the Protection of the National Heritage (ISPAN), a state agency. She is an aide in the Port-au-Prince City Hall with a bachelor's degree in ethnology from the State University's Faculty of Human Sciences. With their hair in dreadlocks and their intellectual energy, they are not unlike hip young urbanites of the moment elsewhere in the West. Before heading to the countryside in the region of saline lakes about thirty minutes northeast of Port-au-Prince, we stop at a street vendor's stand near the airport for candy and bottled water (and cigarettes for the lone smoker in the group). As the vendor, an amiable middle-aged black woman, approaches the vehicle, the cultural impresario lowers the glass of the front passenger door, and the afternoon heat rushes into the air-conditioned cabin.

On the other side of the door by the cultural impresario is stifling sun, dusty sidewalk, and varying degrees of poverty, an environment emblematic of social fields in which the vendor conducts her business and lives her life. As we have done among ourselves before we stopped at her stand, we—organic black-nationalists—address the vendor in Creole unadorned with any French. The younger anthropologist in the car greets her with warm familiarity, and the vendor cheerfully returns the greeting. The young woman inquires after a common acquaintance (another woman). From her chitchat with the vendor, I infer that the acquaintance lives on the same social plane as the vendor. My fellow anthropologist in the car thus knows the vendor at a definite social distance, and the inquiry after her friend's welfare effectively mediates our engagement in her quotidian social universe. In this moment, we enact the unitary Black Republic of the black-nationalist imagination. However, an ideational unity with the vendor in the blackness that unites the five of us in the car would inevitably be a fallacy. The blackness that we share subjectively as nationalist Haitians, the intersubjective terrain of our engagement in the car, is fundamentally defined in dominant cultural modalities of the modern West, in which we are competent, and in which the street vendor and her colleagues on the sidewalk would not be.

After we conclude our purchase, the vendor retreats to her stand, the poet-engineer drives off, the cultural impresario raises the glass of the front passenger door, and again the air-conditioned cabin is sealed from the world outside. We continue toward the countryside with no purpose other than the enjoyment of our camaraderie. At the time, gasoline costs about US$5 a gallon, the amount of the daily minimum wage passed by Parliament in 2009 and bitterly contested by the light-assembly industry. Two recurring themes percolate in our chat the rest of our drive: French as cultural capital and marker of class boundaries, and the significance of the official recognition of Creole as a national language by the Constitution of 1987.

The consensus among my four friends in the car is that the Constitutional affirmation of Creole as an official language of the nation begins to counter the prestige presumptively ascribed to all things foreign, the French language in particular, in preference to the national culture. However, we are *not* speaking the academically sanctioned form of Creole. Formally "proper" Haitian Creole is based on the speech of the monolingual Haitian speaker. Our Creole speech in the car is distinctly the language of a francophone people. The distinction is, for example, in the salience of the "r" sound in a syllable, or in the sounds of "u" and "e" duly closed. Our Creole speech is the dominant spoken form of the language in Haitian spaces of privilege, and privileged Haitians would not generally speak the form of the language that Haiti's intellectual elite has academically codified.

After we hang out in the woods on the outskirts of the town of Thomazeau, we drive back to Port-au-Prince after nightfall. The same themes as when we were coming in the afternoon resurface in our conversation after the poet-engineer tunes in an English-language jazz program on Radio Métropole, a station associated with an elite audience since its founding in the early 1970s. At the sound of the barely accented English of the host, I wonder whether the English-speaking expatriate population is now big enough to be the target audience of a prime-time program on a major station. I am reminded that the program has been on the air for at least thirty years with the same host, a scion of the mulatto family that founded the station. To unanimous agreement, the poet-engineer remarks that quite likely the majority of Haitians who listen to the program do not speak English. The remark prompts the cultural impresario to lament wistfully what he finds to be a crisis of *authenticité* in the Haitian.

Haitians, in the view of the cultural impresario, have lost touch with their culture in their predilection for the foreign. To illustrate the depth of the crisis, he invokes a conversation he had recently with a poor, illiterate woman. Although thoroughly marginalized socially and economically, "uneducated," and a monolingual Creole speaker, the woman reflexively used English phrases such as "y'know" and "I mean" in the conversation. If this woman, of all people, could have so little regard for her culture as to pepper her Creole with English terms, the meaning of which she actually did not know, what hope could there be for Haitians? So reasons the cultural impresario.

I suggest a different reading of the situation to the cultural impresario: could it be that the woman's use of the English terms was an attempt to negotiate the power relations in the encounter? If social prestige and power accrue with knowing French and other foreign modes of culture, I suggest to the cultural impresario, in deploying her very limited repertoire of English, might the woman perhaps just be staking a claim—albeit a hopeless claim—to some Western cultural capital, of a kind amply possessed by the five of us in the car? We mull over the question, and no one ventures an answer. I do not think to ask the corollary question, which, significantly, no one else in the car thinks to pose either: if the cultural impresario equates national cultural authenticity with distance from foreign ways, why is he questioning *her* authenticity and not ours? Not asking the question actually puts us in an intellectual lineage of the black Atlantic.

Frantz Fanon bemoans an inauthentic Antillean with "black skin, white masks" (Fanon 1952), a fellow Caribbean man who wallows incompetently in the vast and complex cultural code of French whiteness. Fanon musters powerful eloquence from his masterly command of the French language to delineate *black* inauthenticity in the fellow's mangling of grammar, syntax, and diction of that very language. Moreover, Fanon critiques this Antillean from within ideologies of the self elaborated very much by a Western intellectuality. As Fanon does not question *his* authenticity, the other Antillean's inauthenticity cannot be due to his *will* to appropriate a culture of whiteness. Rather, the fellow is inauthentic because of his lack of adequate competence in French. Because of his deficient competence, to an elite subjectivity of the black Atlantic, he does not *respectably* integrate white culture in the articulation of his person. Fanon (or the cultural impresario) would not question his authenticity, because his competence in elite cultures of the West is thoroughly naturalized. The inauthentic Antillean is arguably as much his cultural *other* as Europe's, and so is Haiti's monolingual, Haitian Creole-speaking majority population to the nation's privileged, bilingual minority.

Notwithstanding Fanon's fierce critique of European colonialism and the colonized psyche, he deploys his competence in dominant European epistemologies to explicate Europe to Europeans with utter assurance. He will be on the front lines of the post–World War II anticolonial armed struggle in Algeria, but his trajectory from his native Martinique through a French education in medicine to his radical anticolonial engagement will nonetheless have been in a class position of relative privilege, in which inheres his elite Western cultural competencies. However, Fanon is wholly unaware, and so is the cultural impresario, that the acquisition of such competence is the product of determinate sociopolitical practice. The question of authenticity becomes a question of political economy rather than "culture," inasmuch as the inauthentic Antillean, despite his deep aspirations, has not arrived at the competence in dominant cultural ways of the West that mediates belonging in the middle and upper classes of the postcolonial society. Fanon's and the cultural impresario's critical interest in the authenticity of the *other* postcolonial subject displaces the politics of *their* Western cultural competence from the field of critical nationalist engagement.

Four days after our leisurely drive to the outskirts of Thomazeau, the cultural impresario, the poet-engineer, and I had dinner with a common friend, an artist in his late thirties, to the sound of a live jazz trio at Pizza Garden, a hip trattoria in Pétion-Ville. Toward the end of the meal, one of my companions noted a corpulent young black woman at a table across the dining terrace of the restaurant, which by menu, price, and décor would not be out of place in a trendy section of cosmopolitan North America (fig. 8.1).

Figure 8.1. Pizza Garden, June 2016. Photo courtesy of Hugue-Robert Marsan.

My tablemate remarked that the young woman was the daughter of so-and-so, one of the most prominent figures in contemporary Haitian journalism.

As we later walked to our car, I learned further that the father of the corpulent young woman had risen from rather modest beginnings, at which point two random thoughts occurred to me in tandem. Similar thoughts might have occurred to me around the authenticity question on our drive back from Thomazeau earlier in the week, but they did not. Perhaps this time they were facilitated by the tab of nearly US$90, excluding tip, for four small pizzas, three or four bottles of local beer, and three glasses of red wine in a place axiomatically represented in foreign media as the poorest country in the Western hemisphere. It occurred to me first that the young woman's father would have negotiated his current socioeconomic status by professionally deploying his virtuosic command of the French language on a daily basis in Haiti's most prestigious press organization. Then I recalled paternal advice offered to me twenty-five years earlier by the noiriste public intellectual René Piquion, a close friend of my own father and a pugilistic polemicist, if ever there was one: "In this country, if someone tells you not to speak French, he's your enemy. Shoot him."

As I spoke with Piquion at his home that day in the mid-1980s, shortly after my father's funeral, I was enthusiastic about the legitimation of Haitian

Creole as a bona fide language. At the time I left for college a little over four years earlier, as a product of a liberal household, I held an academic respect for the language that had not much to do with actual practice. My current enthusiasm for the speaking of Creole indiscriminately across all spheres of social life was very much an outcome of my years of immersion in a New York University curriculum of inchoate leanings toward the US Left, and in a New York City neighborhood (Manhattan's Greenwich Village) steeped in a history of progressive alternative politics.

Notwithstanding the extreme political and economic violence visited by the Duvalier regime upon poor Haitians, in the 1970s it initiated the movement toward the official sanction of Creole as a national language. Piquion, a classmate of François Duvalier in medical school in the 1930s, was one of the leading intellectuals who turned fulminating anger at mulatto color prejudice in the black middle class into the blistering black nationalism of noirisme. Quite significantly, despite an international reputation resting on masterful expression in French, Piquion did not lapse into a widespread habit of educated Haitians to turn to French periodically during a conversation otherwise conducted in Creole.[3] He spoke entirely in Creole from the time I arrived at his house until I left about an hour later, and he seemed utterly unapologetic for noirisme.[4] I had good reason to expect his unreserved approval of my enthusiastic embrace of the legitimation of Creole. More than baffled, I was intellectually disoriented by his pronounced skepticism. I need not have been. From my ethnographic findings in the privileged classes of Port-au-Prince over two decades later, I came to understand that Piquion was not interested in French-speaking as performative act of privilege but as political tactic.

❧   ❧   ❧

Haiti has been a place of illuminating practice in the politics of knowing the dominant cultural ways of whiteness. In French, the word "education" denotes more than scholastic knowledge; it also refers to good breeding, good manners. When Haitians use the word in conversation, the subject is almost always class, and the object is almost inevitably the position of someone or some group in the social pecking order. The referent of "education" in Haitians' conversation is often the whole spectrum of bourgeois values, however locally adapted, from morals to table manners to diction. A man in his late 30s made typical use of the term, while he related to me a business partnership gone sour.

The man came of age in the orbit of socioeconomic privilege as a son outside the marriage of an army officer who was briefly Haiti's president, but he now lives in much reduced economic circumstances in a working-class neighborhood of a US city. He started a business enterprise with a partner, who provided the financing based on a "handshake" agreement. However, he quit the venture after the partner unceremoniously changed the terms of the arrangement. After he finished telling me the history of the project in a mix of Creole and English, with particular emphasis on the partner's lack of grace in violating the terms of the partnership, he added with disdain: "Y'know, education," the second word said pointedly with the French pronunciation in a sentence otherwise spoken in English. The man's schooling had stopped after he briefly attended a US community college, but the referent of "education" here was bourgeois cultural attributes in toto. While the partner drove a late-model luxury SUV and dressed nattily, and the man lived an economically precarious life, his practiced use of "education" would indicate to me all that the partner lacked which he possessed, and which presumably would situate him higher in the Haitian social order relative to the partner.

The bourgeois schema of the world is central to privileged life in both of Haiti's colorized formations and irrespective of political ideology. This fact transpired to me in a dismissive assessment of Wyclef Jean's aborted candidacy in the 2010 presidential elections. I was speaking with the director of a medical NGO, a practicing physician, and he told me (in Haitian Creole), "Wyclef pa pale okenn lang. Li pa pale anglè. Li pa pale fransè. Li pa pale kreyòl" [Wyclef doesn't speak any language. He doesn't speak English. He doesn't speak French. He doesn't speak Creole]. Jean, an international music star who immigrated to the USA with his family around age ten, manifestly speaks English and is fluent in Haitian Creole. However, the physician was not interested in Jean's linguistic skills; he was assessing a different practical reality. He did not find Jean adequately prepared in the West's elite modes of rational discourse. In effect, he found Jean so lacking in knowing white that Jean's aspiration to the nation's presidency was notionally a joke.

The physician grew up and attended school in his native town in southern Haiti until the middle of the secondary level, the limit of the local institution. He then went to live with kin in Port-au-Prince, the capital, to continue his studies. A son of the provincial proletariat, his parents would not have been able to support him through school in the capital. The support came from his aunt, his father's half-sister. His paternal grandmother was eking out a living in the informal economy of their hometown, and his father was already born, when, in the 1930s, the grandmother began a relationship with a man from Port-au-Prince. The man's family was well connected to the political elite since at least the middle of the nineteenth century. The man had settled in the town to work in the management of a major US enterprise in the area. Two children—a daughter, then a son—were born of the relationship, younger half-siblings of the physician's father. Although the physician's paternal grandmother and the father of her two younger children were not married, the father recognized the children, and they bore his last name. The man died an early death, when the children were barely out of their toddler years. The daughter was one of my collaborators, along with the physician, her nephew.

The physician's aunt told me, "By my mother's incredible foresight, despite her poverty and lack of education, she sent [my brother] and me to live with our father's [family] in Port-au-Prince after his death." The matriarch of the father's family was a nineteenth-century daughter of the provincial mulatto petite bourgeoisie who married a man from the black political elite. She barely tolerated the presence of her deceased son's two children in her household, because of their mother's social origins. However, one of the matriarch's other sons, an engaged black nationalist, embraced both children and looked after them. In the early 1960s, the daughter left to study in Europe on a state scholarship secured through the family's connections in the political elite and never returned to Haiti to live. She had a long career at the World Bank and the International Monetary Fund, and she financially supported her nephew, the physician, from the time he left his hometown to finish secondary school in Port-au-Prince until he found his footing as a doctor after medical school.

After medical school at the State University of Haiti, the physician continued with five years of specialization in France on a scholarship. Fluent in English, several years ago he successfully led an application for a grant from the United States Centers for Disease Control, with which he founded a medical-service project that became the NGO that he runs today. Based on figures he provides, it is now a multimillion-dollar agency funded by the CDC, and it operates under the auspices but independently of the Haitian state. He is cognizant of working through the state apparatus but protected from the vagaries of Haitian politics.

When I asked the physician why he chose to return to Haiti after the specialization in France, he seemed genuinely baffled as he answered, "But I'm Haitian!" He expresses himself impeccably in spoken and written Haitian Creole, and without self-consciousness. At work, he speaks French or Creole, or French and Creole alternately in a conversation, presumably according to prevailing norms of code-switching. After he introduces me to a manager of an operational unit of the agency, a youthful and amiable man neatly dressed in "business casual," the three of us discuss their work at length in Creole. He describes with understated nationalist passion how the agency provides an essential service without which great numbers of Haitians across age, sex, and class lines die every year: "Without this, scores of women die in childbirth every month, and nobody pays attention. Imagine what the media would make of it if twice a month on a regular basis a small plane full of passengers crashed and everybody died." He says he is on schedule in gradually expanding the coverage area of his agency across the country and expects to make its service accessible nationally within the next five years.[5]

Within the constraints of the global neoliberal moment, the physician is arguably a model of black-nationalist engagement with the Haitian condition. He nonetheless finds Wyclef Jean, a highly successful black professional in his forties, to be a Haitian who does not yet speak. The physician's dismissal of Wyclef Jean as a potential president of Haiti was arguably classist as it was based on what he considered Jean's cultural deficiencies. Yet to see it as mere elitism would be to miss the profound implications of the personal socio-political histories that informed his (the physician's) subjectivity. He would understand Piquion's cautionary insistence on knowing French. Moreover, his position on Jean's candidacy suggests that elite competence in Western ways of being is not reducible to mere fluency in this or that language. His assessment that Jean could not "speak" expressed a concern that Jean was not adequately familiar with privileged modern ontologies. He did not believe that Jean could adequately engage with the human experience on the global stage in normative vocabularies proposed by the symbolic systems of Western political economic powers. This is again an assessment consistent with Robotham's (2000) finding of the global articulation of political economic power with cultural prestige.

The importance of knowing French in Haitian social life is the global political-economic instrumentality of French writ small. Yet again, if the contestation of Haiti's elite classes requires *knowing* French rather than the mere speaking of French, the requirement is an *organic*—naturalized, seemingly effortless—competence in French and Western bourgeois cultures in general. At the most mundane levels of everyday experience, linguistic competence as vector of elite power is intrinsically entwined with management of the bodily self and other nonverbal symbolic projections of personhood. This point revealed itself to me in a fleeting instant of a conversation with a female writer on social etiquette at her tastefully decorated villa in Pétion-Ville. During our conversation, she is wearing shorts and a sleeveless top. The top shifts slightly and for a few moments reveals an edge of undergarment. The woman eventually notices the thin strip of exposed bra in her reflection in a wall mirror. In an instantaneous action that is as seamless as it is precise and inconspicuous, she pinches the edge of her top between thumb and index finger, the other fingers curved just so, and matter-of-factly pulls it over the bra, still with full engagement in the conversation at hand. Elegant is the word that comes to mind as I absorb the artful precision of the woman's managerial intervention on the garment.

The woman's adjustment of her body covering did not mark just any mode of being social. The "proper" form of her intervention on the strap of her bra was an object of her education in the bourgeois way of being in the world. From her studied insouciance to the architecture of her fingers while snapping the top back over her bra, her cultural skills in this instant of being social were inseparable from her competence in French and other modalities of bourgeois culture. It was a determinate cultural way, a *bourgeois* way of intervening in the management of the body. The point is that in Haiti's postcolonial bourgeois society, privileged Haitians arrive at bourgeois ways of being social through organic experiential apprenticeship in everyday life, a fact that states the depth of the problematic of inequality in Haiti beyond the already vexing question of competence in the French language.

Michel DeGraff forcefully makes the point that Haitian Creole ought to be the language of schooling in Haiti. Children learn best in the language that permeates their quotidian social life, and the overwhelming majority of Haitian children in Haiti are, across class lines, by far most linguistically at home in Creole. DeGraff also invokes the enormous lack of French-competent instructors in his argument against French as medium of instruction (DeGraff 2010, 2017). The argument is certainly sound because, schooled through the medium of Haitian Creole rather than French, children of Haiti's monolingual Creole-speaking majority would be more efficaciously literate and more viably educated in mathematics and the natural sciences (DeGraff and Stump 2018). There yet remains in local class stratification the import that the French language and culture inexorably obtain from global processes. If the construction of Haiti's elites and middle classes is to be contested by today's monolingual descendants of the bossales, who will teach them the cultures of whiteness?

CONCLUSION

LIBERAL POLITICS IN A FAILURE OF HERMENEUTICS— *YON TRAVAY JIGANTÈS*

Elite and middle-class Haitians constituting Haiti's minority francophone population are enmeshed in a layered problematic of hermeneutics that inheres in the "color question," and it encumbers the formation of a relatively coherent liberal politics in the privileged classes. Through their nation's presumptive Blackness, progressive bilingual black Haitians see themselves a priori in unity with the country's—generally dark-skinned—monolingual Creole-speaking population, and a priori in disunity with mulattoes, who are otherwise fellow subjects of the privileged classes. Yet, among the privileged, the black liberal and the mulatto liberal realize their social situations in the enactment of norms of Western bourgeois modernity, and they do so in common fields of social practice that are radically closed to the nation's monolingual Creole speakers. Moreover, judged by state attention to their needs and interests, the latter continue not to matter to the political process (cf. Fass 2004). In the contradiction, the privileged black liberal and the privileged mulatto liberal fail to realize the commonality of their bourgeois experience of the historical moment. They become mutually unintelligible on the national condition in the tension between the mulatto's color prejudice and the nation's ideational Blackness. This hermeneutic failure is of critical import to Haiti's national development, inasmuch as it is a failure to negoti-ate a mutual nationalist intelligibility by classes of Haitians who would lead the national project (cf. Price-Mars 1919).

As the poet-engineer and I discussed the possibility of alliances across lines of class and color one afternoon in October 2012, we came to reflect on the engaged artist in society. He told me then of his acquaintance with the fair-complexioned Haitian writer and storyteller Mimi Barthélémy.[1] He deeply respects her work. Barthélémy, to him, seeks a cultural *rattrapage*, a remediation that would open the cultures of Haiti's socioeconomic elites to the nation's vernaculars. He also knew Barthélémy's late husband, the (white) French anthropologist Gérard Barthélémy. With European Union funding that the latter secured, they once built a well that brought drinking water to a slum. The poet-engineer points to their collaboration as exemplary grassroots politi-cal engagement. He is also an acquaintance of one of the couple's daughters, an artist born and reared in Europe. He invoked with clear appreciation a series of works by her that speak to the plight of Haitians so desperately poor, they resorted to eating patties of clay, fat, water, and salt baked in the sun.[2]

I asked the poet-engineer whether he could see himself acting politically together with Mimi Barthélémy on the national condition. Despite his posi-tive social and intellectual connections to her, he did not find that a viable proposition. He argued that was impossible because she "belongs to a cat-egory of Haitians" and as a result "is limited by her class." He added, "Just like you and me: we are limited in what we can do within the class." He is skeptical of dogmatic noiriste positions, and in our conversation, he located the limit of our political agency, as well as that of Mimi Barthélémy, in the class situ-ation. Yet, to him, Barthélémy's color was, prior to her class, an immutably negative index of *her* agency on the national project. While he found her to be a commendable agent of Haitian *culture* whose work he identified with, he effectively saw Barthélémy the political subject through the prejudice of color that underpins the endogamy that underpins the reproduction of the mulatto formation. About a year before that conversation, I had asked him whether he might have any views on the condition of Haiti in common with the fair-complexioned executive, who lived about a ten-minute walk from his house. He answered succinctly then that he could not see such a thing happening. I asked him whether he might in fact speak with her to find out. "No," he said. "Paskeu l se w mulat?" [Because she's a mulatto?], I asked. "Wi" [Yes], he answered.

Mulatto color prejudice ultimately expresses itself conspicuously in the perennially dominant visibility of mulattoes in the national economy. Thus, the poet-engineer's black-nationalist subjectivity could not conceive of anyone in their "category of Haitians" acting in concert with him in a progressive political nationalism, because their identitarian formation controls the transcendent economic vectors of inequality in the nation. I pressed him on the point that afternoon of October 2012. He and I had been talking color, class, nation, and politics in Haiti since I first arrived in the field over a year and a half earlier. I suggested that, since he was in fact cognizant of the possibilities of subjective agency, privileged Haitian nationalists might just be capable of creating a transcendent space (intellectual, cultural, practical), where he, Barthélémy, the erudite clair businessman, and I might negotiate our distinctions of class and color within a liberal vision of the human condition in Haiti. "Se yon travay jigantès" [It's a gigantic task], he said matter-of-factly, a laconic mode of responding that he tended to reserve for particularly intractable issues. His pessimism eventually motivated me to conclude this study with a critical focus on the relationship between the "color question," the global valuation of whiteness that informs it, and liberal politics in Haiti's bourgeois society.

I continue the conclusion below by first situating the poet-engineer's categorization of Mimi Barthélémy—a Haitian apart from the two of us—in the black-nationalist anger at mulatto color prejudice. I then delineate the problematic fragmentation of liberal politics by the politics of color. Seeking practical and theoretical pathways out of this dilemma, I conflate black-on-black classist colorism together with mulatto color prejudice as a praxis of privilege, the better to revisit critically, and reject, the black-nationalist tradition that views Haitian liberalism as a *mulatto* politics. I then tease out of the Lavalas movement of the 1990s the possibilities of a coherent liberalism across the boundary of color. I also find in the moment the immense difficulty of realizing those possibilities due to the privileged Haitian's preoccupation with the "color question." I read the scope of Haiti's problematic of color in the global valuation of fairness of complexion and other "white" somatic traits. I posit Haitian black-on-black colorism and mulatto prejudice as derivative effects of the significance of whiteness in postcolonial economies historically engaged with the global West. While colorism must be confronted locally, I argue, ultimately, it will continue to obtain without a systematic global devaluation of "white" skin. Finally, I suggest theoretical political-economic pathways toward that devaluation.

❦   ❦   ❦

The latent anger of the privileged black Haitian toward the mulatto as political subject is understandable, because mulatto color prejudice is indisputably evocative of the colonial white racism that undergirded the slavery system. This fact does make it analytically and practically daunting to reconcile Haitian political liberalism from its disruption in the field of color. Mulatto prejudice is nonetheless only part of a broader praxis of color, which also articulates the social blackening of poor Haitians by subjects of the black formation of privilege. Moreover, privileged blacks participating in the economy of color are inherently colorist as they consider potential partners' relative lightness of complexion in assessing possible romantic relations. While mulatto prejudice is manifest and resisted, black-on-black colorism remains to be demystified and to be made an object of active critical engagement and resistance.

If black-on-black colorism and mulatto color prejudice were routinely and visibly critiqued and resisted together as one ecumenical problematic of privileged-class formation, the rupture of liberalism in the tension between mulatto prejudice and black nationalism would begin to subside as the "color question" began to stand separate and apart from political-economic ideology in Haitian civil society. This would also be a viable point of departure to rethink Haiti through the meanings and ramifications of the Founding Fathers' withholding of citizenship from the African former slaves in the new nation. There is a need for a new narrative of Haiti that positively foregrounds the bossales' distinctive agency alongside the Creoles' project of Independence in the uncompromising confrontation with white supremacy in Revolutionary Saint-Domingue. Such a national narrative might generate effective critical thought and action on the myriad kinds of everyday violence perpetrated by the bilingual, privileged minority on the monolingual, marginalized majority, the sociocultural descendant formation of the bossales, who were also nascent Haiti's majority population. The Black Republic narrative has not been and could not be such a generative context, because it works to mystify the foundational degradation of the bossales inscribed in the Act of Independence by the Revolutionary creole alliance.

Narrators of Haiti's Blackness and subscribers to the postulates of the narrative have proven themselves incapable of acknowledging that the Founding Fathers, in the text of their founding document, effectively made a stateless people of the native Africans on the national territory in the moment of its creation. The legacy of that foundational violence could indeed be the object of a corrective liberal politics in the contemporary nation, but Haitian liberalism would need first to be reclaimed from the colorized fragmentation of the body politic among the privileged. The justification of the delegitimation of Haitian liberal politics by Trouillot (1990a), Acacia (2006), and other engaged black-nationalist scholars is hardly evident. The premise, stated or unstated, is that Haitian liberalism, at its roots in the nineteenth century Parti libéral, is essentially a hollow mulatto political strategy in the contestation of national leadership. This might be correct, if the work of the iconic black intellectuals Anténor Firmin and Edmond Paul, pivotal theorists of the PL, could be seen as a legacy of the mulatto formation, a proposition that is a manifest absurdity.

More broadly, Haitian liberalism tends to be caught in a problematic of temporality. Progressive thinkers and actors of Haitian national politics who imagine new futures of Haiti in the postcolonial present tend to measure them against an imagined postcolonial future at the conclusion of the epic victory over Napoleon Bonaparte's army. In this imagined past future, the new nation would realize the potential of universal liberty for its people. That, as is clear in the historiography, did not happen. From Louverture to Dessalines to Christophe, state agrarian policies created a regime of plantation agriculture not unlike that of slavery for now ostensibly free agricultural workers. Their bondage, to a significant extent, was in fact legally re-codified under Boyer nearly a quarter of a century after Independence. Between Christophe and Boyer, Pétion's shift to small-scale agriculture only shifted state policy to an indirect mode of unfair agricultural surplus labor extraction through taxation (Trouillot 1990a). Moreover, Pétion made himself the first president for life of the Republic, with commensurate dictatorial powers.

The encroachment of the imagined post-Independence Haitian future in the political imagination is not without cost, because it does not leave much space besides utopia—or magical thinking—in which to envision new possibilities of the national project within present postcolonial realities (see Scott 2014 on "postcolonial futures past"). It can lead students of Haiti taking the Saint-Domingue Revolution as historic backdrop of their reflections to approach the Haitian condition through "progressivist axiomatics" that posit the "consoling, anticipatory teleology" of a revolutionary renewal that must be (44). An inchoate longing thus often suffuses engaged scholarship and activist discourses alike, a wistful hope for some possibilities of the Saint-Domingue Revolution that were *not* realized and that might yet be reclaimed. Bourgeois liberalism does seem then ruefully lacking.

If the postcolonial present must be lived "amid the ruins" of the postcolonial future promised by the anticolonial struggle (Scott 2014, 2), contemporary Haiti's sociohistorical reality must be apprehended within the actual ruins of the *Pères Fondateurs'* seminal—and intentional—entry in the bourgeois order of the global West, not amid the presumed ruins of some imaginary project of universal freedom. As we accept that the victorious Revolutionaries of Saint-Domingue founded a protobourgeois society at the dawn of the West, a reformist Haitian liberal politics becomes eminently imaginable in the line of their legacy. The political agency of privileged Haitian liberals similarly becomes meaningfully measurable in the moral economy theorized by E. P. Thompson (1971), which has perhaps yet to be given the critical attention it warrants (Edelman 2012; Fassin 2012). Democratic liberalism may well deserve in Haiti the "deficit of legitimacy" that it has earned within the dominant nations of the West (Grenier 2001, 174). Nonetheless, in the global North, the Left continues to operationalize postulates of a liberal politics—in courts of law, for example—to generate resistance to new waves or new forms of social inequality (Tejani 2004). In Haiti, a liberal tradition retrieved and duly recalibrated might be similarly useful. In the context of the modernist bourgeois moral economy, liberal politics would appear usable toward change for the better in the Haitian condition, while it is axiomatically dismissible in the context of the nebulous promise of transcendent freedom so often presently imagined in the Saint-Domingue Revolution.

The Haitian state has stood against the nation since Independence (Trouillot 1990a), and it remains today "a predatory State facilitating an exceeding accumulation of rent" (Jean 2013, 24).[3] Yet, in 1946, in an arguably revolutionary moment, the country's intractable sociopolitical problematic of color splintered a movement of progressive politics into a multitude of "left" parties that defined themselves in color (Smith 2009). In so doing, the Haitian left unwittingly rendered itself ineffectual and irrelevant (see Trouillot 1990a). The colorized splintering of liberalism in that moment was to the benefit of the alliance between the economic oligarchy and the "right" of the political elite. Much later, through much of the 1990s, the Lavalas movement held the possibility of a transformative politics of popular democracy. By the middle of the 2000s, the alliance of the oligarchy and the political elite had broadly recovered from the brief Lavalas interlude. The Haitian state could not be transformed without a break through the hermeneutic cul-de-sac in which liberal politics finds itself in Haiti's privileged classes.

Segments of Haiti's economic elite, embodied by the clair executive, the erudite clair businessman, and the chronically broke mulatto entrepreneur, share with progressive, privileged black nationalists their opposition to the state's clientelist relations with the oligarchy. Those relations are loci of political rent that encumbers economic agency in the business sector outside the oligarchy and intensifies impoverishment in the lower classes (Fass 2004), a central concern of progressive activists. Yet, in the hermeneutic conundrum, the opposition remains splintered at the boundary of the two identitarian formations. An anthropology of Lavalas that actually investigates the articulation of class and identitarian politics in the movement remains to be made, and it is beyond the scope of the present work. Rather, I invoke the movement for its visible interclass coalition, which suggests the possibilities of a relatively coherent and cohesive liberalism—that is, a meaningful political liberalism circulating across the boundaries of color—in Haiti's privileged classes.

Lavalas was a "social democratic and radical populist" movement (Fatton 1999, 215). However, an alliance of nationalists from both colorized formations of privilege represented its political organization in seeking and gaining control of the state with Aristide's election in 1990. That was hardly a postcolonial precedent. Popular resistance to postcolonial political economic oppression had well before that found form and content through positive engagements with sectors of Westernized local elites (cf. Wolf 1969). The Lavalas coalition in effect suggests the possibility of multimodal alliances in Haitian progressive politics, across color lines among liberal segments of the privileged classes, across class lines between privileged liberal formations and popular organizations. Such alliances might arrive at an appreciably popular-democratic state with a modicum of accountability to the nation and some functional attention to the interests of the rural and urban poor. However, privileged black and mulatto progressive actors did not become a distinct political faction beyond—perhaps even within—the evanescent Lavalas moment. From my participant-observation in the lives of privileged Haitians, I found that, despite their spontaneous crossing of lines of color and class to act politically together in the movement, there remained a lack of practical and discursive structures that would reproduce such mobility.[4]

An anthropology of the Lavalas movement grounded in the lived experience of its actors could open pathways toward a formation of progressive politics in Haiti's privileged classes. However, the current study already reveals that the demystification of the sociopolitical uses of color in Haitian life is a precondition of any viable liberal politics in the country. It is also already evident that Haiti's problematic *question de couleur* is externally rooted in the foundational binary racialism of Western modernity. Because of that, if the construction of a formation of progressive political actors across the boundaries of color would be "yon travay jigantès," the immensity of such a task may be yet more daunting than it first appears.

The dominant construction of blackness in modern Haiti is one part of a dual site in which obtains the enormity of a project to rethink the Haitian nation out of the Black Republic narrative; mulatto colorism is the other. As abhorrent as mulatto color prejudice is to a certain bourgeois modernist ethos, it is not aberrant. The logic of mulatto prejudice is aligned with the pairing of the "international division of labor [with] a hierarchy of races [and] cultures" (Trouillot 1990a, 110), which actively favors "white" appearance. This is also true of black-on-black colorism, because the racial hierarchy twinned with the economic hierarchy is as actively prejudicial to "black" (cf. Robotham 2000). Locally as globally, the pairing of hierarchies of economy and race in Western modernity ultimately entails the articulation of political economic power with prestigious European *cultures* (Robotham 2000), not with racialized somatic characteristics. Somatic appearance nonetheless remains the most immediate signal of a potentially white *sociocultural* subject, and the phenomenon makes sites of postcolonial socioeconomic contestation bewilderingly complex. It is tactically rational that Haiti's mulattoes operationalize an endogamy to preserve visible tidemarks of whiteness on their bodies. It is as tactically rational that blacks of privilege seek to control the blackness of their persons, and to bestow it irreducibly on Haitians bearing the relatively dark body without the requisite cultures to contest the construction of the middle and upper classes.

To succeed in combating the colorism of privileged Haitians, an anticolorist intervention would need to identify, then negate, the discursive and practical points at which the societal valuation of lightness of complexion, or alternately the devaluation of a relatively dark skin, arises phenomenally. The theoretical and empirical efforts to locate those phenomenal moments in Haitian social economy—when and how the social subject comes to see higher value in a relatively light skin and lower value in a relatively dark skin—would be hard enough. The full magnitude of the difficulty is in the fact that colorism in Haiti is pegged to the global value of whiteness and fair complexion continues to retain dominant currency in social economies of the Atlantic as a signal of potential whiteness.

The mechanisms of privilege reproduction in Haiti's postcolonial bourgeois society should alert one that the entry of a nonwhite people in spheres of privilege hitherto reserved for whites does not announce the defeat of racism, even when such entry was the result of a radical Revolution that defeated white supremacy. The corollary insight is that, in Western postcolonial societies, racial justice does not announce social justice. In Haiti, similarly to the experience of class through race in the West (Hall 1980), black and mulatto privileged Haitians clearly live their class situations through normative practices and ideologies of their respective color formations. Class is a prior modality that contains color. In the class, the forms of color and concomitant forms of colorism are historically specific to it. Bilingual light-skinned Haitians of means and bilingual dark-skinned Haitians of means become, respectively, mulattoes and blacks only in the privileged classes. Similarly complexioned people in the working classes and the lumpen proletariat are simply *malere*, poor people, whose skin tones are socially invisible to the privileged. Arguably, by extrapolation, as the privileged classes in the global West would also contain their specific forms of race and racism in the historical moment, racial justice in spheres of privilege would not necessarily entail racial justice beyond, or social justice for all.

Judging by the Haitian experience, it would seem, within the elite and middle classes of the bourgeois West, subjects of "color" viably contest sociopolitical economic privilege by deploying values other than lightness of skin in quantities sufficient to control racialist effects that favor whites within the class. To say this differently, in the elites and in the middle classes, whites and people of color live race as elite and middle-class people, and, as they must, they combat a historical racism that is deployed against elite and middle-class people. Similarly, colored subjects in the working classes and the lumpen proletariat live race with whites within the class, and, as they must, they combat forms of racism historically deployed against working-class and disenfranchised people. Moreover, as elite subjects of color imbue their persons with some degree of lightness of complexion acquired in a spouse in exchange of other forms of capital in the marriage alliance, every such exchange reaffirms the dominant valuation of fair complexion. In a movement of social justice, the case of Haiti reveals, racist or colorist privileged people of color who themselves must confront the racism or colorism of elite and middle-class lives must yet be held accountable for their articulation of a classist racism that injures those below socially, politically, and economically.

The Haitian example suggests that postcolonial movements of social justice in the Atlantic world might benefit in effectiveness, if they ultimately bypassed the issue of racism altogether to confront "white" skin as an actual socioeconomic currency. We may not yet know precisely the vectors of the valuation—thus also of the potential devaluation—of lightness of complexion. However, in the negotiation of class situations, the privileged of Haiti do make salient that light skin is but another exchange value being negotiated.

The devaluation of a currency in bourgeois modernist economies is not only *imaginable*, it is in fact routinely achieved in political economic practice. With borrowings from the literature on fiat money, anthropologists could well begin to blaze a trail of research that might inform a systematic devaluation of lightness of complexion. Since the abolishment of the gold standard in 1971, money is nothing but "pieces of paper" backed by nothing, and this innovation is neither disinterested nor necessarily in support of "justice or economic efficiency" (Hoppe 1994, 49). Fiat money is created by the state out of self-interest (Ritter 1995, 134). Through what economists have termed *seigniorage*, the state intrinsically keeps for itself a portion of the value stated on the face of the currency, leaving the unsuspecting public with an actually lesser value than what the money that it holds ostensibly represents (see Ritter 1995).[5] One may begin to imagine here contours of the field in which the colonial state in Virginia invented "white" skin out of the light complexion of Europeans wretchedly impoverished in indentured servitude(Buck 2001). Poor Europeans had sought better terms for their labor. Without any higher valuation of their labor-power, they were instead motivated to identify with European elites in a commonality of somatic appearance and geographic origins. In effect, by arbitrary power, the colonial state privileged the somatic appearance and geographic origins of subaltern Europeans within the broader subaltern population, vesting with relative value the constructed "white" condition of the European worker within the broader population of workers. Thus, making fair skin by fiat a value that substitutes for an increase in the value of labor-power, Virginia's colonial elites continued to appropriate labor from the fair-complexioned laborer without paying more for it. This mode of labor appropriation and the modern state's appropriation of some of the nominal value of fiat money through seigniorage are arguably two of a kind.

If dominant modern states can intentionally manage the exchange value of their national fiat monies, albeit with varying degrees of success, the valuation of lightness of complexion can presumably be an object of intentional interventions as well. The ethnographic method in anthropology has demonstrated an immense capacity to uncover underlying phenomenal effects in social thought and action. Its dedicated application might pinpoint actual moments in which fairness of complexion concretely accretes the social economic currency of "white" skin, making the white person concomitantly a favored person in determinate social encounters. Conversely, it might locate moments in which social conditions devalue the relatively dark complexion into "black" skin, quite possibly from processes that the state devolved to its agents, making the black person the object of racism and racial discrimination.

The ethnographic method might similarly tease out the moments in which privileged colored subjects, by controlling their existential degradation, relatively controls the blackening—or some other racialization—of their persons, or the moments in which they generate existential degradation of *other* colored subjects to advance their movement toward blackness or other forms of racial otherness. Or else dominant Western states could outlaw the circulation of fair complexion as value—that is, as "white" skin—and concomitantly ensure that statutory penalties are adequately robust to deter its fraudulent circulation as currency in social economies. A high enough cost for perceiving some kind of value in fairness of complexion might, for example, deter a landlord from preferring white house hunters in racially mixed pools of house hunters, or a police corps from being more inclined to brutalize people of color relative to whites.

Ultimately, the bourgeois experience in Haiti suggests, without ceasing to confront racism and white supremacy by any viable means, an effective antiracist movement in the West would seek not so much to preempt racist thought and action but rather to destabilize the moment in which lightness of complexion phenomenally accretes concrete value as currency of social economies. With fairness of skin no longer an exchangeable value, postcolonial privileged people of color would cease to experience the racism that currently proceeds from their *natural* deficit in lightness of complexion as they and fair-complexioned people otherwise contest class situations through *cultural* modalities. In the laboring classes and in capital's lumpen "reserve army," without the fallacious substitution of a value of labor by the value of a skin color, the [de]valuation of labor-power would be experienced more accurately, and more commonly, by hitherto "white" workers alongside their "colored" peers. This vision evidently entails not merely a new vocabulary of race as social category but new epistemologies and new ontologies of the West, which dominant Western states might not wish to produce. Nonetheless, as nonwhite people in "centers" of the West routinely attain what may yet be called "white" privilege, the case of Haiti reveals the urgency of rethinking the politics of race and class in the Atlantic, to imagine new ways of combating the conjugated work of those two operators in the reproduction of gaping social inequalities. However a project to devalue the currency of "white" skin may be instantiated globally, its success will have to precede the local defeat of colorism in Haiti. Such a project is in fact bound to be *yon travay jigantès*.

NOTES

Preface: Positionality, Method, and the Haitian Vocabulary of Color

1. The state had a monopoly on sugar distribution, not on production.

2. My translation of Merleau-Ponty.

3. In the late 2000s, the top 10 percent of earners shared nearly 50 percent of national income, while the bottom 20 percent earned slightly more than 1 percent (Dupuy 2010).

4. BNRH became Banque de la République d'Haïti (BRH) with the spin-off of the BNC.

5. *Négritude* was launched in Paris by the Martinican Aimé Césaire, the Senegalese Léopold Sedar Senghor, and the French Guyanese Léon Damas in the 1930s in their short-lived journal, *L'Étudiant Noir*.

Introduction: Privilege in Haiti and the Caribbean's Modernity

1. The band also had a Creole name, Wanga Nègès (Hummingbird). It played *twoubadou*, a pop genre itself evocative of popular experience. Ti Coca, the band leader and lead singer, generally performed with a red kerchief evocative of vodou rituals wrapped around his neck, when he wasn't twirling it about. The space also included an art gallery, which I never visited.

2. I would dine at La Plantation myself the next evening as the guest of a thriving black couple and their daughter. The husband suggested that we go there after I asked him and his wife about it in order to contextualize what the gynecologist had told me about his meal there. Throughout the text, as my collaborators, I refer to the husband as the "engineering contractor" and the wife as the "math teacher."

3. The Duvalier regime lasted from the inauguration of François in October 1957 to Jean-Claude's forced departure from Haiti on February 6, 1986, amidst growing popular protests. The latter had inherited the regime upon the death of the former, his father, in April of 1971.

4. For example, to obtain a mortgage on a property, in addition to committing the property as collateral, the borrower is generally required to maintain throughout the duration of the mortgage a life insurance policy for the original amount of the loan, with the lender as beneficiary, together with a separate property damage policy also for the original loan amount. One of my collaborators once quipped, "In Haiti, banks lend money to people who don't need to borrow money."

5. Geggus estimates that in 1789 "probably less than 55 percent" of the slaves were Africans (Geggus 2016, 13n); Dubois estimates the African-born at 330,000 (66 percent) of a half-million slaves in 1791 (Dubois 2012, 21).

6. Matthew Smith (2009, 58, 88) speaks of René Salomon, a physician who founded the Parti socialiste haïtien in 1946, as a grandson of Lysius Salomon. However, I have found no suggestions anywhere else that Salomon might have grandchildren other than the children of his daughter Ida. Her children bear the last names of Laraque (a daughter by her first husband) and Faubert (a son by her second husband). Ida, retained in historical memory as the poet Ida Faubert, is invariably the only one mentioned or alluded to in publications or public records as a child of Lysius Salomon. The Association de généalogie d'Haïti's compilation of Lysius Salomon's genealogy proceeds from his father, Pierre-Etienne Salomon, through the seventh generation. The AGH presents a distinct genealogical line that starts at René Salomon and his wife, proceeds to their children, and stop at the latter's children. There are no linkages between the two clusters.

7. Both the son and grandson of Ida Faubert were born and reared in France.

8. While Thompson demonstrates a definite moral calculus informing ideological position and political action in the eighteenth-century English "mob," he remains silent on a no less "moral" economy in the English elite, which his analysis implicitly points to.

Chapter One: Historical Context: Class, Race, and Nation

1. My translation.

2. The creoles were generally Saint-Domingue natives, but Henri Christophe, the Founding Father, was born in Grenada.

3. Three of the Founding Fathers who were signatories of the Act of Independence subsequently gave the nation five Constitutions. None revisited the status of the nation's residents who were natives of Africa present in the colony and at Independence. The first three (Dessalines's in 1805, Pétion's in 1806, and Christophe's in 1807) presumed the existence of a Haitian "citizen" without defining the underlying citizenship. Most conspicuously, Pétion's Constitution of 1816 specifically states that "any African, Indian and those issued from their blood, born in the colonies or in foreign countries, who [come] to reside in the Republic will [be] Haitians, but [not] until after a year of residency" (in Janvier 1886, 117). Pétion would grant citizenship to African immigrants one year after they arrived in the *Republic*, which he founded in 1806, but he did not at all revisit the question of citizenship for the native Africans actually in the nation at its founding. Neither "citizen" nor "citizenship" appears in Christophe's 1811 Constitution. It was not until 1843 that the state formally alluded to the question of citizenship relative to the nation's foundational bossale population. However, the 1843 Constitution actually sidesteps the question in simply stating: "Are Haitians all individuals born in Haiti or descendant of Africans or Indians" (in Janvier 1886, 155). This definition, granting citizenship to the bossales' descendants, but not to the

bossales themselves, is reprised in Constitutional texts enacted in 1846 and in 1849 (and amended in 1850 and 1860).

4. Dubois puts the total bossale population at 330,000, with 40,000 new arrivals within the previous year, and the total slave population is generally at half a million in the historiography.

5. The silence is notable in the work of the late nineteenth-century black intellectual Louis Joseph Janvier, a prominent theorist of the Parti national, which claimed power for the black elite by virtue of its identification with the nation's majority "black" population. He included the third section of the Act of Independence, which grants "dictatorial power [to] Dessalines," in his edited anthology of Haitian Constitutions (Janvier 1886, 29). Although he does not attribute the text that he uses to any source, he cites "Madiou, *Histoire d'Haïti*, tome III, page 171" in his contextual comments (Janvier 1886, 30n). Page 171 of Madiou's original (1849) edition of his *History of Haiti*, volume 3, precisely supports the citation, and the full text of the act appears on pages 115–18. Janvier nonetheless remains silent in his extensive body of work on the significance of "indigène" in sections one and two of the act.

6. Through the 1760s, particularly in the southern peninsula, wealthy mulattoes had been undifferentiated racially in their integration of the planter elite (see Garrigus 2006, 1–2).

7. It is generally said that the Act of Independence was written by Boisrond-Tonnerre, Dessalines's secretary and a mulatto from the slaveholding colonial planter class, though he does not seem to have himself held property in the colony. However, Deborah Jenson persuasively casts doubt on his authorship of the Act. She reminds us that the texts are Dessalinian through and through, because "Dessalines, not Boisrond, was the crucial conceptual voice in the main sections of the [Act of Independence] as he was in his other proclamations from late 1803 through the final months of 1804" (2009, 76).

8. The proclamation of November 29, 1803, was first published in the US press on January 7, 1804, and by February 22, it had appeared in no fewer than thirty-nine US newspapers (Jenson 2009). Similarly, the Act of January 1, 1804, appeared simultaneously in two US newspapers on the following May 7, then "began to circulate widely" (Jenson 2009, 90).

9. See Madiou (1988b, 146) on Dessalines's precious-stone jewelry; see Turnier 1989 on his leased property).

10. The law of the "milliard" in the end actually cost the French state 630 million francs (Gain 1929, 433). In Bordeaux, 70 percent of those indemnified were nobles (Franke 1997, 234).

11. In addition to Dessalines, The Heroes of Independence customarily comprise Toussaint Louverture, Henri Christophe, Alexandre Pétion, and Capois La Mort.

12. Although the phrase "République noire" [black Republic] has been used since at least the last quarter of the nineteenth century, through this period the usage seems to be a banally metaphorical reference lacking the solemnity that seems attached to it in later official and academic discourses. In 181 substantive pages (pp 7–187, including indices) of a history textbook approved by the Department of Public Instruction in 1906, only once, on the 144th page, does one read "République noire" (Bellegarde et Lhérisson 1906, 152). Justin Lhérisson, a coauthor of the schoolbook, was also the author of a poem (also called "La Dessalinienne") that won the competition for the lyrics to the national anthem. For examples of the usage in the late nineteenth century, see Janvier's *La République d'Haïti et ses visiteurs* (1883, xxi), Anténor Firmin's *De l'égalité des races humaines* (1885, 111), and Hannibal Price's *De la rehabilitation de la race noire par la République d'Haïti* (1900, 1, 145).

13. Alexis's Proclamation is reproduced in full on the front page of the January 2, 1904, issue of *Le Nouvelliste*; my translation.

14. My translation.

15. The Déclaration appeared in the July-August-September 1938 issue (the first) of *Les Griots*.

16. My translation. Duvalier elaborated his position most comprehensively with Lorimer Denis in Le problème des classes à travers l'histoire d'Haïti (Denis and Duvalier 1965).

17. The indigenous Taino population was exterminated by the Spaniards before the end of the sixteenth century. However, its size varies widely in the history of the extinction. The nineteenth-century Haitian historian Thomas Madiou (calling the extinct indigenous inhabitants "Haitians") puts the population at two million at the time of Columbus's landing in December 1492 (1988a, 6) and at sixty thousand in 1507 (1988a, 16). Noble David Cook writes that "by 1542 [native populations] were virtually extinct" (1998, 16), and he quotes estimates published between 1971 and 1993 that range the island's 1492 population from sixty thousand to nearly eight million people (1998, 23). Whatever the numbers would have been, among the slave population of Saint-Domingue there was historical memory of the genocide as they reclaimed the island's Taino name in calling the new nation "Haiti."

18. *Avan n vote* means "Before we vote."

Chapter Two: Snapshot of a Western Place: Modern and Racialized, Unequal and Moral

1. Asad's argument proceeds from Stanley Diamond's insight that "'acculturation has always been a matter of conquest. [A] civilization shatters a primitive culture [standing] in its historical right of way, or a primitive social economy, in the grip of a civilized market, becomes so attenuated [that its] foundering groups may adopt the standards of the more potent society. [They] are conscripts of civilization, not volunteers'" (Asad 1992, 333).

2. At the time, the results of the second round of the elections, held days before my departure for Port-au-Prince, had not yet been announced.

3. For conditions in IDP camps after the earthquake and their broader sociopolitical contexts, see Mark Schuller (2016) and the volume edited by him and Pablo Morales (2012).

4. Leslie Manigat had deep roots in the political elite. His grandfather, Saint-Surin François Manigat, was a scion of the northern landed elite, who studied in France and was an influential member of Lysius Salomon's cabinet. His grandmother, Marie Magny, was a granddaughter of Etienne Magny, a key figure in the defense and evacuation of the fort Crête-à-Pierrot during the War of Independence, and a signatory of the 1805 Constitution creating Dessalines's Empire and the Constitution of 1811 creating Christophe's Kingdom of the North.

5. Martelly, if he had a program, would have no clue how to control the old-school "magouyeu" (racketeers) who constituted his political organization, the physician told me, while Manigat would know how to navigate treacherous currents to implement the program she professed to hold to better living conditions in the country. Martelly was to prove adept at revitalizing what I would call Jean-Claude Duvalier's decolorized Duvalierism. Through the time of this writing in the summer of 2014, he would have consistently attempted to bring back a Duvalierist authoritarianism to the executive branch.

6. Cf. Shore (2002, 10–11) and Nugent (2002, 72) on the practical and methodological challenges of studying up.

7. As mentioned in the introduction, I use, for example, "neuf" rather than "nèf" (nine) and "suicidé" rather than "swisidè" to reflect the French-inflected speech of a privileged

Haitian subject speaking Haitian Creole. I will note further instances only when the distinctive speech is of import in the significance of the moment.

8. She stopped the donations, she also told me, when one of her drivers was indeed grievously wounded in accident and his care at the hospital was no different from the usual far-from-adequate level.

9. The wife lived in Haiti for nearly two decades before leaving after the second coup d'état against Aristide, saying she could no longer cope with the chronic political instability and increasing insecurity.

10. Aristide was prevented by the Constitution from running for reelection in 1995.

Chapter Three: *Noirisme* and the Political Instrumentality of Blackness

1. "I swear before God and before the Nation to be its uncompromising and fierce guardian. Let it flutter in the azure to remind all Haitians of the exploits of our sublime martyrs of Crête à Pierrot, of Butte Charier, and of Vertières, who attained immortality under cannonballs and volleys of bullets to found for us a fatherland where the Haitian negro truly feels sovereign and free" (my translation).

The recitation of this text did not generally happen at private institutions. The ritual continued after Jean-Claude Duvalier came to power following his father's death in 1971 before gradually fading. It stopped completely after the collapse of the regime in 1986.

2. The publication of Aimé Césaire's poem "Cahiers d'un retour au pays natal" in 1938 is generally considered the starting point of the Négritude movement. Speaking of his experience as a student in Paris around that time, he says: "'I felt very quickly that I was not a European, that I was not a Frenchman, either, but that I was a Negro. That's all. It's not more complicated than that'" (in Louis 2004, 28; my translation). The Negro is asserting his cultural humanity but is not yet insisting on the more complicated matter of retribution for his degradation hitherto.

3. The groundbreaking ceremony on September 22, 1967, was one of a series of ritualized moments marking the tenth anniversary of the regime. In his speech for the occasion, Duvalier's Minister of Information, Paul Blanchet, exulted about the maroon: "Glory to this Blacksmith of the Fatherland," and thanked Duvalier for undertaking the project to bring the figure back to national memory: "Glory to You, Excellency, Dr. François Duvalier, President for Life of the Republic" (my translation). The speech appeared in the September 25 issue of *Le Nouvelliste*.

4. Mangonès does not seem to have been present at the groundbreaking (see note 11 below). He retraced the history of his submission of the project proposal and of Duvalier's enthusiastic approval in a speech at the unveiling of the Monument on December 6, 1968. The full text appeared in the December 10, 1968, issue of *Le Nouvelliste*.

5. The events are described in a series of brief announcements on the front page of the day's issue of *Le Nouvelliste*.

6. According to the announcement of the groundbreaking in *Le Nouvelliste*, "it fell to [Minister of Information Paul Blanchet] the task of bringing out the significance and the patriotic dimension of the manifestation" (my translation). Duvalier does not seem to have been present at the ceremony. *Le Nouvelliste* did not report any remarks by Duvalier at the groundbreaking either in the September 22 issue or the one of September 25, in which the speech of the Minister of Information was published in full.

7. My translation.

8. "The monument erected to the memory of the Unknown Maroon of St-Domingue is a dream cherished by me long before acceding to the presidency of the Republic, because no Chief of State thought of bringing out from obscurity the sublime unknown whose struggle over three centuries remains the most vivid prefiguration that would create for us in valiance and glory this eternal fatherland that will be returned to no one" (my translation). The plaque bearing the text was still attached to the base of the statue when I visited the monument in June 2016 and in a photograph taken in April 2018. When I returned in November 2018, it was missing.

9. Geggus is methodically concerned with the distance between the evidence and various claims of relationships between Marronage, Voodoo, and the Saint-Domingue Slave Revolt.

10. My translation. Mangonès described the logic of his symbolic and architectonic choices in his speech at the unveiling of the monument on December 6, 1968.

11. My translation from Duvalier's speech at the unveiling ceremony on December 6, 1968. His and Mangonès's speech for the occasion were published in full in the *Le Nouvelliste* issue of December 10.

Duvalier is possibly in error in taking the bossales Petit Noël Prieur and Lamour Dérance to have been maroons (cf. Geggus 1992). However, what is significant is that he is justifying their murder by Dessalines because they did not support the vision of a nation-state.

12. My translation.

13. See Béchacq (2006) on the resonance of "mawon" in various vernacular registers.

14. To express the notion of "a taken-for-granted" during our conversation (otherwise in Creole), I used the French phrase "un ça va de soi," which can be translated as "an it-goes-without-saying."

15. The man nevertheless found that "things were better now than under Duvalier, because if I bad-mouth [President] Martelly, no "makout" would come to take me away."

16. I specifically used the Creole phrase to remain in the linguistic schema of the man's quotidian life. In general, even while otherwise speaking Creole, Haitians inevitably use the French "République noire," which marks a modicum of educational—thus, in Haiti, privilege—attainment.

17. When I asked the man whether he ever discussed Haiti being a black country with people in his native village on his visits there, he dismissed my question with irony. "What people?" he asked. "When someone dies in the countryside, there's no one to carry the body," he added, alluding to rural migration.

18. Official documents use the towns' French names. I use Fondènèg (Creole for Fond-des-Nègres) as the minibus driver spoke in Creole. At the time, I thought perhaps, like the post-Independence Polish settlement in nearby Fond-des-Blancs, that town had a settlement of Germans. That turned out to be incorrect.

19. He left his hometown of Saint-Marc to finish the last three years of secondary school in Port-au-Prince.

20. The fifth and fourth grades in the Haitian school system at the time (based on the French model) would correspond to the eighth and ninth, respectively, in the United States. The second and first grades would be the US eleventh and twelfth, while "philosophie" ("philo" in its short form), the final year following first grade, would more or less represent the curriculum in the first year of a US college.

Chapter Four: Class and Black-Nationalist Sociality

1. Long known as "la bière nationale" [the national beer], Prestige has been known as "la bière haïtienne" since it was purchased in 2011 by the Dutch company Heineken.

2. At the end of our brief chat at his table, the senator, Jocelerme Privert, gave me his telephone number. Although I followed up with a courtesy call and we spoke briefly again within the week, I never got to speak with him substantively in the context of my project. A little more than four years after we were introduced at Presse Café, now president of the senate, he successfully negotiated the departure of Michel Martelly at the end of his term in a moment of constitutional crisis. With no clear constitutional path toward a successor, the negotiated settlement made him *Président Provisoire* [Interim President] of the Republic. At the time of this writing, another year later, he has overseen a tortuous path toward what were generally peaceful presidential elections but is now coping with increasingly violent street protests organized by losing parties since the results were announced about three weeks ago.

3. According to the presentation on its website, Fokal is funded primarily by the US-based financier George Soros's Open Society project with additional financing from France and the European Union.

Chapter Five: Mulatto, Prejudice, and Other White Tidemarks of the Nation

1. See Trouillot on the fluidity of what he calls "color-cum-social categories" (1990a, 109–13). The fluidity transpires in various analysts' divergent categorizations. Thus where Trouillot makes "clair" (light) (112) the broad category that holds various color subclassifications, Price-Mars (1966) makes mulatto the broader classification. Both are correct, as in quotidian practice a speaker might alternatively use "clair" or "mulâtre" as the broader category. In Price-Mars's classification of Haitian presidents, he speaks of placing "Boisrond Canal among the mulattoes, however, [my] only meeting with him . . . gave me the impression that he was rather a griffe" (37). The instability of color classification is particularly remarkable here as "griffe" is arguably applicable to someone somewhat darker than the international human rights activist and actor Harry Belafonte.

2. See chapter 4 in Trouillot (1990a).

3. Haiti's Constitution does not allow dual citizenship.

4. The one substantive result was a review in an online French publication of the book *Restavec: From Haitian Slave Child to Middle-Class American* in translation. Translating the English text, the reviewer cites the description of a Haitian character in the tale as "blanc," white. The book was written for an American audience by a Haitian author long established in the United States.

5. A fifty-minute documentary released on YouTube in August 2010 was the only artifact yielded by the queries that presented a Haitian, a fair-skinned, middle-aged man who had lived in North America since the 1980s, referring to people born and living in Haiti as whites. Two native-born, fair-skinned Haitians living in Haiti are interviewed (in English) in the video. They might be taken for whites in the USA or Europe, but neither speaks of or alludes to being white. Of the two, one is the chief executive of Haiti's best known publishing house and the other a transnational *konpa* music star based in Florida. The publisher talks about

race, color, and being Haitian in a reasoned, dispassionate commentary. Invoking French and German ancestry and "Haitian roots as well, going back all the way to Independent time and colonial time," he speaks of "fellow countrymen" who have dealings with him and do not consider him to be fully Haitian. He and the other three native-born interviewees speak qua Haitians of their relation to Haiti. In any event, the documentary was well outside Haiti's public sphere and did not engage Haitians in a national conversation. Even on Haitian community sites, as far as I could tell, online discussions about them were exclusively in English, occasionally mixed with Haitian Creole. No comments related the video to any sociopolitical process of the moment in Haiti. As a complete work, it treads very different discourses from those of the interviews (apparently taped in 2009). The Haitian subjects interviewed speak of their unexceptional integration in national life. The documentary, through the syntax of audiovisual narrative, situates the interviews in the trope of rational whites civilizing sensuous, primitive blacks. It is twinned with *Forgotten Faces of Jamaica* as a unitary project, which presents itself on its official website as "a video documentary project [that] celebrates the minority ethnic groups of the West Indies . . . These ethnic groups . . . have experienced racism and discrimination [and] have a story to tell about their hardships and about their accomplishments." The project on the whole, in a North Atlantic vocabulary of white reaction, is reminiscent of resistance in North America and in Europe to public initiatives that grapple with historic social injustice to peoples of color. The author of the project (the producer-director of the Jamaica and Haiti videos) is a white American from Methuen, Massachusetts, with family ties in Jamaica, who "has spent much of his life between time in the West Indies and here in the Merrimack [Valley] due to his mixed family background," according to the *Haverhill Gazette* of August 6, 2010. Accessed March 30, 2014, https://www.hgazette.com/news/lifestyles/haverhill-filmmaker-documents-forgotten-faces -of-haiti/article_9c1b85a5-c7b9-57fb-8412-32351d41c231.html

The Haiti video was on YouTube in six segments. Accessed February 16, 2012. http:// www.youtube.com/watch?v=F6HU8MMPXpY, http://www.youtube.com/watch?v=sOxbY yk7tGM, http://www.youtube.com/watch?v=rtH907l7zIo, http://www.youtube.com/watch? v=z7hTFHawOHA, http://www.youtube.com/watch?v=7jFPAA5f4_0, and http://www.you tube.com/watch?v=i_AiIJsXUSM. The project's website, the sites of its constituent videos, and the page of the Gazette are interlinked. Accessed, respectively, February 16, 2012. http:// forgottenfaces.info/, http://forgottenfaces.info/jamaica.html, http://forgottenfaces.info/haiti .html, and http://www.hgazette.com/arts/x2064742154/Haverhill-filmmaker-documents -Forgotten-Faces-of-Haiti.

6. Other meanings of "pè" include afraid, priest, pair, and peace.

7. I did not arrive to the mulatto entrepreneur as a subject of the fieldwork through snowball sampling. I knew of him in high school and reached out to him through social media, and he agreed to participate in the study, before I left for the field. He put me back in touch with his younger brother, whom I knew fairly well as a teenager, although we had had no contact in the decades since we both left Haiti.

8. Bush attributes the insight to Richard Alba.

9. *Mete krèm nan kafe a* is a Creole saying. *Améliorer la race* is French.

10. I should note that, although I identify that household as a "mulatto family," neither the poet-engineer nor his brother invoked or identified them as such. They both consistently used the surname to refer to them.

11. Like the poet-engineer and his brother, when the Duvalier in-laws' daughter and the clair man invoked or identified the mulatto family, they consistently used the family surnames. Neither spoke of a "mulatto family."

12. He hinted that he voted for Martelly but was never willing to tell me explicitly whom he voted for.

13. PAIN's president, Hébert Docteur, served as agriculture minister under Duvalier for a little more than a year before the collapse of the regime in February 1986 and again for six months under Martelly. The party endorsed Martelly in the second round of the elections after the failure of a negotiation to endorse Mirlande Manigat, according to a report by Radio Kiskeya ("Le Parti Agricole Industriel National (PAIN) soutient la candidature à la présidence de Michel Joseph Martelly"). Accessed April 30, 2014. http://radiokiskeya.com /spip.php?article7541.

Chapter Six: Unity in Colorism and Class Ideologies

1. "Leu w nan peyi blan ou wè tout figu yon seul kouleu/Nanpwen mulatrès, bèl marabou, bèl grifonne kreyòl/Ki renmen bèl wòb, bonne poud e bonne odeu/Ni jeune bèl negrès ki konn di bon ti pawòl"—my transcription from a recording of uncertain date by Les artistes de Port-au-Prince. I deviate several times from academically correct Creole orthography to reflect the speech of the singer in the linguistic habitus of the elite and middle classes. The academically correct spelling of the words in question, which reflects typical speech of monolingual Creole-speaking Haitians, would be as follows: "lè" for "leu"; "figi" for "figu"; "sèl" for "seul"; "koulè" for "kouleu"; "milatrès" for "mulatrès"; "grifonn" for "grifonne"; "bon" for "bonne"; "odè" for "odeu"; and "jenn" for "jeune."

2. The eldest went to medical school at the State University of Haiti.

3. The social situations of his patients range far up the socioeconomic ladder (and across the colorized spectrum), although he did not speak of noticing signs of skin lightening in his middle-class and upper-middle-class patients.

4. By her public photographs, Claudinette Fouchard's characteristics would fit the somatic indices of "peau intermédiaire" (intermediate complexion) and "cheveu intermédiaire" (intermediate hair) used by Labelle. In any event, like the mulatto intellectual who found Fouchard to be "black" (chapter 5), Labelle assessed her subjects' somatic appearances not their belonging to one or the other color formation. Fouchard is of the mulatto elite.

5. In *Le Nouvelliste*, December 22, 1959; my translation.

6. *Le Nouvelliste* and the English-language weekly *Haiti Sun* are two publications with accessible archives containing issues covering the moment. *Le Nouvelliste* covered it in varying degrees in seven issues, those of December 22, 1959, and January 8, 9, 11, 14, 15, and 16, 1960. *Haiti Sun* covered it on December 20, 1959, and on January 10, 17, and 24, 1960.

7. See "Le Retour de Claudinette Fouchard" [The Return of Claudinette Fouchard] on the front page, *Le Nouvelliste*, January 11, 1960.

8. Front page of *Le Nouvelliste* of January 14, 1960; my translation.

9. The poems appear on page 2 of *Le Nouvelliste*, January 11, 1960; my translation.

10. The poem, "Claudinette," appeared on the front page of the January 9, 1960, issue.

11. *Le Nouvelliste*, January 11, 1960; my translation.

Chapter Seven: Material Unity in Privilege

1. The engineering contractor's skin tone is more or less comparable to that of the US Supreme Court Associate Justice Clarence Thomas or the cinema icon Sidney

Poitier; the civil engineer is distinctly darker than the retired American basketball superstar Michael Jordan.

2. At the time of my fieldwork, the Duvalier in-laws' cousin was deceased.

Chapter Eight: The Political Economy of Knowing White

1. Bourdieu's *Langage et pouvoir symbolique* (2001) is the author's revised French edition of *Language and Symbolic Power* (1991), which itself was the English translation of the original text as *Ce que parler veut dire* (1982); my translation.

2. My translation.

3. Piquion was a champion of négritude in Haiti and was a contributor to thematic encounters around the movement in Europe, Africa, and the Americas.

4. I was at Piquion's house to pay my respect after over four years away at school. As a friend of the family, he had shown interest in my intellectual development since my boyhood. The visit took place a week or so after my father's funeral, at which, he would tell me with satisfaction, he was the first to arrive.

5. A Pan American Health Organization report on the period of 2007–2009 supports the broad lines of his representation of the agency's progress.

Conclusion: Liberal Politics in a Failure of Hermeneutics—*Yon Travay Jigantès*

1. Barthélémy, who had lived in France for several decades, died six months later in April of 2013.

2. The recipe is taken from a report in the *New York Times* issue of May 5, 2004. Accessed March 6, 2014. https://www.nytimes.com/2004/05/05/world/deepening-poverty-breeds-anger-and-desperation-in-haiti.html.

3. My translation of Jean.

4. See J. Christopher Kovats-Bernat's ethnography of post-Duvalier political violence on Aristide's failure through his two presidencies (1990–1995, 2000–2004) to engage in a promised national dialogue on poverty-reduction and on the hollowing out of the Lavalas promise in general (Kovats-Bernat 2006, 124–25). On the same theme, see also Robert Fatton's analysis of the structural underpinnings of "processes of intense class formation and differentiation *within* . . . the emerging Lavalas leadership issued from the lower middle classes and the 'petite bourgeoisie'" (2000, 21). On debilitating factionalism in Lavalas, see Kovats-Bernat (2006, 127–29), Fatton (2000, 22–26), and Maguire (2002, 30–33).

5. Essentially, in modern seigniorage, the state appropriates value in the difference between the nominal value of banknotes and the direct and indirect costs of producing them. Paper money not backed by a commodity retains public credibility to the extent that the state sufficiently internalizes "macroeconomic externalities" that offset the potential of seigniorage (Ritter 1995, 147).

REFERENCES

Acacia, Michel. 2006. *Historicité et Structuration Sociale en Haïti*. Port-au-Prince: Imprimeur II.

Allen, Woody, dir. 1979. *Manhattan*. Hollywood: United Artists.

Appadurai, Arjun. 1990. "Disjuncture and Difference in the Global Cultural Economy." *Theory, Culture and Society* 7 (2–3): 295–310.

Asad, Talal. 1991. "From the Colonial History of Anthropology to the Anthropology of Western Hegemony." Pp. 314–24 in *Colonial Situations: Essays on the Contextualization of Ethnographic Knowledge*, edited by George W. Stocking Jr.. Madison: University of Wisconsin Press.

Averill, Gage. 1997. *A Day for the Hunter: A Day for the Prey: Popular Music and Power in Haiti*. Chicago: University of Chicago Press.

Barthélémy, Gérard. 1989. *Le pays en dehors: essai sur l'univers rural haïtien*. Port-au-Prince: Éditions Henri Deschamps.

Barthélémy, Gérard. 1996. *Dans la splendeur d'un après-midi d'histoire*. Port-au-Prince: Éditions Henri Deschamps.

Béchacq, Dimitri. 2006. "Les parcours du marronnage dans l'histoire haïtienne: Entre instrumentalisation politique et réinterprétation sociale." *Ethnologies* 28 (1): 203–40. doi:10.7202/014155ar.

Bell, Madison Smartt. 2007. *Toussaint L'Ouverture: A Biography*. New York: Pantheon.

Bellegarde, Windsor, and Justin Lhérisson. 1906. *Manuel d'histoire d'Haiti : conforme aux programmes officiels a l'usage des ecoles de la république*. Port-au-Prince: n.p.

Bernard, Joseph, Jr. 2010. *Histoire des colonies arabe et juive d'Haïti*. Port-au-Prince: Éditions Henri Deschamps.

Bernard, Joseph, Jr. 2011a. *Histoire de la colonie allemande d'Haïti*. Port-au-Prince: Éditions Henri Deschamps.

Bernard, Joseph, Jr. 2011b. *Histoire de la colonie italienne d'Haïti*. Port-au-Prince: Éditions Henri Deschamps.

Berrou, Raphaël, and Pradel Pompilus. 1975. *Deux poètes indigénistes: Carl Brouard et Émile Roumer*. Port-au-Prince: Éditions Caraïbes.

Bourdieu, Pierre. 1979. *La distinction: critique sociale du jugement*. Paris: Les Éditions de Minuit.

Bourdieu, Pierre. 2001 [1982]. *Langage et pouvoir symbolique*. Paris: Éditions du Seuil.

Bruun, Maja Hojer, Gry Skrædderdal Jakobsen, and Stine Krøijer. 2011. Introduction to Theme Issue, "The Concern for Sociality: Practicing Equality and Hierarchy in Denmark." *Social Analysis* 55 (2): 21–44. doi:10.3167/sa.2011.550201.

Buck, Pem Davidson. 2001. *Worked to the Bone: Race, Class, Power, and Privilege in Kentucky*. New York: Monthly Review.

Buck-Morss, Susan. 2009. *Hegel, Haiti, and Universal History*. Pittsburgh: University of Pittsburgh Press.

Bush, Melanie E. L. 2004. *Breaking the Code of Good Intentions: Everyday Forms of Whiteness*. Lanham, MD: Rowman & Littlefield.

Casimir, Jean. 2000. "La suppression de la culture africaine dans l'histoire d'Haïti." *Socio-anthropologie* 8. doi: 10.4000/socio-anthropologie.124.

Casimir, Jean. 2009a. "From Saint-Domingue to Haiti: To Live Again or To Live at Last!" In *The World of the Haitian Revolution*, edited by David Patrick Geggus and Norman Fiering. Bloomington: Indiana University Press.

Casimir, Jean. 2009b. *Haïti et ses élites: L'interminable dialogue de sourds*. Port-au-Prince: Éditions de l'Université d'État d'Haïti.

Cauna, Jacques de. 2004. *Toussaint L'Ouverture et l'indépendance d'Haïti: Témoignages pour une commémoration*. Paris: Karthala.

Charles, Asselin. 2002. "Haitian Exceptionalism and Caribbean Consciousness." *The Journal of Caribbean Studies* 3 (2): 115–30.

Clitandre, Nadège. 2011. "Haitian Exceptionalism in The Caribbean and The Project of Rebuilding Haiti." *The Journal of Haitian Studies* 17 (2): 146–53.

Cook, Noble David. 1998. *Born to Die: Disease and New World Conquest, 1492–1650*. Cambridge: Cambridge University Press.

Crapanzano, Vincent. 1985 [1980]. *Tuhami, Portrait of a Moroccan*. Chicago: University of Chicago Press.

Dalencour, François. 1944. *La fondation de la république d'Haïti par Alexandre Pétion*. Port-au-Prince: Chez l'Auteur.

Dayan, Colin. 2010. "What is a Metaphor a Metaphor for?" *The Immanent Frame*, Mar. 24. Accessed Jan. 31, 2018. https://tif.ssrc.org/2010/03/24/a-metaphor-for/.

DeGraff, Michel. 2010. "Baryè lang an Ayiti: Kreyòl se lang peyi; se pou sa fòk lekòl fèt an kreyòl." *Le Nouvelliste*, Aug. 30.

DeGraff, Michel. 2017. "La langue maternelle comme fondement du savoir L'Initiative MIT-Haiti: vers une éducation en créole efficace et inclusive." Theme issue, "Diglossies suisses et caribéennes: Retour sur un concept (in)utile." *Revue transatlantique d'études suisses* 6–7: 177–97.

DeGraff, Michel, and Glenda S. Stump. 2018. "Kreyòl, Pedagogy, and Technology for Opening Up Quality Education in Haiti: Changes in Teachers' Metalinguistic Attitudes as First Steps in a Paradigm Shift." *Language* 94 (2): e127-e157.

Denis, Lorimer, and François Duvalier. 1965. *Le probème des classes à traver l'histoire d'Haïti*. Port-au-Prince: Imprimerie de l'État.

Dubois, Laurent. 2004. *Avengers of the New World: The Story of the Haitian Revolution.* Cambridge: Harvard University Press.

Dubois, Laurent. 2012. *Haiti: Aftershocks of History.* New York: Metropolitan Books.

Du Bois, W. E. B. 1935. *Black Reconstruction in America 1860–1880.* New York: Free Press.

Dupuy, Alex. 1989. *Haiti in the world economy: Class, race, and underdevelopment since 1700.* Boulder: Westview Press.

Dupuy, Alex. 2004. "Class, Race, and Nation: Unresolved Contradictions of the Saint-Domingue Revolution." *Journal of Haitian Studies* 10 (1): 6–21.

Dupuy, Alex. 2010. "Disaster Capitalism to the Rescue: The international Community and Haiti After the Earthquake." *NACLA Report on the Americas* 43 (4): 14–19.

Dupuy, Alex. 2015 [2014]. *Haiti: From Revolutionary Slaves to Powerless Citizens: Essays on the Politics and Economics of Underdevelopment, 1804–2013.* New York: Routledge.

Duvalier, François. 1969. *Mémoires d'un leader du Tiers Monde: Mes négociations avec le Saint-Siège ou Une tranche d'Histoire.* Paris: Hachette.

Edelman, Mark. 2012. "E. P. Thompson and Moral Economies." Pp. 49–66 in *A Companion to Moral Anthropology,* edited by Didier Fassin. Malden, MA: John Wiley & Sons.

Fanon, Frantz. 1952. *Peau noire, masques blancs.* Paris: Éditions du Seuil.

Fanon, Frantz. 1991 [1961]. *Les damnés de la terre.* Paris: Gallimard.

Fanon, Frantz. 2011. *Œuvres.* Paris: La Découverte.

Fass, Simon M. 2004 [1988]. *Political Economy in Haiti: The Drama of Survival.* New Brunswick, NJ: Transaction.

Fassin, Didier, ed. 2012. *A Companion of Moral Anthropology.* Malden, MA: John Wiley & Sons.

Fatton, Robert, Jr. 1999. "The Impairments of Democratization: Haiti in Comparative Perspective." *Comparative Politics* 31 (2): 209–29.

Fatton, Robert, Jr. 2000. "Constitution Without Constitutionalism: Haiti and the Vagaries of Democratization." *NWIG: New West Indian Guide* 74 (1–2): 5–32.

Ferrer, Ada. 2012. "Haiti, Free Soil, and Antislavery in the Revolutionary Atlantic." *The American Historical Review* 117 (1): 40–66.

Fick, Carolyn E. 1990. *The Making of Haiti: The Saint-Domingue Revolution from Below.* Knoxville: University of Tennessee Press.

Firmin, Anténor. 1885. *De l'égalité des races humaines.* Paris: F. Pichon.

Franke, Almut. 1997. "La loi de l'indemnité de 1825 dans l'arrondissement de Bordeaux." *Annales du Midi : revue archéologique, historique et philologique de la France méridionale,* 109 (218): 223–45.

Gaffield, Julia, ed. 2016. *The Haitian Declaration of Independence: Creation, Context, and Legacy.* Charlottesville: University of Virginia Press.

Gaillard, Roger. 1998 [1928]. Introduction to Jean Price-Mars, *Ainsi parla l'Oncle: Essais d'ethnographie,* vii–xxxiii. Port-au-Prince: Imprimeur II.

Gain, André. 1929. "La Restauration et les biens des émigrés." *Revue d'histoire moderne* 4 (34): 431–34.

Garrigus, John D. 2006. *Before Haiti: Race and Citizenship in French Saint-Domingue.* New York: Palgrave Macmillan.

Garrigus, John D. 2009. "Saint-Domingue's Free People of Color and The Tools of Revolution." Pp. 49–64 in *The World of the Haitian Revolution,* edited by David Patrick Geggus and Norman Fiering. Bloomington: Indiana University Press.

Geggus, David. 1992. "Marronage, Voodoo, and the Saint-Domingue Slave Revolt of 1791."
     Proceedings of the Meeting of the French Colonial Historical Society 15 (1992): 22–35.
Geggus, David. 2014. *The Haitian Revolution: A Documentary History*. Indianapolis:
     Hackett.
Geggus, David. 2016. "Haiti's Declaration of Independence." Pp. 25–41 in *The Haitian
     Declaration of Independence: Creation, Context, and Legacy*, edited by Julia Gaffield.
     Charlottesville: University of Virginia Press.
Girard, Philippe. 2010. "Trading Races: Joseph and Marie Bunel, a Diplomat and a Merchant
     in Saint-Domingue and Philadelphia." *Journal of the Early Republic* 30 (Fall): 351–76.
Girard, Philippe. 2012. "Jean-Jacques Dessalines and The Atlantic System: A Reappraisal."
     The William and Mary Quarterly 69 (3): 549–82.
Girard, Philippe. 2016. *Toussaint Louverture: A Revolutionary Life*. New York: Basic Books.
Grenier, Yvon. 2001. "The Romantic Liberalism of Octavio Paz." *Mexican Studies* 17 (1):
     171–91
Hacker, Andrew. 1992. *Two Nations: Black and White, Separate, Hostile, Unequal*. New York:
     Ballantine Books.
Hall, Stuart. 1980. "Race, Articulation and Societies Structured in Dominance." Pp. 305–45
     in *Sociological Theories: Race and Colonialism*, edited by United Nations Educational,
     Scientific and Cultural Organization. Paris: UNESCO.
Holt, Thomas C. 2002. *The Problem of Race in the Twenty-first Century*. Cambridge:
     Harvard University Press.
Hoppe, Hans-Hermann. 1994. "How Is Fiat Money Possible? Or, The Devolution of Money
     and Credit." *The Review of Austrian Economics* 7 (2): 49–74.
Hurston, Zora Neale. 1990 [1938]. *Tell My Horse: Voodoo and Life in Haiti and Jamaica*. New
     York: Harper & Row.
International Delegation to the Haitian General Elections. 1991. *The 1990 General Elections
     in Haiti*. Washington, D.C.: National Democratic Institute for International Affairs.
Jacobs-Huey, Lanita. 2002. "The Natives Are Gazing and Talking Back: Reviewing the
     Problematics of Positionality, Voice, and Accountability among 'Native' Anthropologists."
     American Anthropologist 104 3: 791–804.
James, C. L. R. 1963 [1938]. *The Black Jacobins: Toussaint L'Ouverture and the San Domingo
     Revolution*. New York: Vintage Books.
Janvier, Louis Joseph. 1883. *La République d'Haïti et ses visiteurs*. Paris: Morpon et
     Flammarion.
Janvier, Louis Joseph. 1886. *Les Constitutions d'Haïti (1801–1885)*. Paris: C. Marpon and E.
     Flammarion.
Jean, Fritz A. 2013. *Haïti, la fin d'une histoire économique*. Port-au-Prince: Ayiti Rasanble.
Jenson, Deborah. 2009. "Dessalines's American Proclamations of the Haitian
     Independence." *The Journal of Haitian Studies* 15 (1&2): 72–102.
Johnson, Ronald Angelo. 2014. *Diplomacy in Black and White: John Adams, Toussaint
     Louverture, and Their Atlantic World Alliance*. Athens: University of Georgia Press.
Joseph, Mario, and Jeena Shah. 2012. "Combating Forced Evictions in Haiti's IDP Camps."
     Pp. 138–43 in *Tectonic Shifts: Haiti Since the Earthquake*, edited by Mark Schuller and
     Pablo Morales. Sterling, VA: Kumarian Press.
Kovats-Bernat, J. Christopher. 2006. "Factional Terror, Paramilitarism and Civil War in
     Haiti: The View from Port-au-Prince, 1994–2004." Theme Issue, "La guerre et la paix."
     Anthropologica 48 (1): 117–39.

Labelle, Micheline. 1987 [1979]. *Idéologie de couleur et classes sociales en Haïti*. Montréal: Les Presses de l'Université de Montréal.

Linnet, Jeppe. (2011). "Money Can't Buy Me Hygge: Danish Middle-Class Consumption, Egalitarianism, and the Sanctity of Inner Space." Theme Issue, "The Concern for Sociality: Practicing Equality and Hierarchy in Denmark." *Social Analysis* 55 (2): 21–44. doi:10.3167/sa.2011.550202.

Louis, Patrice. 2004. *Aimé Césaire, rencontre avec un nègre fondamental*. Paris: Arlea.

Lynelle, Amy. 2015. "The Chains of Pitit Pierr': Colonial Legacies and Character Linkage in Oswald Durand's Rires et pleurs." *The French Review* 88 (3): 163–75.

Madiou, Thomas. 1988a [1848]. *Histoire d'Haïti*, t. 1: 1492–1799. Port-au-Prince: Henri Deschamps.

Madiou, Thomas. 1988b [1848]. *Histoire d'Haïti*, t. 3: 1803–1807. Port-au-Prince: Henri Deschamps.

Madiou, Thomas. 1988c [1848]. *Histoire d'Haïti*, t. 6: 1819–1826. Port-au-Prince: Henri Deschamps.

MADRE, Cuny School of Law, Bureau des Avocats Internationaux, Institute for Justice and Democracy in Haiti, and Lisa Davis. 2012. "Our Bodies Are Still Trembling: Haitian Women Fight Rape." Pp. 157–61 in *Tectonic Shifts: Haiti Since the Earthquake*, edited by Mark Schuller and Pablo Morales. Sterling, VA: Kumarian Press.

Magloire, Gerarde, and Kevin A. Yelvington. 2005. "Haiti and the Anthropological Imagination." Theme issue, "Haiti et l'anthropologie." *Gradhiva* 1: 127–52 [pdf: 1–35. Accessed Aug. 5, 2013. https://gradhiva.revues.org/335].

Maguire, Robert. 2002. "Haiti's Political Gridlock." *Journal of Haitian Studies* 8 (2): 30–42.

Marcus, George E. 1995. "Ethnography In/Of the World System: The Emergence of Multi-Sited Ethnography." *Annual Review of Anthropology* 24 (1): 95–117.

Meehan, Kevin. 1999. "'Titid ak pèp la se marasa': Jean-Bertrand Aristide and the New National Romance in Haiti." Pp. 105–21 in *Caribbean Romances: The Politics of Regional Representation*, edited by Belinda Edmonson. Charlottesville: University of Virginia Press.

Meehan, Kevin, and Marie Léticée. 2000. "A Folio of Writing from 'La Revue Indigène' (1927–28): Translation and Commentary." *Callaloo* 23 (4): 1377–1380.

Merleau-Ponty, Maurice. 1999 [1945]. *Phénoménologie de la perception*. Paris: Gallimard.

Middleton, Richard. 1990. *Studying Popular Music*. Milton Keynes, UK: Open University Press.

Miller, Frances. 1981. *"Tanty"—The Darling Decades*. Sag Harbor, NY: Sandbox Press.

Mintz, Sidney. 1996. "Enduring Substances, Trying Theories: The Caribbean Region as Oikoumene." *The Journal of The Royal Anthropological Institute* 2 (2): 289–311.

Nader, Laura. 1972. "Up the Anthropologist: Perspectives Gained from Studying Up." Pp. 284–311 in *Re inventing Anthropology*, edited by Dell Hymes. New York: Pantheon Books.

Nagel, Joanne. 2000. "Ethnicity and Sexuality." *Annual Review of Sociology* 26: 107–33

Narayan, Kirin. 1993. "How 'Native' Is a Native Anthropologist?" *American Anthropologist* 95 (3): 671–86.

Nicholls, David. 1974a. "Ideology and Political Protest in Haiti, 1930–1946." *Journal of Contemporary History* 9 (4): 3–26.

Nicholls, David. 1974b. "A Work of Combat: Mulatto Historians and the Haitian Past, 1847–1867." *Journal of Interamerican Studies and World Affairs* 16 (1): 15–38.

Nicholls, David. 1996 [1979]. *From Dessalines to Duvalier: Race, Colour and National Independence in Haiti*. New Brunswick, NJ: Rutgers University Press.

Nugent, Stephen. 2002. "Gente boa: elites in and of Amazonia." Pp. 61–73 in *Elite Cultures: Anthropological Perspectives*, edited by Cris Shore and Stephen Nugent. Milton Park, UK: Routledge.

Pan American Union. 1911. "Haiti." *Bulletin of the Pan American Union* 32 (2): 364-372.

Péan, Leslie J.-R. 2003. *Haïti, économie politique de la corruption: De Saint-Domingue à Haïti 1791–1870*. Paris: Maisonneuve & Larose.

Perrot, Marie-Clémence. 1997. "La politique linguistique pendant la Révolution française." *Mots* (52): 158–67. doi: https://doi.org/10.3406/mots.1997.2474.

Piketty, Thomas. 2013. *Capital au XXIᵉ siècle*. Paris: Éditions du Seuil.

Piquion, René. 1966. *Manuel de Négritude*. Port-au-Prince: Éditions Henri Deschamps.

Price, Hannibal. 1900. *De la réhabilitation de la race noire par la République d'Haïti*. Port-au-Prince: J. Verrolot.

Price-Mars, Jean. 1919. *La vocation de l'élite*. Port-au-Prince: Imprimerie E. Chenet.

Price-Mars, Jean. 1967. *Lettre Ouverte au Dr. René Piquion, Directeur de l'Ecole Normale Supérieure, sur son « Manuel de la Négritude » Le Préjugé de couleur est-il la question sociale?* Port-au-Prince: Les Editions des Antilles.

Price-Mars, Jean. 1998 [1928]. *Ainsi parla l'Oncle: Essais d'ethnographie*. Port-au-Prince: Imprimeur II.

Reinsel, Amy. 2008. *Poetry of Revolution: Romanticism and National Projects in Nineteenth-century Haiti*. PhD diss., Faculty of Arts and Sciences, University of Pittsburgh.

Ribeiro Thomaz, Omar. 2005. "Haitian Elites and Their Perceptions of Poverty and of Inequality." Pp. 127–56 in *Elite Perceptions of Poverty and Inequality*, edited by Elisa P. Moore and Mick Moore. Cape Town: David Philip.

Ritter, Joseph A. 1995. "The Transition from Barter to Fiat Money." *The American Economic Review* 85 (1): 134–49.

Roberts, Neil. 2015. *Freedom as Marronage*. Chicago: University of Chicago Press.

Robotham, Don. 2000. "Blackening the Jamaican Nation: The Travails of a Black Bourgeoisie in a Globalized World." *Identities: Global Studies in Culture and Power* 7 (1): 1–37.

Rosenblatt, Helena. 2018. *The Lost History of Liberalism: From Ancient Rome to the Twenty-First Century*. Princeton: Princeton University Press.

Sanjek, Roger. 1991. "The Ethnographic Present." *Man* 26 (4): 609–28.

Schuller, Mark. 2010. "'Mr Blan,' Or, the Incredible Whiteness of Being (an Anthropologist)." Pp. 105–30 in *Fieldwork Identities in the Caribbean*, edited by Erin B. Taylor. Coconut Creek, FL: Caribbean Studies Press.

Schuller, Mark. 2016. *Humanitarian Aftershocks in Haiti*. New Brunswick, NJ: Rutgers University Press.

Schuller, Mark, and Pablo Morales, ed. 2012. *Tectonic Shifts: Haiti Since the Earthquake*. Sterling, VA: Kumarian Press.

Scott, David. 2004. *Conscripts of Modernity: The Tragedy of Colonial Enlightenment*. Durham: Duke University Press.

Scott, David. 2014. *Omens of Adversity: Tragedy, Time, Memory, Justice*. Durham: Duke University Press.

Senghor, Léopold Sedar, ed. 1948. *Anthologie de la nouvelle poésie noire et malgache de langue française*. Paris: Presses Universitaires de France.

Shannon, Magdaline. 1996. *Jean Price-Mars, the Haitian Elite and the American Occupation, 1915–35*. New York: St. Martin's Press.

Shore, Cris. 2002. "Introduction: Towards an Anthropology of Elites." Pp. 1–21 in *Elite Cultures: Anthropological Perspectives*, edited by Cris Shore and Stephen Nugent. Milton Park, UK: Routledge.

Smith, Matthew J. 2009. *Red & Black in Haiti—Radicalism, Conflict, and Political Change 1934–1957*. Chapel Hill: University of North Carolina.

Sylvain, Normil. 1927. "Un rêve de Georges Sylvain." *La Revue indigène* 1 (1): 1–10.

Tejani, Riaz. 2004. "Liberalism Repatriated: Prospects of an Anthropology of Antiracism." *Anthropological Quarterly* 77 (2): 331–38.

Thomas, Deborah. 2004. *Modern Blackness: Nationalism, Globalization, and the Politics of Culture in Jamaica*. Durham: Duke University Press.

Thompson, E. P. 1971. "The Moral Economy of the English Crowd in the Eighteenth Century England." *Past & Present* 50 (Feb.): 76–136.

Trouillot, Michel-Rolph. 1990a. *Haiti, State Against Nation: The Origins and Legacy of Duvalierism*. New York: Monthly Review.

Trouillot, Michel-Rolph. 1990b. "The Odd and The Ordinary: Haiti, the Caribbean and The World." *Cimarron: New Perspectives on the Caribbean* 2 (3): 3–12.

Trouillot, Michel-Rolph. 1995. *Silencing the Past: Power and the Production of History*. Boston: Beacon.

Turnier, Alain. 1989. *Quand la nation demande des comptes*. Port-au-Prince: Le Natal.

Ulysse, Gina. 2007. *Downtown Ladies: Informal Commercial Importers, a Haitian Anthropologist, and Self-Making in Jamaica*. Chicago: University of Chicago Press.

Vanneschi, Myriam. 2013. "The Many Contradictions of a Ghetto Biennale." *Hyperallergenic*. Accessed Feb. 28, 2019. https://hyperallergenic.com/100563/the-many-contradictions -of-a-ghetto-biennale/.

Verdery, Katherine. 1993. "Whither 'Nation' and 'Nationalism'?" Theme issue, "Reconstructing Nations and States." *Daedalus* 122 (3): 37–46.

Wolf, Eric. 1969. *Peasant Wars of the Twentieth Century*. New York: Harper and Row.

Wray, Matt. 2006. *Not Quite White: White Trash and the Boundaries of White Trash*. Durham: Duke University Press.

INDEX

References to photographs appear in **bold**.

ABOUT THE AUTHOR

Photo by Joanne Marius

Dr. Philippe-Richard Marius received his PhD in cultural anthropology at the Graduate Center of the City University of New York (CUNY). His research interests include race, class, culture, privilege, and inequality in Western bourgeois societies. He teaches in the Department of Sociology and Anthropology at the College of Staten Island, where he is also the director of assessment for student affairs.

www.ingramcontent.com/pod-product-compliance
Lightning Source LLC
Chambersburg PA
CBHW031126270326
41929CB00011B/1518